asian martial arts

in literature & movies

An Anthology of Articles from the *Journal of Asian Martial Arts*
Compiled by Michael A. DeMarco, M.A.

Disclaimer

Please note that the authors and publisher of this book are not responsible in any manner whatsoever for any injury that may result from practicing the techniques and/or following the instructions given within. Since the physical activities described herein may be too strenuous in nature for some readers to engage in safely, it is essential that a physician be consulted prior to training.

All Rights Reserved

No part of this publication, including illustrations, may be reproduced or utilized in any form or by any means, electronic or mechanical, including photocopying, recording, or by any information storage and retrieval system (beyond that copying permitted by sections 107 and 108 of the US Copyright Law and except by reviewers for the public press), without written permission from Via Media Publishing Company.

Warning: Any unauthorized act in relation to a copyright work may result in both a civil claim for damages and criminal prosecution.

Copyright © 2016
by Via Media Publishing Company
941 Calle Mejia #822, Santa Fe, NM 87501 USA, E-mail: md@goviamedia.com

All articles in this anthology were originally published in the *Journal of Asian Martial Arts*.
Listed according to the table of contents for this anthology:

Grady, J. (2000), Vol. 9, No. 4, pp. 52-75
Grady, J. (1998), Vol. 7, No. 2, pp. 86-101
Donohue, J. (1992), Vol. 1, No. 2, pp. 84-93
Bates, C. (1993), Vol. 2 No. 4, pp. 28-39
Maliszewski, M. (2000), Vol. 9 No. 3, pp. 58-77
Maliszewski, M. (2001), Vol. 10 No. 2, pp. 76-87
Mok, O. (2001), Vol. 10 No. 3, pp. 16-23
Maliszewski, M. (2002), Vol. 11 No. 3, pp. 50-65
Donohue, J. (2003), Vol. 12, No. 2, pp. 56-63
Gilbey, J. (2003), Vol. 12 No. 3, pp. 52-67
DeRose, J. (2004), Vol. 13, No. 1, pp. 78-85
Graebner, P. (2005), Vol. 14, No. 3, pp. 64-71
Sheridan, B. (2009), Vol. 18, No. 1, pp. 64-71
Bailey, T. (2009), Vol. 18, No. 3, pp. 70-73
Dalia, A. (2011), Vol. 20, No. 3, pp. 8-21

Book and cover design by Via Media Publishing Company
Edited by Michael A. DeMarco, M.A.

Cover illustration

Artwork by Chang Jung Shan • http://jung-shan.blogspot.com

ISBN: 978-1893765320

w w w . v i a m e d i a p u b l i s h i n g . c o m

contents

iv **Preface** by Michael DeMarco, M.A.

CHAPTERS

1 **Fist of Fantasy: Martial Arts and Prose Fiction** by James Grady, B.A.

29 **Celluloid Katas: Martial Arts in the Movies — A Practitioner's Prejudices** by James Grady, B.A.

45 **A Sort of Swordsman** by John J. Donohue, Ph.D.

59 **Wang Wu Notices the Commotion on Music Hall Street: An Excerpt from Tales of Chivalrous and Altruistic Heros** by Christopher Bates, M.A.

71 **Inside Interview with Curtis Wong: Extraordinary Contributions to Martial Arts Popularization** by Michael Maliszewski, Ph.D.

94 **Don Wilson: Kickboxing Champion and Film Star Shares His Perspectives** by Michael Maliszewski, Ph.D.

108 **Dianxue: A Genre-Specific Form of Attack in Martial Arts Fiction** by Olivia Mok, Ph.D.

117 **Film Producer Andre Morgan and the Evolution of Asian Martial Arts in Movies** by Michael Maliszewski, Ph.D.

135 **Heiho: A Tale of Strategy** by John J. Donohue, Ph.D.

144 **The Master: Chinese Boxing Accounts in an Envelope** by John F. Gilbey, M.A.

162 **Again! Practicing for Perfection** by John Richard DeRose

171 **Samurai Geometry: A Story of Values** by Peter Graebner, M.A.

178 **From the Tatami Mat to the Printed Page: Author Barry Eisler Keeps His Fiction Real** by Brian R. Sheridan, M.A.

186 **Arthur Rosenfeld: Martial Artist and Storyteller** by Thomas H. Bailey, Jr., L.M.P., A.P.

192 **Fighting Heroes: The Core Values of the Xia Tradition in Early China** by Albert Dalia, Ph.D.

203 **Index**

preface

Most learn about martial arts through movies and print publications, primarily fictional. "Fiction is drama, the blood of drama is conflict, and martial arts are rooted in conflict," writes James Grady in chapter one. Good fiction uses martial arts well, while poor writing skills can be plain boring!

This anthology is a collection of fifteen articles that cover the richness and depth of Asian martial arts in both movies and literature. After looking over the array of topics, I decided to utilize writings by James Grady for the two introductory chapters.

Grady is an internationally renowned writer and investigative journalist known for his nail-biting thriller novels. His early novel was adapted to film as *Three Days of the Condor* (1975) starring Robert Redford. Grady has since written over a dozen wonderful novels and in between wrote two excellent pieces for the *Journal of Asian Martial Arts*: one dealing with movies and another with literature.

The following chapters are greatly enriched by the informative contents in Grady's chapters. Details about movie-making are provided in the interview with producer Andre Morgan (*Enter the Dragon, Walter Texas Ranger, Martial Law*, etc.), plus the inside scoop in the publishing and film industries in the interview with multifaceted Curtis Wong. Actor/producer/kickboxing champion Don Wilson provides insights from both sides of the camera in his interview.

Among the chapters are Albert Dalia's exposition of China's "wandering martial hero" stories that have roots reaching back two thousand years; Christopher Bates' excerpt from Xiang Kairan's *Tales of Chivalrous and Altruistic Heroes*; and Olivia Mok's research and translations of sections of *Fox Volant of the Snowy Mountain*, a Louis Cha's novel of 1959. In the latter, Mok extricates references to *dianxue*—the methods of attacking vital points.

We also have fiction focusing on Japanese and Chinese martial traditions by John Donohue, Peter Graebner, John DeRose, and John Gilbey's (aka, Robert W. Smith)—each highlighting combative experience, theory and technique with cultural trimmings. Interviews with Barry Eisler and Author Rosenfeld give insight into scholar/practitioners whose published novels contain text colored by their knowledge of the martial arts and culture.

We hope you'll find this book captivating, exciting, heroic, spellbinding, content rich, fascinating, penetrating . . .

Michael A. DeMarco, Publisher
Santa Fe, New Mexico, August 2016

chapter 1

Fist of Fantasy: Martial Arts & Prose Fiction ~ A Practitioner's Prejudices

by James Grady, B.A.

Adam Hall
David Hunt
Charles Johnson
Jay McInerney
Peter O'Donnell

"Literature's only excuses [are] exploring the questions of innocence and experience, good and evil."
– Stephen King (1999)

"Action is character."
– F. Scott Fitzgerald (Bruccolli, 1978)

Photo by Akiko O. Dykhuizen.

Our lives breathe fiction. Stories tell us how we lived and how to live, then let us escape life's daily grind. Stories shape our psyches as dreams or fantasies for Freud and Jung to quarrel over like critics at a Soho art gallery. The stories/lies we tell are our armor as Tracy Chapman sings: "There is fiction in the space between you and me ... fiction in the space between you and reality."[1] Sages from Joseph Campbell to Bruce Springsteen record how myths/stories drive cultures and consciousness.[2]

Stories—fictions—pack potent punches for martial artists.

Most martial artists, certainly most Americans, first learn about martial arts through fictional mediums.[3] While most of such contemporary educational initiation comes through motion pictures and television, many living American martial artists had their first exposure to systematic Asian combat systems through literature like Ian Fleming's 1959 novel, *Goldfinger*. Until tale-tellers jack in to some cyber/holographic creative medium *a la The Matrix* or late 20th Century cyberpunk novels[4] to develop fictional experiences directly from their cerebrum, written tales, be they screen plays (the architectural blueprints for the film medium's creative teams), poems, short stories, or novels, will constitute the basis of fiction.

Additionally, much of how we learn and train as martial artists comes from fictional construction. The activities we engage in with titles like karate, gongfu, and aikido are predicated learning systems set against the hypothetical story of battling an attacker. Indeed, the kata, poomse, and forms we use in training are dramatizations of such encounters. Whether it is the Yang style taiji form or taekwondo's Kwang Gae, we act out our responses to an imagined foe, and spend years training in this fictional construction to hone our spirits, minds, and bodies for an ambush of such reality.

Perhaps our koan is: *To survive the truth, master a lie.*

Exploring the nexus between martial arts and prose fiction requires a disclosure. As I confessed in a previous *Journal of Asian Martial Arts* (JAMA) (1998) essay on martial arts and movies, for a working author to critique others' prose efforts veers close to a conflict of interest; for a feeble student of martial arts to pontificate about them borders on the absurd. These are truths I admit again, and still have the gall to proceed.

Our nexus of martial arts and fiction shimmers with both process and product.

Writing fiction feels like Western boxing's sparring, karate's kumite, judo's randori, taiji's pushing-hands: a dance of co-operation and opposition with a muse whose face is much like yours; where your next move is not so much "thought out" as it is "sensed" or "intuited"; where years spent learning, practicing, and experiencing the success and failure of skills like paragraphing and verb-noun configuration come together in a reaction that dictates a keystroke on a computer screen or pen scratch on a virgin page. Just as sensei and sifu caution their well-trained students about "over-thinking" a fight, I argue that for a writer, too much building-block linear thought inhibits fruitful reaction to a fictional moment, just as too little concept of literary strategy and consciousness creates a second-rate sentence.

Time and place fall away when you are at your best in sparring. You become one with your opponent, engage in a violent dance akin to lovemaking. The more you release/focus into "there," the "better" you will do and that "there" will become. Zen mind, no-mind, *wu wei*: these are not esoteric terms, they are physical/spiritual/mental realities martial artists approach in our best moments even as some other person in the "there" attempts to slam his non-esoteric fist into our forehead.

Writers like ball players talk of being in the zone, of slipping into an altered state of reality where "it" just happens, and what results is their best fiction. Just as Yang Chengfu might spontaneously burst into laughter while holding a taiji posture,[5] writers can be overwhelmed by emotions they experience because of the "there" they create out of ether. Tears rain on keyboards. When you are there, kicks and punches blasting in, a push attacking your slamming heart, electricity crackling up your spine, your whole being flowing with the moment, zero borders between you and the "there," ask: "Are you writing or fighting?" and the answer is: "Yes."

Perhaps the preceding paragraph makes you feel like you've been sucked into insanity. Possibly that's true, but probably that journey is necessary to understand the process of fiction writing. Not coincidentally, whether it's a 49-year-old man whispering to a ten-year-old boy as they agonize through an eight-hour taekwondo black-belt exam, or an otherwise practical woman trembling as she sinks all her weight through one screaming leg for a Squatting Single Whip taiji posture in a windowless concrete basement classroom that's vibrating from the blaring speakers in the rock-n-roll CD store upstairs, martial arts students routinely doubt their own sanity: "We gotta be crazy to do this."

Art is rebellion against pure sanity.

That wink of light on the process of fiction writing leaves us back alone in the darkness if we do not consider the product of the process: the fictions themselves.

Fiction loves martial arts, at least, in theory.

Fiction is drama, the blood of drama is conflict, and martial arts are rooted in conflict. Add to that Fitzgerald's observation about action defining character, and fiction's attraction to martial arts screams louder than any kiai.

However, as martial arts prove daily, theory and reality are two different things.

Fictionally writing about martial arts is a challenge where failure creates the deadliest criticism a writer can hear: "Boring!"

"John clobbered Paul." Who cares? And really, who cares much how John did it? Written on the page as opposed to depicted on the silver screen, martial actions are flat and uninteresting unless they occur in a context that the reader cares about and involves characters he likes in a setting that has aroused his curiosity or concern. Making a reader care about the overall story doesn't mean finding a tonnage of words to describe a razzle-dazzle combat technique that might (or might not) succeed in a Detroit alley. In fact, the more time spent on such details, the greater the danger that the reader's attention will drift off the whole of the story, thus diluting the work's *raison d'etre* and power, and glazing the reader's eyes. Consider our three-word tale: "John clobbered Paul." Does it make the story more interesting to say: "John back kicked Paul"? Perhaps a little. However, compare those two stories with: "Mary clobbered Paul." The drama of story number three hooks more readers more deeply than either of the other two, and the "hooking" element is not the depiction of martial acrobatics, but an enhancement of the classic elements of fiction.

Fiction works because of magic beyond the sum of its parts. An over emphasis on any one part dilutes that magic. That's one reason why "male adventure novels" or "blood and guts" bombasts barely climb to the popcorn level on the literary food chain. Most of them are just-for-the-money charades written with junior high locker room smugness, shotgunned with clichés, choked with overly technical description of semi-possible action, crippled by a lack of any profound ethical stance, poorly plotted with cardboard characters, and implanted with a heart that is absurd.[6]

All of which leads to a central premise: The concept of a "martial arts story" is doomed at birth. Considering whether or not such an effort is "good" is like searching for phrases to praise a corpse. Dead is dead.

Which leaves us with the concept of good fiction that uses martial arts well. Luckily, such fiction exists.

Critiquing fiction to find examples for our concern is an overwhelming task. There are too many books and stories to consider. Moreover, criticism is in large part a question of taste: what I find worthy may horrify you.

Following wiser minds than mine, my "critical criteria" for praising stories using martial arts avoided "getting stuck in structural analysis,"[7] and strove to keep in mind Henry James's dictum: "Be one on whom nothing is lost."[8] I sought stories and writers who caught the magic that makes good fiction—and who portrayed martial arts within that magic. For martial arts, I stuck to the Asian systems that are the focus of JAMA, though there are wonderful fictions involving Western boxing. I avoided stories propelled by weapons or empowered by surr/supra/magic realism (thus *a priori* eliminating some fine novels like Carolyn See's *Golden Days*, 1987), and sought only work worthy of praise: savaging anyone's efforts from the safety of the critic's seat is too easy and gains JAMA readers nothing.

What I offer is a fist of fiction, five writers and their works worthy of your time to read.

Fiction abounds with cartoon characters proclaimed to be "the world's greatest martial artist" or "the deadliest man alive." Such absurd hyperbole too often sets the tone for the rest of the story, and thus dooms the tale from word one. Consider the realities of luck, timing, and circumstance that shape every combative encounter. A heavyweight hero with stellar black-belt rankings in a dozen martial arts (who somehow is still vibrantly young despite the expenditure of time necessary to have attained all that education) only has the fighting ability of a seven-year-old if he's in the fevered grip of Hong Kong flu. Even on his best day, a banana peel or a sucker punch from a little old lady can flatten our stellar fighter.

Centering fiction on "the best" character means the drama of his encounters with other characters is nonexistent. If he is "the best," then he cannot lose in any encounter, and therefore no drama exists. At most, his adventures portray as mayhem manuals, a prose creation that probably only satisfies the Marquis de Sade.

That leaves our fictional superstar with only two possible dramas: the existential battle against (or for) himself, or the surprise opponent who will "best the best." The existential battle exists for all characters in good fiction, but is especially true in warrior fiction, where the character must convince himself (and thus the reader) that risking one's life in painful encounters is somehow better than staying home with a sweetheart and/or a cold six pack and a warm TV. The surprise opponent plot runs the risk of begging the question, of merely creating a successor to "the best" and thus leaving us in the same old dull swamp of superlatives.

But fiction loves irony, and our irony is that one of the five fingers of our martial arts and fiction fist involves the cartoonish character of "the greatest martial artist alive" opposing a heroic creation brought to life not only in novels, but also in movies, TV shows, and newspaper strip cartoons. While the magic for this work comes in part from its creator's fertile imagination and solid talent, fantastic though this story and character are, its real power comes from its inspiration of experienced truth.[9]

Peter O'Donnell

Northern Persia (Iran) near the Caucasus in 1942 was a blood-soaked geography. A young British Army sergeant named Peter O'Donnell commanded a mobile radio detachment battling the Third Reich's death-head minions for the oil fields. As they had for thousands of years in hundreds of wars, shattered refugees staggered through that wasteland. O'Donnell's unit camped by a stream. As the soldiers cooked their evening stew, the young sergeant looked up.

A lone barefoot girl of about twelve appeared nearby wearing a rag of a dress, all her belongings wrapped in a blanket she balanced on her head. From a thong around her neck dangled a piece of wood, lashed to it with a wire was a long nail. This was her weapon, her existential statement to the world that she would not accept victimhood.

"She had been on her own for some time, because she wasn't phased, she was her own person, this little kid," remembers O'Donnell. He had one of his men take a mess tin of stew and a mug of tea to her. As she ate, O'Donnell put tins of food with a can opener near her so she could get them without coming too close to the foreign male soldiers. She spoke in a language none of the

Brits understood, though they knew it wasn't Arabic. She washed the utensils in the stream and brought them back to the tins of food. Her gestures asked if the supplies were for her. After the Brits nodded yes, she put the food in her bundle.

"She stood there for a few seconds," says O'Donnell, "then she gave us a smile [that] could have lit up a small village.... She said something and walked off into the desert going south.... She was on her own [but] she walked like a little princess."

Gone. Vanished into the chaos of war and history. But seared into O'Donnell's heart.

Twenty years later, as "Bond, James Bond" heroes swelled through entertainment fiction, writer O'Donnell "thought it was about time someone came up with a female who could do all the things the males had been doing. But for me she had to be plausible, so I had to give her the kind of background that would make her plausible."

With plausibility in mind and the gutsy refugee girl scarred on his heart, O'Donnell created Modesty Blaise.

In the fad and product tie-in driven entertainment blitz of our 21st Century, it's difficult to recognize how "big" Modesty Blaise was in the last third of the 20th Century. O'Donnell's creation lived in a dozen internationally successful books, a movie, a TV series, and a London newspaper cartoon strip. Now forty years after her creation, she has fan-driven Web sites. Though "politically correct" and refined cultural mavens will not give her this due, Modesty represents a feminist literary milestone: never before had a series female protagonist received such global acceptance for living a fictional violently adventurous life in which gender was merely a facet of her existence. Modesty bested competent men on the fictive battlefields males had ruled since Adam and Eve fled the snake-poisoned garden. And she did so with brains, athleticism, courage, honor—all without losing her heterosexual femininity. She had a male who was her best friend and lieutenant, not her lover or boss. Though vulnerable (a rape survivor), she was victorious.

O'Donnell made her a refugee child/reformed thief, a rogue who stumbles onto the side of the angels largely through alliances with British intelligence. While his novels usually pit her against bizarre villains in outlandish plots (thus avoiding formulaic Cold War confrontations prevalent in that era) and utilize a now-dated British prose cadence/style, Modesty's stories are powered by that strain of "plausible" action and vibrant character.

Extensive research helped O'Donnell shape Modesty, whether it's the thirty years of *National Geographic* magazines in his office bookcase or consultations with the British Amateur Fencing Association, or his work in creating her martial arts skills.[10]

During a trip to Haifa, Israel, in 1962, when he was developing Modesty, the now-eighty-years-old O'Donnell told JAMA he stumbled across a paperback edition of *Zen Combat* by Jay Gluck (New York: Ballantine Books, 1962). Subtitled "A Complete Guide to the Oriental Arts of Attack and Defense— Karate, Kendo, Zen Archery, Aiki," the book also discusses Chinese kenpo, judo, bushido, fire walking, ki, and weapons—especially the *kongo*, a six-inch long dumbbell shaped weapon favored by Modesty, who also studied numerous unarmed combat styles.

"I've had no martial arts training [other than his WWII army schooling]," says O'Donnell, "but have quite often watched workouts in the dojo. A girl called Christine Child, who was British judo champion and also a film stunt girl, wrote to me as a fan, and later introduced me to Brian Jacks, British middleweight champion. My greatest need was to have shots of combat moves that I could send to Romero [artist/illustrator for O'Donnell]. Christine and Brian put on an hour-long performance in the dojo for me, and I had a photographer who took scores of pix. Apart from this, my research has been in books and magazines such as *Combat*—the latter mainly for further pix...."

O'Donnell's talent and imagination bow in at top form in *The Silver Mistress* (1965), the second Modesty Blaise book and the one most germane to this essay. To rescue her kidnapped friend and mentor Tarrant, the head of the British Secret Service, Modesty must face Sexton, the self-proclaimed world's greatest martial artist, our cartoon character if ever one existed. Except O'Donnell brings Sexton to life—and has Modesty use the very cartoonesque nature of Sexton's character to defeat him.

Illustration by Enrique Romero
from *The Silver Mistress*.

Escaping from captivity, Modesty and Tarrant flee pursuing villains through an underground cavern. She pauses, strips, and hands him a can of scavenged machine oil:

> She stood up naked, holding her shirt and wrapping it about both her hands, then said sharply, "Grease me. I can't do it myself. I've got to keep my hands dry. Grease me all over. Hurry."

Tarrant complies. In the half-light of the cavern, the grease gives Modesty a silver sheen (hence the title). Sexton had given the captives a martial arts demonstration in his gym to intimidate them, but all the while, Modesty was thinking. As she sets her ambush in the rocky cavern, she tells Tarrant: "This isn't a surface for fancy kicks and chops, so he'll want to get hold of me, and I need an edge there."

Her Sherlock Holmes analysis of Sexton's character have given her another slim but credible edge. She uses that edge to set-up Sexton and, in the ensuing one-on-one unarmed challenge combat, she kills him. Modesty tells Tarrant:

> "He was the best I've ever seen. I could never have taken him on his own ground."
>
> "On his own ground," Tarrant repeated slowly. She was no doubt right about that. But the ground and the situation were all part of the battle, any battle. A point Sexton had missed and she had not.

And that's a point hundreds of authors miss with their "greatest martial artist" creations.

Women in fiction have been empowered by martial arts just as have been women in life. Modesty Blaise has fictional sisters who share her martial arts study, some dating back to Chinese legends of the woman warrior *Mulan* (whether in the Disney movie of the same name or as revised in Maxine Hong Kingston's *The Woman Warrior* [1976]). But the degree to which martial arts figures in those stories tends to be minimal, whether the characters are serial figures in several books or not. For example, notch-below-black-belt-herself, author S.J. Rozan's well-written fictional private eye character Lydia Chen has a taekwondo black belt, but is more inclined to fill her hand with a pistol than a fist, and her martial arts background is more important as a cultural/family issue than a character point (Lydia's girlhood New York City neighborhood gongfu school wouldn't take females as students, even Chinese girls like her).

David Hunt

Using martial arts to develop a character and doing so over multiple books is a technique exemplified by author David Hunt (a pseudonym for William Bayer) in his two Kay Farrow novels. Unlike Modesty Blaise or numerous other fictional martial artists male and female, Kay's life and profession are not geared toward confrontation: she's a photographer—not portraits, commercial work, or journalism, but art. That core of work defines her life, making her more a recording witness than an activist. Her stories reflect how she is drawn into adventure and confrontation as much as what happens when she gets there. Kay is also defined by a medical condition startling for a photographer: she's an achromat—completely color blind, and suffers from photophobia (an aversion to bright light). From the moment she opens her eyes, her world is radically different from the rest of us, a perceptive reality that is reflected in her photographs, her attitudes, her adventures.

Hunt writes in what *Publisher's Weekly* called "a vibrant, melancholy narrative voice" and that *The New York Times* says creates an ambiance for the reader that's "strange, seductive ... as eerie as a midnight walk in the fog." Hunt also chose to define Kay by making her an aikido student, emphasis on "student."[11]

"I felt that it was important that Kay's aikido skills not be a constant," Hunt told JAMA, "rather that she should develop them through the two books. In other words, I didn't want her to just be an aikidoist who goes to class, but a person training to improve and working toward the black belt exam. This required a lot of commitment on her part, and reflected the kind of self discipline and striving that was essential to her character."

And that choice by the author is a key to the quality of Hunt's work: his character's aikido is not just an add-on or an empowering device, not just a party trick for our heroine, but is instead an integral, integrated, and living part of her being. Using martial arts in that fashion reflects its best use in real life, and makes for better fiction.

Hunt has no martial arts training, yet his authorial vision compelled him to do more than choose a combative art at random.

"I decided to make Kay an aikidoist after reading a book, *Women in Aikido*, by Andrea Siegel [North Atlantic Books, 1993]," says Hunt. "It just seemed the 'right' martial art for the character. I was especially intrigued by the concept of blending as opposed to punching or kicking.... Since Kay is very petite, 106 lbs., but feisty and puts herself in dangerous situations photographing the hustler scene at night, I wanted her to have defensive skills.... She is gentle and vulnerable and also doesn't take any shit. All this worked well with a character seriously committed to aikido training. I also enjoyed creating the character of her sensei (Rita), a black woman, a former kick-ass Marine, not one of those metaphysical Northern California Zen-utterance sensei types, but a real direct type person who likes Kay a lot and with whom Kay identifies."

Hunt attended classes by Robert Nadeau Sensei in San Francisco, and classes on Martha's Vineyard.

"And then," says Hunt, "to get the black belt exam right, I attended an aikido summer retreat at Colgate College."

Many non-practicing martial arts writers would have stopped their research after reading one book and perhaps watching a few Bruce Lee or Steven Seagal movies. But not Hunt, and his extra effort shows. His thoughtful approach to blending martial arts into Kay Farrow flowers in the second novel, *Trick of Light* (1998), a story whose through-line is an intertwining of her personal crises, the plot's driving evil force, and Kay's final preparations for her black-belt exam. After Kay's horrible experiences, that exam blossoms to end the book:

> Everything feels "right" this afternoon. I have found my center. I own the place where I stand, and a good-sized area around me. Rita has counseled me many times: "When you step onto the mat, take possession, make it your own."

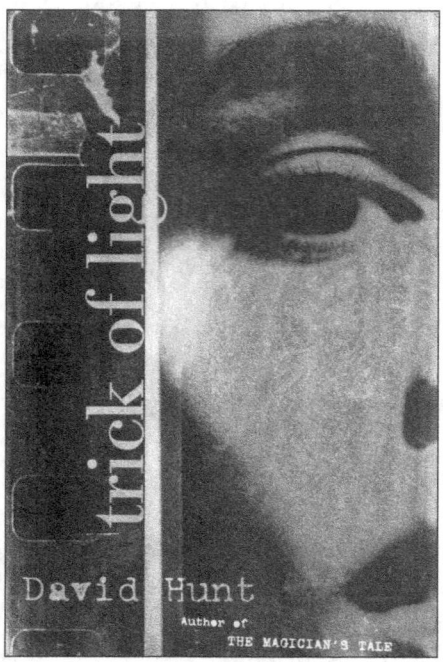

Book cover of *Trick of Light*.

Kay comes to the multiple-attacker portion of her test:

> I stand ready to take them on, claiming my space, drilling my legs down into the mat, preparing to blend. And then, just as they come at me, I enter a trance state. Even the bright sunlight that floods the field house doesn't distract or blind me now.
>
> I don't think about anything, don't calculate, don't prepare, simply take them on as they come ... I float.... No gesture is wasted....
>
> I am at the center of a whirlpool of energy, aware of everything around me yet fazed by nothing. Time is warped. Actions that appear to others as sudden are for me orderly and slow.... I am at the center of it all, she-who-harmonizes, she-who-is-the music, blending effortlessly, cleanly, in tune with the cosmic process, every breath clearly drawn, every move structured as in a dance.

The exam serves as an epiphany for Kay:

> I did it, and now I have regained my life. My time of mourning and anger is over. Once again my life belongs wholly to me.

What more could any character expect?

Adam Hall

The "serial" approach to literature—the same character appearing in successive novels—leads us to our third author/example, another pseudonym: Adam Hall, one of nine pen names used by the amazingly prolific British writer Elleston Trevor, slain by cancer in 1995.[12]

The British-born and educated Hall pictured himself as a writer from age five. A dropout from sadistic British schools, Hall wanted to be a Spitfire pilot in World War II, but vision problems made him only a Royal Air Force (RAF) mechanic. He began seriously writing at nineteen, while still battling the Nazis. One of his best-known "Trevor" works is the book adapted to a movie of the same name, *The Flight of the Phoenix*, but what we praise here is Adam Hall's decades-long book series about a British spy named Quiller.

Adam Hall in a Shotokan style X-block.

Photo by Ted Hill.

Influenced in part by John Le Carre (pseudonym for British writer David Cornwell), in 1965, Hall published *The Quiller Memorandum*, the story of a British agent—"shadow executive"—employed by a heartless covert government organization called The Bureau, a bureaucracy with its own language, mores, and arrogance of mission, the classic never-admitted-to-exist secret agency that populated both the fiction and fact of the Cold War.[13] Quiller is a paradox, an organization man who operates as a lone wolf, a falcon launched into one crises after another, a man who thinks in terms of nerve synapses and tactical esoterica, a troubleshooter who refuses to carry a gun, because guns create a false sense of confidence. Better, thinks Quiller, to rely on instincts, intelligence—and unarmed combat skills.

Yet when Hall began writing the Quiller series, his only martial arts training was whatever rough-trade tricks he'd learned in the RAF.

"The early books, when they mentioned any kind of karate, were cheats," said Hall in 1982.[14]

He invented Asian sounding terms for techniques and action segments and wrote best sellers. *The Quiller Memorandum* became a George Segal, Alec Guinness, Max Von Sydow movie written by Harold Pinter that disappointed Hall, but did not deter him from continuing the series. Nor did a short-lived BBC TV series.

Hall was a fanatic for accuracy and research: he wrote the Hong Kong police to get a copy of a parking ticket so the few words he'd use to describe it would not be false. That drive for precision, plus a lifetime of adventure (race car driving, among other pursuits), led him, to begin studying martial arts at age fifty-eight, an educational journey so profound that when a reporter asked him to list the most important events that had a lasting effect on his life, besides moving from one country to another (Britain, Spain, France, and finally to the United States), Hall mentioned only studying karate.[15]

A longtime student of yoga, Hall's first formal martial arts training was in "Chinese kenpo" (*quanfa*), but then scheduling conflicts led him to JKA Shotokan karate, an art he practiced with his son, Jean-Pierre Trevor. In 1984, at age sixty-four, Hall received a black belt under Koyama Shojiro in Arizona. Hall dedicated a Quiller novel to his sensei, and once noted that "karate fines down the environment to this one, personal attack on one's own limitations.... I know myself better. I know other people better. There's nothing quite like karate to reveal character."[16]

Evolution in Hall's personal life and martial arts study reflected in Quiller. Like many classic serial heroes, on one level Quiller never changed, never aged from the veteran operative in his 1965 debut through the seventeen books that ended in 1995 with a novel finished three days before Hall's death. On other levels, Quiller grew. He became more compassionate, and his cynicism adopted a modest world-embracing rather than condescending world-weary view. And martial arts became a deeper, more realistic force in Quiller's life. His battle scenes and tactics were not pure Shotokan, but as Hall progressed in his own studies, the fictions began to feel more real.

One of the central ironies of the Quiller *oeuvre* is Hall's prose style. Most so-called "action/espionage/thriller genre" novels are written in straight-ahead, traditional linear prose. Hall defied such popular stylistic simplicity. At times the Quiller books spew out in a maddening, almost James Joycean first person stream-of-consciousness machinegun prose, with run-on sentences shotgunned by undefined terms. Chapters and scenes often begin with the aftereffects of the action that defines the plot, and then unfold on a serpentine time line that forces the reader to pay strict attention—and propels him deeper into the book. A lesser writer couldn't ape Hall's style; most who tried would inspire readers to hunt them down and beat them to their knees with the book. But Hall was not a lesser writer. A winner of a Mystery Writers of America Edgar Award and the French Grand Prix de Litterature Policiere, his powerful talent of adrenalized style, character and ethic caught the magic that is great prose, attracting legions of fans who cherish his work beyond the author's mortal time.

For sheer totality of elegance, my personal Quiller favorite is 1994's morally complex, vividly written *Quiller Salamander*. However, to illustrate Hall's use of martial arts, consider this opening segment of *The Warsaw Document* (1971):

There would be no warning, I knew that.

In the total darkness I thought I could see things: the glint of his eyes, his bared teeth; and in the silence I thought I could hear his breath and the soft tentative padding of his feet as he looked for me, but all I saw and heard was in my imagination and I knew that soon my nerves were going to start playing up because of the worry; the worry that there'd be no warning when he came at me. He'd come the instant he found me.

Breathing was difficult because this place wasn't very big and we were so close that one drawn breath would be a giveaway; also, it would have to be expelled before the next inhalation and I was afraid of being caught with empty lungs. I breathed tidally, right near the top, part of my conscious mind registering the smell of hemp and coconut.

It was worse than I'd thought, the waiting. There was nothing to go on: no means of orientation. He was only a man but he was invisible and inaudible and these were the attributes of a phantom and my scalp was raised. It needn't be true that he was where I thought he was: somewhere in front of me where my hands could get at him. Even in the dark there's comfort if an enemy can be faced: the real dread is of being taken from behind.

That was where he came for me: from behind. We hadn't touched; we had simply come so close that the instincts were triggered and the nerves galvanized and I was already in a throat lock with my knees buckling to a flat kick before I could hook at him, but my hands were free and I caught him and reached his thumb as we pitched down, breaking the hold while he used his foot again and missed and tried again and connected a fraction too late, his breath grunting as I forced him over. We fought close, neither wanting to lose the other in the unnerving dark. My shoulder hit the wall and I used the chance, going down low and recoiling against him, but the momentum wasn't enough, and he deadened the spring and forced me into a spine-bending *yoshida* that paralyzed the arms. Then some fool came in and switched the light on.

Jay McInerney

Radical prose style, controversial subject matter, and discipline learned from martial arts propelled our fourth author into prominence. Jay McInerney debuted in 1984 with a huge commercial and cultural hit novel. *Bright Lights, Big City*, a stream of consciousness saga/satire about oh-so-cool, self-absorbed young Manhattan hipsters who turbo charge their lives snorting lines of cocaine as they taxi down neon streets they call success. Written in a frenzied, immediate second person style—"You are not the kind of guy who would be at a place like this at this time of the morning. But here you are, and you cannot say that the terrain is entirely unfamiliar, although the details are fuzzy...." The book chronicled a time and place before basketball star Len Bias's overdose death alerted sixties-jaded America that cocaine—as writer George Pelecanos (2000) puts it—"was the drug that always drove the car and never gave up the keys."[17]

But *Bright Lights* was not McInerney's first attempt at fiction, nor is it either his work of focus here or, in my view, his best book of that era in his career. That credit belongs to his novel, *Ransom* (1985).

"I lived in Japan from 1977 to 1979," McInerney told JAMA.[18] "I started writing a novel about Japan when I returned to the States and worked on it for two years in grad school studying creative writing and English at Syracuse University. Whether or not it was *Ransom*, I'm not sure—but parts of it survived. Finally, out of frustration at my inability to make a novel about Japan, I turned to more recent experience and wrote *Bright Lights* ... quickly; it was done in six months. Finally, while waiting for its publication, I returned to the idea of a Japan novel and started almost from scratch. *Ransom* is the result."

What a fine result. *Ransom*—"exactly the kind of book I expected to write all along.... *Bright Lights* came out of nowhere, in a way"—is an ex-pat novel in the tradition of Ernest Hemingway, a crime novel in the tradition of James Cain, and a martial arts novel in the tradition of... well, in the tradition of the other four writers in our fantasy fist.

While living in Japan, McInerney studied JKA Shotokan karate in Tokyo for six months, then Goju-ryu in Kyoto for a year and a half. Though that education was crucial to his novel, it is perhaps more important to McInerney realizing his life as an author: "I absolutely believe that it was the discipline of karate which got me disciplined about fiction. The lesson was very simple really—if I didn't practice every day, I lost ground. I finally realized writing fiction was as fierce a discipline as karate."

Reading *Ransom* feels like riding in a jetliner as it plummets towards earth, an odd kind of exhilaration and fascination in which you wonder whether your marvelous flying machine will pull up safe at the last moment.

The novel recounts the life of American ex-pat Christopher Ransom, who came to Asia to escape a domineering, manipulative father and "looking for freedom in the homeland of fatalism, looking for he didn't know what—but something more vital than the pallid choice of career."

His story begins and ends in Japan, but with a slipstream timeline that reveals Ransom's early days in Asia, a time zone of love and horror near the Khyber Pass in Pakistan, when he becomes mesmerized by fellow ex-pats Annette and Ian. The gravity of their narcissism sucks the troubled, questing Ransom into their intertwined orbits as he mistakes their hollow self-assurance for the kind of self-empowerment he craves. Convinced of their own supreme self-importance, Annette and Ian graciously allow Ransom to pledge them his soul and survival, a classic act of a passionate young man who's pure of heart but fogged of mind. Such characters in such a place face an inevitability that McInerney builds with exacting, keenly spaced suspense.

With those scars etched on his already-battered heart and suffering from "Asia burn," the novel begins as Ransom opens his eyes after having been knocked out sparring in his karate class, which meets outdoors on an asphalt courtyard. His sensei tells him he was dropped by a reverse roundhouse kick from Ito, "the monk," the sublime karateka who Ransom yearns to equal.

Upon arriving in Japan, Ransom by chance happened upon the class:

> Every night for a week Ransom watched them practice. He had not noticed the fighting so much as the grace of movement…. They conveyed an extraordinary sense of self-possession. For months Ransom had drifted across landscapes in a fevered daze, oblivious to almost everything but his own pain and guilt. The dojo with its strange incantations and white uniforms seemed to him a sacramental place, an intersection of body and spirit, where power and danger were ritualized in such a way that a man could learn to understand them. Ransom had lost his bearings spiritually, and he wanted to reclaim himself.
>
> His first lessons are in bowing and sweeping the courtyard.
>
> The school was Goju-ryu: "hard-soft," based on a notion of alternating tension and relaxation, systole and diastole. The style combined the hard Okinawan techniques with the more flexible Chinese Kenpo.

Ransom's school and his self-effacing attempts to find his center make him a target for Frank DeVito, an ex-Marine bully, "current Bruce Lee clone," who studies with a teacher known for his brutality and thuggish movies he made starring himself. DeVito is another narcissist, a martial arts practitioner who's drawn half the circle. He realizes that training to fight and face death conveys a type of freedom, but fails to grasp that the point of freedom is to celebrate life.

DeVito worships the glorious power of death, receiving it is ultimately unimaginable for him, but delivering it to someone else is his obsession.

And looming in his eyes is Ransom, a quiet, refusing-to-engage/fight fellow American who studies with a sensei who thinks the grand award of a black belt is of little importance.

Conflict within conflict, crisis within crisis, Ransom moves through his fate.

McInerney takes us on that journey with karate/martial arts as our pilot. The novel is filled with a score of fight scenes, in fact, far more than most "blood and guts" prose atrocities or quality "genre thrillers." He writes such action moments in flat, factual, non-dramatic language, and therefore conveys them with engaging, empathetic accuracy:

> Now it was Ransom's turn [to spar]...fixing his eyes on the Monk's, holding the gaze through the bow. The Monk settled back, way down in cat stance, all of his weight back on the rear leg, folded nearly double, while the lead foot barely touched the pavement. He made an L with his forearms in front of his chest, the left vertical, the right horizontal. It seemed to Ransom that Ito's eyes were like pools in which no fish were showing; he would have to throw out some bait. He kicked. The Monk swept the kick away with his forearm. Ransom threw another kick, two jabs, and got knocked sideways by a kick in the ribs.
>
> His breath was short and there was a dull pain in his ribs. The sensei told him to straighten up and fight. The ache in his ribs was either going to slow him down or serve as his weapon. He straightened up, then lowered himself into a crouch facing the Monk. When he inhaled, he drew the ache into a fine, hot wire extending from his side up into his right arm. He aimed it at the Monk's chest. When the Monk came at him he drove it home, feeling the impact of his knuckles against the Monk's sternum travel back to its point of origin in his ribs. The pain dissipated and then it was gone, as if it had traveled from his own body into the Monk's.
>
> The sensei called the point, the first time Ransom had ever scored on the Monk. He was trying to remember how he had done it as they squared off, when the Monk kicked him in the chest for the match.

The kick in your chest from *Ransom* is worth it. The novel should be shelved with timeless period literature catalyzed by the Vietnam-to-Ronald-Reagan era, along with such gems as Kent Anderson's *Sympathy for the Devil* (1987), Joan Didion's *Play It as It Lays* (1970), Richard Farnia's *I've Been Down So Long It Looks Like Up to Me* (1966), Ken Kesey's *One Flew Over the Cuckoo's Nest* (1962), Greg McDonald's *Running Scared* (1964), Tim O'Brien's *The*

Things They Carried (1990), Richard Price's The Wanderers (1974), and Robert Stone's Dog Soldiers (1974). And for any martial artist searching for an entertaining way to explain this thing of ours to a friend, Ransom offers some good—and disturbing—insights to share.

Charles Johnson

Sharing our last writer with JAMA's readers is a privilege to relish. Charles Johnson is one of America's major writers, a serious martial artist, and a wonderful human being.

Consider the following true story. Former *Chicago Tribune* reporter Johnson rose through the ranks of American literature and academia to win the National Book Award for his work, *Middle Passage* (1990). If ever there was a justifiable moment for a writer to put modesty aside and bask in the spotlight as the audience and world cheered, that 1989 awards dinner night was it for Charles Johnson. But instead of self-congratulation, Johnson walked to the podium and delivered an awe-struck tribute to seventy-six-year-old writer Ralph Ellison, as that icon sat in the audience listening.

> "Like the day of my marriage, the days my children were born, and that night of my first martial-arts promotion," says Johnson, "I count the experience of reading that tribute [to Ellison] as one of the finest moments of my life."[19]

That first martial arts exam Johnson took was in the late 1960's came after he found a martial arts school in Chicago called Chi Tao Chuan of the Monastery. College boy Johnson had "long wanted to systematically study a fighting art, partly because what I'd seen of Japanese karate impressed me ... and partly because the Chicago area in the late 1960's was a pretty dangerous place for Blacks [like Johnson] and 'longhairs.'"

Johnson's sifu eventually steered him to the Tiger animal style of the school's version of gongfu. The training was arduous: "Often I wondered if I'd exit the studio alive."

And that promotion?

"I'm at a loss to explain how I felt," says Johnson, "at nineteen, as we received our membership cards and congratulations. The room was aglow.

Though tired in every cell, my body felt transparent; my mind, clear as spring water. I couldn't have cared less if I missed my train and spent all night roaming downtown Chicago—I just wanted someone to jump me—before the next train at 8:00 a.m. I count this as one of the best nights of my life, a rare kind of rite-of-passage that showed me, as a young man, something about my capacity for discipline, enduring pain, and pushing myself beyond my expectations."

Charles Johnson practicing with the staff.
Photo courtesy of C. Johnson.

Martial arts is a powerful influence on Johnson. In that Chicago *guan* (studio; sometimes written *kuan* or *kwoon*), he met the Buddhist path he now walks. And call him artist: besides writing and martial arts, MacArthur "genius award" winner Johnson is an accomplished visual artist who's worked in mediums ranging from pen and ink sketches to television's PBS.

For Johnson, the linkages between martial arts and writing are clear:[20] "I've always been intrigued by Yukio Mishima's devotion to *bunburyodo*, what he saw as the dual way of the martial and literary arts. I do think ... there is a connection, first and perhaps foremost in the sense of the discipline martial art practice demands—that discipline of total physical and mental engagement in the here and now serves well to strengthen the discipline any writer (or artist) must have. My friend [screenwriter and author] Steven Barnes ... begins his day with weights and martial arts practice before writing. I guess I do much the same, working out before I write (which is usually late evening and the wee hours of the morning) because after practice both mind and body are relaxed, clear, and I can approach the page with something like "beginner's mind," unconcerned about my performance the day before or even with past literary performances....

"When I was a young philosophy student, it occurred to me life was, of course, a whole, but one could speak of it as flowing in three streams that come together. The streams were Mind, Body and Spirit.... And one could—or should—develop each stream to its full (Aristotelian) potential. For the Mind's development I chose philosophy. For the Body's, martial arts. And for the Spirit, literary and visual arts (later I added Buddhism to this). To separate any of these is (to me) engaging in a kind of existential apartheid, for one stream feeds the other, and all together enrich human life."

Like many martial artists, Johnson's education was in part dictated by geography: the college he attended was far from any gongfu guan, so he took the available path and studied karate. He's currently rated as an instructor in Choy Li Fut (*Cai Li Fo*)—"I haven't had the time to become a sifu." His Seattle guan is called "Blue Phoenix," and also teaches both long and short form Yang Taiji, which Johnson also practices. Beyond his own writing, he holds a professorship for Excellence in English at the University of Washington.

But there is no need to go beyond Johnson's writing to appreciate his artistry. Consider two short stories (available in various collections), two fists of excellence that (in what I humbly think is the proper and best pattern of literary conception) "forced" themselves upon Johnson rather than being products of a purely intellectual literary decision.

Consider *Kwoon*, first published in 1991.

"One afternoon when I was working out at home," says Johnson, "right in the middle of a heavy sweat, the story's premise came to me—what if tomorrow a truly talented, devastating killer dropped into a martial arts school and beat the stuffings out of a good teacher in front of his students, and suppose that teacher is a good transmitter of his school's tradition, and not a bad fighter but simply not as good as [the visiting challenger]?"

Johnson wanted to examine what it means to be a teacher, what it means to be a student, what it means to be a person, and how life can force one to change. In that martial arts setting, with a traditional straight-ahead prose style, he succeeds admirably.[21]

Not to take anything from the wonderfulness of *Kwoon* or disparage Johnson's fist of any of its power, but Johnson's other fist is so electrifying it must be our focus.

Consider *China*, first published in 1980.

And consider it one of the finest short stories in American literature.

China began as an attempt by Johnson to get his mentor, the novelist John Gardner, who was "*very* Western, Protestant, etc.," to understand, to "see ... where [Johnson] lived" in regards to Buddhism and Eastern thought, a process triggered after Gardner read Johnson's novel *Oxherding Tale* (1982). Gardner and Johnson exchanged a series of letters until Johnson realized that Gardner "much preferred reading stories to reading arguments...."

This is how *China* came into being—a first draft in about twelve hours, which Gardner loved, even decided to add two [minor] sentences to, and which he published in his literary magazine.... I'd not planned on doing *China*.

The story *happened*. And happens for every reader:

Evelyn's problems with her husband, Rudolph, began one evening in early March—a dreary winter evening in Seattle—when he complained after a heavy meal of pig's feet and mashed potatoes of shortness of breath, an allergy to something she put in his food perhaps, or brought on by the first signs of wild flowers around them. She suggested they get out of the house for the evening, go to a movie. He was fifty-four, a postman for thirty-three years now, with high blood pressure, emphysema, flat feet, and, as Evelyn told her friend Shelberdine Lewis, the lingering fear that he had cancer. Getting old, he was also getting hard to live with. He told her never to salt his dinners, to keep their Lincoln Continental at a crawl, and never run her fingers along his inner thigh when they sat in Reverend William Merrill's church, because anything, even sex, or laughing too loud—Rudolph was serious—might bring on heart failure.

That opening paragraph serves as a textbook for fiction writers. The first sentence creates suspense—"problems ... began"; establishes specific time and place in a tactile fashion, "March ... dreary winter evening in Seattle" contrasted with "first signs of wild flowers"; creates and defines characters and sets them in opposition to each other; tantalizes the reader's all-important visceral senses of taste and smell with food and flowers; taps into readers' primal emotions, fear of aging and cancer, and does so with humor; contrasting the primal sexual sensation (again, shown tactually with a finger stroked along the inner thigh) of liberation with the stuffy inhibiting setting of restrictive church. The whipsawing of common images and outlandish truths—*sexual desire can truly lead to lethal heart attacks/do you want to give up all sexual possibilities/do you want to die*—exhilarates readers with tension but without them sensing an author's heavy hand. The scene is so intensely *ordinary*, so *common*, the reader immediately identifies with it and with both characters. Yet the suspense created by the second word sucks the reader into hungering to know what uncommon drama these characters will face. The portrayal of characters contains empathetic "mini" scenes: Evelyn commiserating with her friend Shelberdine and Rudolph and Evelyn "crawling" along in traffic in their Lincoln Continental (no doubt in the street ahead of you as you're late for work).

All that is accomplished without a wasted or superfluous word, like an aikido or taiji adept letting the eyes/push of a reader flow into the writer's space and then with a feather touch rocketing him out through the story. Try accomplishing that in twelve hours. Or twelve years. Thus is defined the word "artist."

Charles Johnson practicing an Eagle Claw technique.
Photos courtesy of C. Johnson.

Johnson blends the techniques of omniscient author and unreliable narrator to unfold his story. Poor Evelyn chooses "a peaceful movie for their Saturday night outing," a low-key satire that puts Rudolph to sleep.

Until the previews of coming attractions that feature ... some sort of gladiator movie, Evelyn thought ... pretty trashy stuff at that. The plot's revenge theme was a poor excuse for Chinese actors or Japanese (she couldn't tell those people apart) to flail the air with their hands and feet, take on fifty costumed extras at once, and leap twenty feet through the air in perfect defiance of gravity. Rudolph's mouth hung open.

When that movie comes to town, Rudolph sneaks off to see it, stays for the martial arts demonstration afterwards, then races home to a frantic, worried wife.

"Wonderful." Evelyn screwed up her lips. "I'm calling hospitals and you're at a Hong Kong double feature."

"Listen," said Rudolph. "You don't understand." He seemed at that moment as if he did not understand either.

Rudolph horrifies her when he announces he has signed up for martial arts lessons.

> "You're fifty-four years old, Rudolph."
> "I know that."
> "You're no Muhammad Ali."
> "I know that," he said.
> "You're no Bruce Lee. Do you want to be Bruce Lee? Do you know where he is now, Rudolph? He's dead—dead here in a Seattle cemetery and buried up on Capital Hill."

But Rudolph has moved beyond thoughts of the cemetery to thoughts of life, visions of what he can do, what he might do. He is a character choosing change and transformation, a character seeking to define—redefine—himself. Such is the essence of drama.

Drama it is, especially for poor Evelyn, through whose horrified eyes we witness the transformation, as her Rudolph who can't do a push-up spends their money for equipment and lessons in an activity that for her is as comprehensible as Martian opera. Her friend Shelberdine comforts Evelyn with the wisdom that Rudolph's obsession is merely a mid-life crisis. But Evelyn senses:

> .... a dark vision ... a dangerous vision, and in it she whiffed something that might destroy her. What that was, she couldn't say, but she knew her Rudolph better than he knew himself. He would see the error—the waste of time—in his new hobby, and she was sure he would mend his ways.
>
> In the weeks, then months that followed, Evelyn waited, watching her husband for a flag of surrender. There was no such sign. He became worse than before.

That "worse" of course is irony: he improves his diet, his health, his mind, even his soul and spirit through mediation and study. What one person does affects all others: a choice of change by Rudolph forces that unsettling process on his wife, who reacts to it by targeting the agent of change, Rudolph, rather than facing herself. She insists that he return to "being himself."

> "I can only be what I've been?" This he asked softly, but his voice trembled.... "I only want to be what I can be, which isn't the greatest fighter in the world, only the fighter I can be...."

Reviewers and critics always face an ethical and practical dilemma. The best goal of critical reviewing is to lead people to fiction they will read, challenge and absorb into their own lives. Doing that usually means obeying the obvious marketing rule: Don't give away the ending, dummy! But this is not a usual author/story by any measure, nor would this conversation do the author/story justice to package an analysis of *China* with a cliffhanger synopsis. While the goal here is to seduce every one of you to rush to acquire a copy of Johnson's story so you can experience the whole process of his enlightening prose, teasing you by following the obvious marketing rule undercuts the worth of that story and this article's heart: the examination of the nexus between martial arts and prose fiction. The conclusion of *China* at the Saturday tournament in Seattle's Kingdome where a frantic, panicked, yet dutifully loving Evelyn watches her husband spar in the far ring represents the apogee of that nexus:

> Yet it was not truly him that Evelyn, sitting down, saw.... She caught her breath when, miscalculating his distance from his opponent, her husband stepped sideways into a roundhouse kick with lots of snap—she heard the cloth of his opponent's gi crack like a gunshot when he threw the technique. She leaned forward, gripping the huge purse on her lap when Rudolph recovered and retreated from the killing to the neutral zone, and then, in a wide stance, rethought strategy. This was not the man she'd slept with for twenty years.... She did not know him, perhaps had never known him, and she never would, for the man on the floor, the man splashed with sweat, rising on the ball of his rear foot for a flying kick—was he so foolish he still thought he could fly?—would outlive her.... And then Evelyn was on her feet, unsure why, but the crowd had stood suddenly to clap, and Evelyn clapped, too, though for an instant she pounded her gloved hands together instinctively until her vision cleared, the momentary flash of retinal blindness giving way to a frame of her husband, the postman, twenty feet off the ground in a perfect flying kick that floored his opponent and made a Japanese judge who looked like Oddjob shout "ippon"—one point—and the fighting in the farthest ring, in herself, perhaps in all the world, was over.

What better apogee, what better climax could we reach?

Endnotes

Beyond specific citation, the following individuals contributed greatly to this effort and deserve special thanks and recognition: Warren D. Conner, Michael Dirda, Bonnie Goldstein, Nathan Grady, Kent Hedlundh, Jeff Herrod, Larry Hicks, Chris Holmes, John Holloway, Sidner Larson, Otto Penzler, Jon Peralez, Carolyn See, Lisa See, Robert Smith, Nat Sobel, Joseph Svinth, Georgi "Yegor" Tolstiakov, Chaille Trevor, Jean-Pierre Trevor, Helen Tworkov, Amanda Urban.

[1] Tracy Chapman, from the CD, *Telling Stories*, Electra Entertainment Group/Time Warner, 2000 (Purple Rabbit Music-ASCAP), lyrics from "Telling Stories."

[2] The body of writer Joseph Campbell's work speaks to the power of myths and stories, as does Bruce Springsteen in his eloquent anthem, "Backstreets," off the *Born To Run* album (Columbia, 1975): *"Remember all the movies, Terry / We'd go see / Trying to learn to walk like the heroes / We thought we had to be...."*

[3] The groundbreaking study on this topic remains *Warrior Dreams* by John J. Donohue (1994).

[4] The novels of William Gibson and Neal Stephenson are good examples.

[5] Anecdote repeated several times during the author's course of study with Robert Smith, and attributed by Smith to Yang Chengfu's student/Smith's teacher, Professor Zheng Manqing.

[6] Such fictions may aspire to and perhaps reach what *The Washington Post* movie critic and acclaimed novelist Stephen Hunter calls "a kind of coolness that is beyond morality" (June 22, 1997 *Washington Post Style Section*), but are thus lamentable aesthetically. John Gardner's, *On Moral Fiction*, is instructive to read in this context. For martial artists, the worth of such prose fiction can be judged through the parallel of the poem martial arts pioneer and legend Jon Bluming wrote upon promotion to tenth dan: "Without *kokoro* [spirit] budo is but an empty shell" (1998).

[7] Sidner Larson, J.D., Ph.D., associate professor of American Indian Studies and director, American Indian Studies Program, Iowa State University (Ames, Iowa). E-mail to author, June 25, 2000.

[8] Michael Dirda, Pulitzer Prize winning book critic for *The Washington Post*. E-mail to author, June 26, 2000.

[9] Much of the general background information for this section on Peter O'Donnell and his creation, Modesty Blaise, is drawn from an interview with O'Donnell by Simon Moss contained on the Modesty Blaise fans' wonderful Web site (www.cs.umu.se/~kenth/Modesty/podint.html).

[10] Letter from Peter O'Donnell to author, May 9, 2000, plus enclosure of cited book by Jay Gluck, provided martial arts information.

[11] Comments/quotes derived from e-mail from David Hunt to author, May 14,

2000.

12 Most of the information on Adam Hall/Elleston Trevor in this article comes from two sources: (a) The admirable fan-created Web site for Hall/Trevor, www.quiller.net/site/main.html. This site contains a reprint of an article from October 1982's *Fighting Stars* by Dan Hagen called, "The Spy Who Came in From the Dojo." (b) Conversations with Russian journalist Georgi "Yegor" Tolstiakov and his fine in-depth portrait of Elleston Trevor for *The Armchair Detective* entitled, "The Man Who Was Quiller." Correspondence with Trevor family members also was quite helpful.

13 Before dismissing Hall's Bureau as an absurd fictional creation, consider two factual American espionage/covert warfare organizations that operated in the world's shadows unbeknownst to the American public, press, and most of its elected officials during the same time period Quiller was running his early missions: The Defense Department's stand-alone National Reconnaissance Office (NRO), whose still-classified 1974 budget exceeded $1.5 billion, and the Military Area Command Vietnam-Studies and Observation Group (MACV-SOG), an inter-service "unconventional" task force masquerading as scholars, but in reality a consortium of commands dominated by the Central Intelligence Agency and the U.S. Army's Special Forces (Green Berets). SOG warriors operated *at least* throughout Southeast Asia and behind the bamboo curtain into the People's Republic of China on rescue, spy, and other "black" missions. For information on the NRO, see *The CIA and the Cult of Intelligence* by Victor Marchetti and John D. Marks in as late a progressively less-censored revised edition of the 1974 Knopf book as you can find. Information on SOG is now available in several books, but perhaps most fundamentally can be found in Stanton's *Vietnam Order of Battle* (1981). Additionally, this author has significant contact with ex-SOG operatives.

14 From the Dan Hagen interview, previously cited.

15 This assertion from Hall was reported by Yegor Tolstiakov in his "Armchair Detective" article. However, conversations with Yegor and other research lead this author to believe that Hall was deliberately, perhaps instinctively, reflexively, keeping the scope of his answer narrow and protecting his privacy. By all accounts, Hall was deeply involved with his family, and I fail to believe the author in full, reflective candor would not count them as major influences on his life and work.

16 From the Dan Hagen interview.

17 George Pelecanos (2000, *Shame the Devil*). To give the reader a different perspective on current judgments about the drug use/social scene depicted in McInerney's *Bright Lights, Big City*, when this article's author was a national investigative reporter, a high-ranking Drug Enforcement Administration executive, who was a dedicated, anti-narcotics, politically savvy, and conser-

vative crime-fighter, told me on background that, in his view, marijuana and cocaine were going through a phase like alcohol during Prohibition, and that both drugs would be legal "in ten years." He was, of course, wrong.

[18] Author interview with Jay McInerney, e-mail June 22, 2000. Quoted throughout section.

[19] Some of the information and quotes have been multiply published, but the fundamental and best source for material on author Johnson (a source used here) is, *I Call Myself an Artist: Writings by and About Charles Johnson*, edited by R. Byrd (1999).

[20] The quotes from Johnson at and beyond this point are drawn from an e-mail interview of Johnson by the author, February 15, 2000.

[21] *Kwoon* is an interesting example of the non-practicing public's media viewing of martial arts fiction (and perhaps, fact). In an anthology of fiction published by W.W. Norton, martial arts terms used freely in the story are footnoted and defined, though the story has been published elsewhere without them. According to Johnson, the footnotes were added at the request of the anthology's editor who selected the story—author Joyce Carol Oates. Johnson agreed to add them: "I don't think the footnotes were necessary, but if they helped even one reader understand *Kwoon* better, then I don't mind their presence...."

Bibliography

Anderson, K. (1987). *Sympathy for the devil*. Garden City, NY: Doubleday.

Bluming, J. (1998). Without kokoro (spirit) budo is but an empty shell. *Journal of Asian Martial Arts, 7*(2), 74-85.

Bruccoli, M. (Ed.). (1978). *The notebooks of F. Scott Fitzgerald*. San Diego, CA: Harcourt Brace Jovanovich.

Byrd, R. (Ed.) (1999). *I call myself an artist: Writings by and about Charles Johnson*. Bloomington, IL: Indiana University Press.

Didion, J. (1970). *Play it as it lays*. New York: Farrar, Straus, Giroux.

Dirda, M. (2000). E-mail correspondences with author.

Donohue, J. (1994). *Warrior dreams: The martial arts and the American imagination*. Westport, CT: Bergin & Garvey.

Farnia, R. (1966). *I've been down so long it looks like up to me*. New York: Penguin.

Gardner, J. (1978). *On moral fiction*. New York: Basic Books, Inc.

Grady, J. (1998). Celluloid katas: Martial arts in the movies—A practitioner's preferences. *Journal of Asian Martial Arts, 7*(2): 86-101.

Hagen, D. (October, 1982). The spy who came in from the dojo, *Fighting Stars*. From Quiller fan site: www.quiller.net/site/main/html.

Hall, A. (1994). *Quiller salamander*. New York: Otto Penzler Books.

Hall, A. (1972). *The Warsaw document*. New York: Pyramid Books.

Hugo, R. (1979). *The triggering town: Lectures and essays on poetry and writing.* New York: W. W. Norton

Hunt, D. (2000). E-mail correspondence with author.

Hunt, D. (1998). *Trick of light.* New York: G. P. Putnam.

Hunter, S. (June 22, 1997). Nietzsche, Hollywood superman: Tinsel town waxes philosophical—In the worst way. *The Washington Post*, page G1.

Johnson, C. (2000). E-mail correspondence with author.

Johnson, C. (1994). *The sorcerer's apprentice: Tales and conjurations.* New York: Penguin.

Johnson, C. (1990). *Middle passage.* New York: Atheneum.

Johnson, C. (1982). *Oxherding tale.* Bloomington, IN: Indiana University Press.

Kesey, K. (1989). *One flew over the cuckoo's nest.* New York: New American Library.

King, S. (1999). *Hearts in Atlantis.* New York: Scribner.

Kingston, M. (1976). *The woman warrior: Memoirs of a girlhood among ghosts.* New York: Alfred A. Knopf.

Larson, S. (2000). E-mail correspondences and conversations with author.

Lodge, D. (1992). *The art of fiction.* New York: Penguin Books.

McDonald, G. (1964). *Running scared.* New York: Ivan Obolensky, Inc.

McInerney, J. (2000). E-mail correspondence and phone conversation with author.

McInerney, J. (1984). *Bright lights, big city.* New York: Vintage Contemporaries/Random House.

McInerney, J. (1985). *Ransom.* Vintage Contemporaries/Random House.

O'Brien, T. (1990). *The things they carried.* Boston, MA: Houghton Mifflin/Seymour Law.

O'Donnell, P. (2000). Correspondences with author.

O'Donnell, P. (1982). *The silver mistress.* Hampton Falls, NH: Donald M. Grant.

Pelecanos, G. (2000). *Shame the devil.* New York: Little Brown & Co.

Price, R. (1974). *The wanderers.* Boston, MA: Houghton Mifflin.

Stanton, S. (1981). *Vietnam order of battle.* Washington, DC: U.S. News Books.

Stone, R. *Dog soldiers.* Boston, MA: Houghton Mifflin.

Tolstiakov, G. (n.d.). *The man who was Quiller.* Armchair Detective.

Tolstiakov, G. (2000). E-mail correspondence and conversations with the author.

Web Sites

www.cs.umu.se/~kenth/Modesty/podint.html (web fan site for Modesty Blaise).

www.quiller.net/site/main/html (web fan site for Quiller/Adam Hall).

chapter 2

Celluloid Katas: Martial Arts in the Movies ~ A Practitioner's Prejudices

by James Grady, B.A.

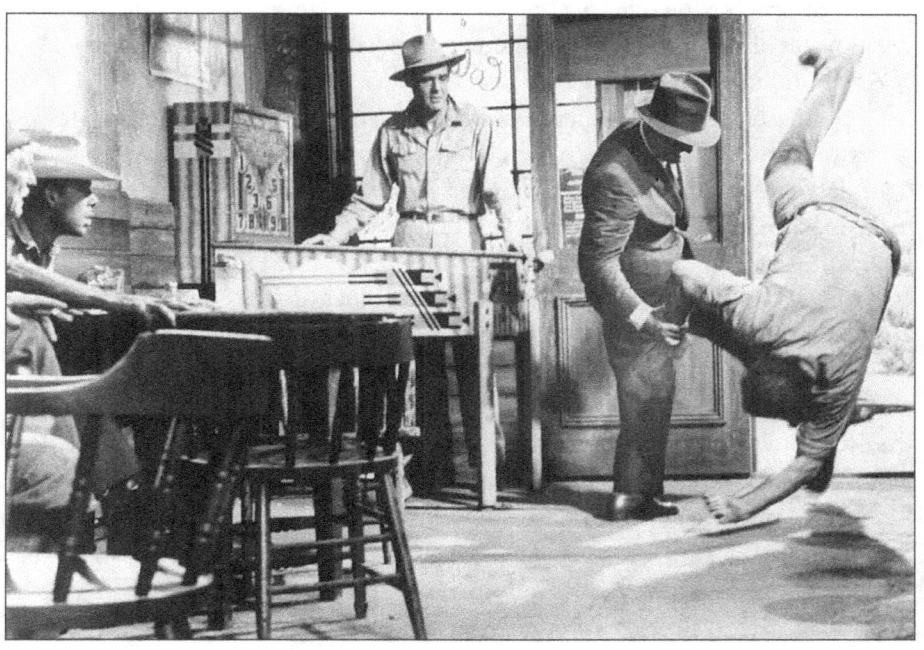

The best fight scene moments from *Bad Day at Black Rock*. That's Spencer Tracy doing the flip on a bar room bully. © *Copyright 1962, Metro-Golden-Mayer Inc.*

"Karate is a form of martial arts in which people who have had years and years of training can, using only their hands and feet, make some of the worst movies in the history of the world."
– Dave Barry

"For most Americans, experience and knowledge concerning the martial arts is obtained passively. The ideas of such 'armchair martial artists' are shaped by movie and television portrayals."
– John Donohue, 1994: 114-115

Stumble into a video store in America and most likely you'll bump into a section hawking "martial arts" movies.[1] What that phenomenon means in terms of both the martial arts and movies is a question that needs clarification more than an answer; undertaking either effort first requires a disclosure: For a working screen writer to criticize others' cinematic efforts veers close to a conflict of interest and wanna be armchair quarterbacking; for a feeble student of martial arts to pontificate about them borders on the absurd and the insulting. These are truths I admit—and have the gall to proceed anyway.

For "martial arts," I want to limit the discussion to the concept suitable for this journal—Asian martial arts. A number of stunning movies have been made about Western boxing—*Raging Bull, Requiem For A Heavyweight*—but to include them in this discussion requires a different author and more space than the *Journal of Asian Martial Arts* provides.

Similarly, I do not wish to discuss movies in which the characters' prowess is defined through weaponry. Once a protagonist employs technology, the boundary of our category blurs: *The Seven Samurai* sword fest slashes straight to its Western remake, *The Magnificent Seven*, where gunfighter Steve McQueen's assertion that "We deal in lead . . ." echoes into Clint Eastwood's *Dirty Harry* cop with a hand cannon hissing, "Do you feel lucky, punk?" a question whose answer rockets to a cowboy hat waving, yee-hawing Slim Pickens riding a hydrogen bomb to its target in the movie *Dr. Strangelove*.

All of which leads to a crucial point: In our Anytown, America, video store, the only category defined by the protagonists' "prowess" is martial arts.[2] Excellent movies have been made about musicians and their music—*Amadeus, Bird, 'Round Midnight*—but those movies are shelved under a "drama," not "musician" category.

With good reason. Movies tell stories, and stories are created by drama, the conflict and cohesiveness between characters. Drama uses an infinity of "means" to express such conflict-cohesiveness; thus, martial arts, endeavors centered on conflict, are gold for cinematic exploitation. The very term "motion pictures" explains another value of martial arts for screen writers and directors: "motion"—dynamic, devastating, ingenious motion—is endemic to martial arts and translates wonderfully through drama onto film and into entertainment. That entertainment may or may not qualify as "art," but often it equals profit, and profit is the pulse of Hollywood.

Beyond such pocketbook practicalities, as Donohue noted in his seminal work, *Warrior Dreams*: "Americans from a broad spectrum find an attraction to the martial arts, precisely because, as art forms, they answer a variety of psychic needs" (1994: 3). Such needs include lone, stoic heroism responding to an internal code rooted in either mentored tradition or noble philosophy, redemption gained through arduous education and experience, then ratified by confrontation—and victory. And it is American movies spawned by Hollywood that this essay focuses on, although the "genre" of martial arts movies is most exemplified by movies created in Hong Kong and other Asian cinema centers, products created from cultural imperatives too complex to be discussed here (Glaessner, 1974; Meyers et al, 1985; Dannen and Long, 1997).[3]

Those primarily Asian movies dominate the "martial arts" section of Anytown's video store, and while they portray the concept of martial arts movies, they also exemplify the weakness of such a genre and the failings of movie makers.

Martial arts can be a fine means to dramatically effect the end ("end" as in "sum total") of a good movie. But precisely because martial arts means are so "filmable," so useable, they are often cinematically perverted, and the means becomes the end of a movie—and its demise as an interesting work of art.

Genre martial arts movies are often lazy exercises in choreography—carefully practiced scenes of "fighting" strung together with a plot perhaps beyond nonsense and cosmeticized by melodrama as opposed to drama. Commercial logistic skills rather than creative talent are necessary to make such movies: round up a cast of flexible bodies who won't freeze up in front of a camera (acting ability is optional), some trampolines, nets and mats for flying kicks and long falls, some wires to help leaden mortals soar, fake blood; a good sound-effects post-production man, and a camera that can be over-cranked for slow motion shots; then pick sufficient words from the following menu to give you both your title and . . . umm . . . plot: *Dragon, Temple, Revenge, Fist, Shaolin, Heart, Death, Ninja, Warrior, Secret*, an animal that might have a wushu or gongfu style named for it, *Master, Tournament, Ultimate, Son/Daughter/Bride, Monk, Game, Fury*.

Instead of being a product of or tribute to martial arts, such movies are hucksetering mockeries of martial arts. They are also the models for what the public thinks of when terms like "martial arts" and "movies" appear in the same breath—or on the same video shelf.

Lest anyone doubt the effect of such movies on American culture, leave Anytown's video store and watch the role-playing mayhem of a grade school playground during recess, where sloppy but stinging acted-out spinning, front and back kicks fly[4] or consider the scene I witnessed in my now-nine-years-old son's taekwondo school. As an upper-belt children's class gathered, a well-dressed mother showed up with her seven-year-old son in tow. She approached the school's founder, John Holloway, a Pan American Games Heavyweight champion, a sixth-degree black belt and Vice President of the U.S. Taekwondo Union to ask about classes for her son:

> He can do all that stuff you see in the movies, so you'll probably just give him a black belt or whatever right away, I mean, he's so into it. Every

morning, he gets out of bed, pops in the video cassette for that movie *Bloodsport*, and does all the moves they do. By the way, he's A.D.D. [attention deficet disorder]: do you think you can handle him?

After Holloway patiently explained how martial arts education works, how he'd taken two A.D.D. kids all the way to black belt, and gave her a packet of printed material, the woman and her son left—never to return.

Leave aside why anyone would let any seven-year-old child repeatedly watch a movie called *Bloodsport*, why a child would be encouraged to pop in a video first thing every morning even if he didn't have A.D.D., and a picture of the nexus between martial arts movies and martial arts education is still all too clear.

The nexus between martial arts movies and "reality" becomes bizarre when considered on a global scale. Terms and concepts already mauled by movie makers are adopted, adapted and transformed yet again in a truly Frankensteinian fashion: according to the October 18, 1997, *Washington Post*, one of bands of "militiamen" battling for control in the Congo Republic called themselves "Ninjas" (other bands were Mambas, Koy-Koy, and Cobras). Perhaps those "militiamen" learned about ninjas from an extensive study of Japanese culture.

That distorted nexus shows up in Hollywood movie development, too, thus spinning the circle. I've been in TV- and movie-development meetings where producers or writers, groping to "build" a character, come up with "he's like a ninja kung fu killer type guy." Other writers have telephoned me for the "right" terms to describe the martial arts prowess and background of the characters they're creating—with no understanding as to the effect on a person's character such training could actually have. Actors who've come from a perceived martial arts background and/or once worked in such a movie can find themselves so rigidly stereotyped that, no matter what their talent, they must battle to convince "the system" to let them play characters who don't know or who in scene after scene don't use martial arts.[5] To show the exotic or action-based dramatic environment of the movie, directors often put a dozen gi-clad black belts in the background of a scene and have them break boards or practice techniques on each other as the hero walks past—for example, when James Bond visits the armorer Q to get his latest lethal gadgets.

When martial arts is portrayed in the standard action or genre movie, fantasy is too pretty a word. To bolster their "character" as tough or brave, or for less coherent reasons, characters stand still to accept repeated kicks and punches from supposedly highly conditioned and trained opponents. Superstar action heroes absorb three or four clean kicks to the head, then go on to defeat the villain. Even Muhammed Ali in his *When We Were Kings* battle with George Foreman did not accept that degree of punishment when he tricked Foreman into "punching himself out" so Ali could triumph. Movie fight scenes are "action packed" and trash the furniture, but until the "stop action" punch lands, almost no human damage materializes. Try falling down the stairs—no, try being thrown down the stairs, then getting up to fight. Anyone who's spent a month with a competent martial arts teacher and who's been attacked by a thug, when envisioning any future non-instructional violent encounter, prays to be able to deliver just one blow as clean as movie characters routinely absorb.

Another interesting cause-and-effect circle of martial arts and movies spins through American culture. What Americans are willing to learn, study and believe is related to what they see on the screen—and what they see on the screen is dictated by the demands of the motion picture medium. When writers and directors in the 40's and 50's discovered judo—an art that creates big and dramatic motion—*seoi-nage* (shoulder throw) and *tomoe-nage* (a falling-backwards, foot-in-the-opponent's-stomach throw) became movie fight scene staples, so much so that I've heard more than one judo sensei describe tomo-nage as "the cowboy throw." In the '80's and '90's, despite any realistic arguments to the contrary, kicks—especially high crescent or spinning kicks—became the movie martial artist's technique of choice. Why? Because, as one producer explained to me, "A hand technique just moves too small and too fast for the camera to catch."[6]

Thus, taekwondo and Northern Shaolin systems and techniques are more likely to be portrayed in movies—no matter what they're called on screen—and, I conjecture, martial arts schools that do not emphasize kicking will have a hard time holding students. Judo and aikido may make great cinematic moments,[7] but, though those arts attract an American student body, they will never dominate the martial arts field, in part because they won't "look real" to cinema-schooled consumers and in part because the first technique students of each art must learn is falling, a physically challenging and ego-deflating education.

There is a chance for improvement in Hollywood martial arts portrayals as more writers, directors, and producers (not more actors) who've studied martial arts assume Tinsel Town power.[8] What becomes of this chance . . . we'll see it on our silver screens.

Given all this, what "good" then can be said about martial arts movies?

That first—and last—thing to say is that "good" comes not from martial arts movies, but martial arts used well in good movies.

The examples of that are sometimes "small" and often surprising.

With Donohue (1994: 96-97), I would argue that history's most commercially successful, entertaining and artistic movie influenced and permeated by martial arts is . . . George Lucas's *Star Wars* saga, the first three parts of which have raked in millions of global fans. The saga is imbued with a concept called "the force"—a martial and life- and health-enhancing power capable of being harnessed by judicious instruction and dedicated study, an entity that pervades the universe and all life. Such a description smacks of qi/ki and Dao with a dash of zen, concepts underlying many Asian martial arts.

Beyond the grand scale of *Star Wars* are a number of movies in which—if only for a few heartbeats—martial arts plays a key role and is portrayed in at least an entertaining, non-insulting fashion. The criteria for my boldly proffered list is simple: the quality of the movie, not the wow's of the martial arts portrayed. I'm sad to say that filling the list sometimes meant stretching the definition of quality.

Before my list, two names must be dealt with, names that appear on martial arts video shelves but who also stand apart from the categorization: Bruce Lee and Jackie Chan.

Bruce Lee is the symbol of martial arts movies, and while none of his movies stand alone as even near great, they created—or were used to create—the very topic addressed here. Not that there aren't good moments in any Bruce Lee film, for example, in Enter The Dragon, when he says of a martial arts dominated, evil cabal: "Why doesn't somebody just pull out a .45 and end it?" he is asking the question that challenges the credibility of every martial arts picture. In that same movie, the sequence in which he stalks a foe through a maze of mirrors is as cinematically wonderful as the split screens pioneered by Elvis Presely in *Jailhouse Rock* (perhaps the only "good" movie starring that karate student). Whatever one thinks of Bruce Lee as a movie maker, actor or martial artist, he has become a larger-than-life cultural force. Ironically, the "best Bruce Lee movie" is not one he made, but rather one made about his life, and discussed below: *Dragon—The Bruce Lee Story*.

Jackie Chan is an artist—a movie artist, an innovator and cinematic risk taker akin to the genius Buster Keaton. While Chan's movies may be too slapstick for action junkies or "serious" movie buffs, they dare to chase art as entertainment —a race in which he puts his life as well as his reputation on the line. Most importantly, Jackie Chan forces martial students to laugh at ourselves. For that alone, he's worth the price of a ticket.

Western audience have been buying tickets to movies that expose them to Asian martial arts since *Outside Woman*, a 1921 flick featuring a jujitsu-skilled, Japanese manservant. Heroes and villains used "judo chops" and other martial arts techniques from then on, including in the string of "big" action films starring various characters, such as Bond, James Bond. But at least one critical source dates the emergence of martial arts as a force in American movies to the 1972 movie *Billy Jack* (Corcoran & Farkas, 1968).

Quite probably true, but *Billy Jack* is a far cry from a good movie—overly sincere and self-important, even though (sadly) it may be as entertaining as a fifth of the features playing at any given 1990's cineplex. Hapkido—an effective martial art—is hero Billy Jack's specialty. But the character's ability to absorb punishment without lasting injury, plus the way his opponents circle him and then wait their turn to be battered (paraphrased by Robert Smith's satirical observation that when Billy Jack takes his boots off to do battle in a park, no doubt strewn with broken glass, sharp rocks and foot-stomping bad guys, "he shows everything he knows about real fighting") keep the movie from my "good" list. But that dramatic act of taking off his boots is precisely the kind of character- and suspense-building visual "business" that movie makers (with good cause) love. So, too, do audiences: even with the artistry of Hollywood accounting, the bargain basement budget *Billy Jack* grossed an estimated \$32 million—in 1970's cash (Corcoran & Farkas, 1968).

That combination of bad and unrealistic plot, flawed character development, over-stated seriousness, self-importance, and/or glib condescension to the audience keeps a number of famous martial arts laced movies off my list—for example, the entire *Lethal Weapon* series (at least, to date). Also, in that series, although Mel Gibson and Danny Glover are wonderful actors in charming combination, and Gibson's ass-kicking paramour in the third movie is a great touch, the martial arts "used" in the movie show . . . umm . . . an interesting knowledge of the field: in the first movie, Glover "builds" the lethality of Gibson's character by telling him that according to his file: "You're also heavy into martial arts, t'ai chi [taiji] and all that killer stuff." Well, t'ai chi can face its challenge as the "supreme ultimate" martial art, but nothing in Gibson's character supports a devotion to t'ai chi; indeed, his commando cop techniques are pure hard style and often egotistically applied. The serial plots of these movie sequels strung together . . . Embrace them at your intelligence's peril. The three movie series grossed hundreds of millions of 1980's dollars.

The works of America's 1990's major martial arts star Steven Seagal make but one appearance on my list (and a qualified one at that) and an important caveat highlighted in Note 8 following this article. Though he can "fill" a screen in much the way John Wayne or Clint Eastwood can, aikido expert Seagal's movies all too often go way "over the top" with self-righteousness, directorial conceits, or plain awful plotting: in *Above The Law*, his cop hero uses Chicago mob-type relatives to fight CIA-linked heroin pushers. The Chicago Outfit as anti-heroin good guys insults the 1,081 victims of unsolved gangland homicides in that city since 1920 (Moldea, 1996: 327). Seagal's first movie, for its multitude of flaws, filled me with expectant hope for him as a major, high quality, martial arts background movie force: I've been exhaling for several cinematic years. The body of Seagal's movies in the 1990's will probably gross close to a billion dollars.

But Seagal—who in February, 1997, was named a reincarnated *Tulku* (roughly, "important teacher") of the Nyingma lineage of Tibetan Buddhism (Time, 1997: 74)—has avoided one curious and troubling cinematic element: in many post-Bond, American martial arts laced movies, the martial arts character is quite often an *a priori* morally reprehensible individual: a professional killer, an urban mercenary, an anti-social (and thus egotistical) rogue, a lethal vessel in search of a soul worth having. Heroes use martial arts and (of course) defeat often "superior" martial artist villains, but well-balanced martial arts characters worthy of a heartfelt bow are rare in contemporary American movies. As *Washington Post* movie critic and author Stephen Hunter noted about "action" movies in the 1990's:

> Ultimately, the philosophy of the Nietszchean superman and the philosophy of this dominant type of American movie boil down to the same unsettling principle. Both preach a kind of coolness that is beyond morality. We may, in the end, understand that one side nominally represents "good" while the other is inherently "bad," but those distinctions are effectively meaningless. The strong win, not the just.
>
> – Hunter, 1997: G1

In defense of "martial arts movies," they often profess that the weak and just can, through diligent striving within some martial art, become the strong and just.

What must be remembered when seeing any dramatic movie is that whatever is portrayed is false: "action" means "act," as in "execute a scripted, rehearsed, artificially lit and staged performance." You can tell almost nothing about a martial art or an actor performing martial arts in any non-documentary movie. What you see is what they're giving you, not what anyone has the ability to do if and when they walk down the wrong alley or toe the kumite line in any dojo. As anyone who's been there knows, reality writes its own script.

Judging movies is next to impossible to do well: there are simply too many movies in existence to be sure you've viewed them all. Some movies with technically "good" martial arts segments and what should be a winning dramatic combination somehow fall apart, perhaps from bad direction, bad acting, bad script, or bad mojo—for example, *Passenger 57*. Other movies simply don't "feel" like they belong in our dramatic category—for example, *Iron and Silk*, a story that's part autobiography, part drama, part travelogue, part wonderful and wholly . . . not there. Where "there" is . . . Well, it's not on my list.

With those cautions carved in your heart, here are two fistfuls of movies featuring martial arts worth watching:

Pushing Hands

Pushing Hands, written and directed by Ang Lee, 1992. From the fade-in moment of an old man's hands slowly rising in a classic taiji opening, this movie does martial arts proud, or rather, martial arts helps make a movie worthy of admiration, the first movie from the man who went on to direct the Oscar winning *Sense And Sensibility*, as well as *The Ice Storm*, *The Wedding Banquet* and *Eat, Drink, Man, Woman*. Ang Lee's story about the septegenarian taiji expert Chinese father (played by Lung Sihung, a masterful actor starring in other Ang Lee stories) who flees post-Red Guard China for Manhattan's suburbs to live with his son, grandson and neurotic novel-writing American wife, is a gem few Americans have discovered. The movie explores Ang Lee's recurring themes of family, fatherhood—and fun, all the while using taiji's "pushing hands" as the story's metaphor. "Pushing hands?" asks the totally, like, American wife. "Yeah," explains her Chinese husband. "It's like taiji for two. A way of keeping your balance while unbalancing your opponent." She replies, "Like marriage." As Lung Sihung's character discovers, "Attaining carefree nothingness isn't easy." As he struggles, we see love lost and triumphant, external "hard style" martial arts, "expelling energy" demonstrations, rooting, and push hands adapted to defeat a quintet of Chinatown thugs. The actors speak both English and Chinese (with subtitles), and while the movie may be hard to find on video cassette, it's worth the hunt.

Above: Star Lung Shihung performing taijiquan's "single whip/tiger's mouth" in *Pushing Hands*. Below: Lung Shihung confronted by co-star Deb Snyder. © *Copyright 1992, Fox Searchlight Productions*.

The Killer Elite, 1975

The Killer Elite is a Vietnam-Watergate era blast of Cold War nihilism, conspiracy, paranoia and existential rage (in that category, see also the espionage wonder *Scorpio*, whose actors crossed paths with the real Watergate burglars, *Nashville*, *The Parallax View*, and *Three Days of the Condor*). Sheer talent shotgunned through *The Killer Elite* saves this movie from itself (though just barely). Directed by Sam Peckinpah of *The Wild Bunch* fame, *Killer Elite* haphazardly mixes cliches and concepts. It is story about the power struggle of unspecified "Asians" featuring Chinese gongfu and ninjas battling their way through San Fransisco in search of safety and/or freedom. A "taiji master" teaches a style with hard strikes, gi's with colored belt levels, and weapons. A hand-to-hand orgy of battle at the airport is at least plausible because of the difficulty in smuggling weapons past security. Fundamentally, this is the story of two hired guns, once partners, now enemies, settling their own score against the backdrop of privatized espionage. The movie paired two *Godfather* stars, James Caan and Robert Duvall (who energizes every frame of film he's ever been in). Bo Hopkins underplays and thus makes us believe him as the psycho marksman cliched in a hundred other movies. Before *The Killer Elite* degenerates into absurd action and smug self-righteousness, there's a great scene in which the daughter of the Asian political leader whom Caan and his team are protecting in a hideout along the docks puts on a ninja suit. Caan asks, "What the hell are you doing?" The maiden replies, "Going out to use the night." Caan tells her, "Hey, look, I got a maniac out there with a thirty-ought-six [rifle]. He's gonna blow you apart if you take ten steps." Snaps the maiden, "He'll have to see me first." "Look kid," says Caan, "do me a favor and go over there and do the Tiger Claw and the Crane Stance and the Chicken Wing and all the other crap in the corner, because out there it's no good."

Commando Clashes

As Donohue and other experts note, the only martial artists indulging the full amplitude of their skills are soldiers, cops, and killers. Hundreds of "war" dramas show recruits being taught hand-to-hand mayhem—not martial arts with uniforms and bowing and respect, martial homicide as best expounded by W.E. Fairbairn. Many of these "war epics" are cans of cliches, but some of them are entertaining and portray hand-to-hand combat in an interesting fashion. Two of the better such movies are *The Devil's Brigade*, a 1968 story about the raiders who were the forerunners of America's modern Green Beret Special Forces, starring William Holden, a movie set in World War II and shot in the midst of the Vietnam war, and one that perhaps consequently ends on an anti-war note. Steven Seagal's 1992 *Under Siege*, with its Navy SEAL hero aboard the hijacked American battleship, is his best movie, in no small part because of wonderfully extreme performances by Tommy Lee Jones and Gary Busey. Seagal's character makes minimal and often unnecessarily graphic use of martial arts and commando skills before filling his hands with high caliber firepower (and thus evolving by our definition beyond this genre), but that progression gives a reality to the movie, one that I bet some executives in Hollywood wanted to ignore by having an unarmed aikido expert Seagal take out a roomful of fully-aware men armed with machine guns. An almost-made-it in this category should be noted: James Cagney's 1946 movie *13 Rue Madeleine*, a story of the Office of Strategic Services, the World War II forerunner of the Central Intelligence Agency, has some great judo/commando tactics moments.

The Karate Kid, 1984

The Karate Kid kicks itself above the sickeningly sweet swamp that drowned its three awful sequels precisely because no one expected the first movie to be so commercially successful. Forget about all its flaws, like the absurdly conceited, supposedly "no can beat" crane stance technique (that fails in the sequel), making the Japanese sensei/mentor of our hero, a Congressional Medal of Honor winner, a cardboard, square-jawed villain. KK succeeds because it winks at itself and at such martial arts staples as belts, because it dares to explore the student-teacher relationship with respect but not too much piety, and because it portrays the pains of adolescence without worshiping that trip. KK is memorable for those of us who remember the pre-pad days of light contact tournaments, when precision and control counted more than brute force. The movie also debuted a star whose light could be seen even in those early days: believable virginal heartthrob Elizabeth Shue, way, way before she was *Leaving Las Vegas*. And if you think the obscene competitiveness portrayed in KK is fiction, stand ringside at a martial arts tournament where trembling, padded, seven-year-old boys and girls toe the sparring line and listen to their mothers scream KK's villainous mantra: "No mercy!"

Dragon: The Bruce Lee Story, 1993

As previously noted, this is the best movie linked to the cultural icon who has everything from restaurants to pirate crews in cyberpunk novels named after him. Remember, this is a dramatic production, not a biography, a production about a legend at that, and thus by definition is a far leap from "just the facts." But there are some wonderful touches: for example, the actor chosen to play Yip Man, Lee's Wing Chun teacher, looks like he stepped out of pictures of the real Yip Man. The choreography is as good as any martial arts dramatization, and the lead actors are a fresh faced, appealing lot, regardless of their skills. The movie portrays martial arts, Hollywood, and the subtleties of racism in ways that can hold the interest of a TV-numbed American audience.

Perhaps most unexpectedly, the movie shows the slip-slide from reality to hallucinogenic vision and dreamlike states with power equal to a more "artistic" movie like *Slaughterhouse Five*.

The Mechanic, 1972

Charles Bronson plays a burnt-out Mob assassin, who seeks rebirth through training a protégé. The metaphor for Bronson and the movie is played out in a segment at the karate dojo where Bronson trains, when a Japanese "master" comes to show a tough American student that "new ways" of karate are insufficient and unworthy. Let me betray the you-would-never-have-predicted-it surprise and tell you that the dojo battle between the greying karate master and the upstart student mirrors the struggles between Bronson and his protégé. Although morally hollow and of shaky realism (mob killers do not work this way), the movie's sum is greater than the holes of its parts.

The Manchurian Candidate, 1962

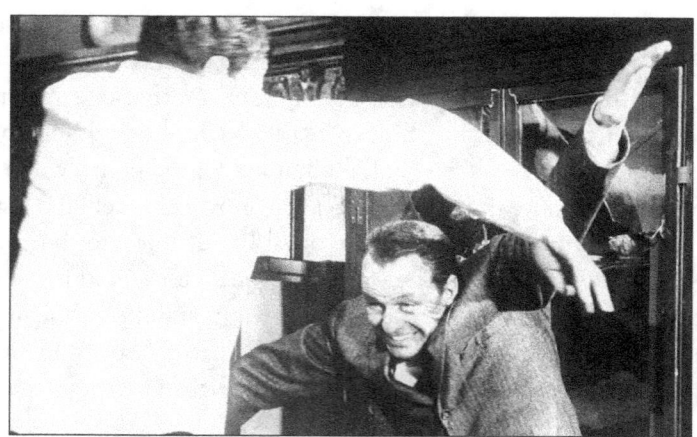

Frank Sinatra battles Henry Silva in the *Manchurian Candidate*.
© Copyright 1962 by MGM. Photo courtesy of Photofest.

This movie from the Richard Condon novel ranks as one of the better American movies ever made. Period. A pulse-pounding attack on McCarthyism and Communism encouraged by President John Kennedy, a scathing attack on image-only politicians, and a classic, suspenseful espionage story, *Manchurian Candidate* is a movie worth owning. Frank Sinatra stars as the commander of an Army squad kidnaped and brainwashed by the enemy in the Korean war. The scenes in which Sinatra "remembers" the brainwashing he went through (scenes at a ladies' garden party interspersed with homicide) are chilling and brilliant.

Years later, when a haunted Sinatra knocks on the door of the man he thinks can save him from what he supposes to be madness, he encounters a face from that nightmarish past, Henry Silva (an "ethnic" actor whom clumsy Hollywood casts here as Korean, elsewhere as Italian, Mexican and American Indian). Sinatra instinctively throws a punch, and the ensuing brawl is a totally believable madhouse of martial mayhem. Indeed, Sinatra broke the little finger of his right hand during the fight scene; the injury gave him a permanent crook in that digit. Also, Sinatra's cross-block of Silva's kick is "real" because Silva kicked with his "wrong" foot. "I wanna tell you something," said Sinatra in a discussion with the movie's director John Frankenheimer and screenwriter George Axelrod that was filmed and tagged onto the video cassette released twenty-eight years later, (when Silva kicked with the opposite foot of the one he'd used in rehearsal) "I never moved so fast in my whole life."

Bad Day at Black Rock, 1954

A sage once noted that all drama starts with the following concept: a stranger comes to town. Seldom is that truth better exemplified than when one-armed Spencer Tracy appears in the windswept nowhereville called Black Rock, stepping off the train into a 1950's sweep of guilt, romance, conspiracy and courage while on a mission that turns out to save his life. When the bad guys finally push Tracy too far, his martial arts counter-attack stuns both the audience and the villains. *Bad Day At Black Rock* was a controversial movie for its time, daring as it did to challenge post-Pearl Harbor, Cold War America's self-righteous image.

Grosse Point Blank, 1997

John Cusack stars as Martin in *Grosse Point Blank*.
© Hollywood Pictures Company. All rights reserved.

Photograph on previous page by Suzanne Hanover, which also is used here as a background for a photograph by Melinda Sue Gordon.

A savage, scathing satire, GPB is the story of professional hitman John Cusack returning to his tenth-year high-school reunion in search of himself and his teenage sweetheart. Cusack commands this movie, a dominance of a highly luminous every-day star, and enormously talented actor that probably was responsible for keeping the picture a pure delight. The movie never backs down from its original hypermoral premise, a courage that must have made studio marketing executives tremble. GPB has two great martial arts moments. The first occurs when Cusack, now a truly lethal weapon, encounters the bully who'd stuffed him into trash cans during high school, an encounter staged in the very halls where the bully had once reigned supreme. What a glorious moment: Cusack can clearly exact revenge that some might call justice; indeed, the loutish bully threatens and taunts him. But Cusack, in a display of maturity, self-discipline and cosmic consciousness, "educates" the bully to the folly of such violence and gets the bully to reveal a gentle side of his soul—all without a whiff of sappiness. That "non-action" reflects the power and responsibilities of choice that can be earned through martial arts study. Moments later, Cusack is attacked by a rival assassin. Their lethal duel in the high school hall is furious, dramatic and realistic—the battle ends in grappling on the floor, as do many true, violent, hand-to-hand encounters, and in an exhibition of penmanship not covered in the average American educational institution. The dialog reflects a sophistication and intelligence rare in modern movies, and is so cleverly machine-gunned through the story that the audience's laughter often drowns out wonderful lines.

Notes

[1] I wince every time I hear the world "film" as a name for motion pictures. "Film" is part of the technology that transmits the product of motion pictures. Using "film" to describe a movie is a pretension born when the art elite discovered that what was happening Saturday nights at the local Bijou could be as interesting—and lucrative—as what was displayed in the local museum. Concepts like "film noir" are more acceptable uses of the term film, but still, when pretension defines, personality suffers. I confess that few people seem to agree with me on this point.

[2] With respect and a great deal of sympathy for the qualms of my teacher Robert Smith about the terms "martial arts" and "martial artist," nevertheless, I'll use these terms.

[3] While the author does not endorse these works (Glaessner, 1974; Meyers et al, 1985; Dannen and Long, 1997), they do present viewpoints worth considering by an interested reader.

[4] Many grade schools now ban their pupils from "playing Bruce Lee," "Ninja Turtles," or other movie and TV "karate/kung fu" games.

[5] Conversation with Steven Seagal's production team and conversations with the late Brandon Lee.

[6] David Levinson, an Emmy winning producer and writer with three decades "in the business."

[7] Steven Seagal's aikido demonstration that opens *Above The Law* exemplifies such drama. Having Seagal narrate the demonstration in Japanese was a wonderful cinematic touch. Judo was lovingly and at times accurately portrayed as a "non-sport" in *Blood On The Sun*, a 1945 James Cagney movie warning of Japanese militarism that, for all its strengths, suffers from an odd mix of racist and anti-racist morality, jingoism, good plotting mixed with absurd coincidences, and Cagney's classic tough-guy character set against cardboard friends, femmes, and villains. Judo—identified as "Japanese wrestling"—also provided a milestone, of sorts, in Ken Russell's 1970, highly

intellectual production of D.H. Lawrence's novel, *Women In Love*. In the movie, two bored British aristocrats square off naked in front of a roaring fireplace for a bizarre parody of randori that exposed American viewers to full frontal male nudity in a "major motion picture." As to the martial arts education marketplace, according to an article in *The Washington Post* (1996: 20), "Karate had the head start, but the Japanese martial art is getting outmuscled in the marketplace by a relative newcomer, Korean taekwondo [sic]." The article quotes officials from the American Athletic Union as well as karate and taekwondo organizations.

[8] For example, Randall Wallace, who wrote the screenplay for the Oscar winning *Braveheart* and directed the 1998 version of *Man In The Iron Mask*, is a first-degree black belt in Shotokan karate.

Bibliography

Corcoran, J. and Farkas, E. (1968). *Martial arts—Tradition, history, people*. New York: Gallery Books.

Dannen, F., and Long, B. (1997). *Hong Kong Bablylon*. New York: Miramax/Hyperion Books.

Donohue, J. (1994). *Warrior dreams: The martial arts and the American imagination*. Westport, CT: Bergin & Garvey.

Glaessner, V. (1974). *Kung fu—Cinema of violence*. New York: Bounty Books.

Hunter, S. Fred (1997, June 22). Nietzsche, Hollywood superman: Tinseltown waxes philosophical—In the worst way. *The Washington Post*, Style Section, p. G1.

Meyers, R., Harlib, A, Palmer, B., and Palmer, K. (1985). *Martial arts movies from Bruce Lee to the ninjas*. New York: Citadel Press.

Moldea, D. (1996). *Dark victory: Ronald Reagan, MCA and the Mob*. New York: Penguin Books.

Time Magazine, (1997, October 13), Buddhism in America, p. 74.

The Washington Post, (1996, November 5), Health Section, p. 20.

The Washington Post, (1997, October 18), p. A16.

chapter 3

A Sort of Swordsman

by John Donohue, Ph. D.

The maw of the school bus swallowed him up. It was a gray, rainy Monday, the kind of weather he loved. The November sky was pulled way down low, the bus windows were fogged up from the heat of adolescent bodies in wet wool, and with a little luck he could maintain himself in his current fuzzy, semi-conscious state until well into Homeroom. Mornings on the bus were normally safe, since the big guys in the back were usually too drowsy to think up anything embarrassing to do to him. As a freshman, however, he knew that the ride home would be vastly different. The overabundant energy and cruel imaginations of the senior guys would have been stoked up by a day of academic repression. He and all the new boys would be pushed around, humiliated and tortured. On the ride home from school, hell was usually in session.

To an adult, the humiliations visited upon him were not earth-shattering. To the fevered mind of the adolescent, however, the minor cruelties of teenagers took on a sinister stature, a malevolent immensity which could make his ears burn in shame just thinking about them later on. These events haunted his dreams: staggering down the long, rubber aisle of the school bus, carefully timing his stagger to fit with the lurch of the vehicle as it began its spastic trek through suburban streets. All eyes are on him as, the last kid on the bus, he searches in vain for a seat. Inevitably, there remains only one place free. In The Back. Freshman no-man's land. Indian country.

He is drawn with a sense of doomed inevitability to the spot. His tormentors wait, breathless. The ordeal takes a number of permutations: he attempts to sit, but has his path blocked by a casually raised leg. A powerful leg, a leg almost adult-sized in its hateful dimensions. The laughter begins and continues sporadically all the way home as he is forced to stand there. In another variation he is allowed to sit. As are the four or five other freshman boys. They are driven with rolling eyes like fear-maddened cattle and packed one on top of the other like pubescent sardines. As the coup-de-grace, the biggest of the seniors takes a running leap and piles on top of them. They moan and squirm until the ride ends. The final scenario is the most terrifying. In a change of pace, it occurs on the ride to school. A freshman is allowed a seat and is left unmolested for the entire ride. The tension, the uncertainty, the sheer absence of harassment is the most horrible thing of all. The bus stops. The doors open. The freshman can see the daylight which signals safety, but sits immobile with terror. Eventually, he rises, pulled to his feet by the tide of inevitability and is doused with flour. It sifts down gently over his hair and clothing to the bovine guffaws of his tormentors. No matter how hard he tries to remove his tormentors' brand, he knows he will emit a shameful puff of flour, a visible wheeze of humiliation, with every mortifying move he makes during the school day. Coming or going, freshmen were relentlessly badgered, tripped, pushed around, and, if the big guys had experienced a particularly bad day in the classroom or playing field, Seamus and his compatriots endured an endless succession of rabbit punches, noogies, and Indian burns.

There were some things about him that made him an irresistible target. He was basically a quiet kid. He liked to read (sometimes he even liked to read the stuff his teachers made him read, but he kept the lid on that). He was also small, a little pudgy, and had a round face with an even rounder nose (one of his distant Irish relatives had seen a picture of him and noted he had a countenance "as Irish as a Dublin pig"). His hairline was so low that, on his birth, his mother had secretly worried that he was retarded. To make matters worse, his parents, with that peculiar form of adult amnesia that blots out an awareness of a kid's need for anonymity, had named him Seamus.

Seamus. The name alone was a well-spring of humiliation for a thirteen-year-old boy. He had asked himself (but never them) why his parents couldn't have chosen something else to call him. Intellectually he knew he was named for a maternal great uncle, but he couldn't quite fathom why they felt this urge to perpetuate such a stupid name. Captain Kirk's parents had resisted the psychotic impulse to call him Seamus (no way you could hear Bones, in a moment of great emotional stress, say "Seamus, you've got to do something!"). Seamus knew that Kirk's parents lived in a more advanced age, but still, was it too much to ask that his own parents just call him James? Then he could have selected from any number of common diminutives and nicknames. Only by dint of great cunning had he fashioned an acceptable variant on his embarrassing moniker.

He had noted fairly early on that anything remotely related to sports was considered manly. He didn't really have much interest in athletics (most of his tormentors through the years had been of the jock persuasion) but he knew the value of a good thing when he saw it. A sporting reference could save you from considerable embarrassment if you used it right. He fell off his bike once and clipped the curb with his rear end. He limped around for days, but instead of telling people (when they asked) that he fell off his bike onto his ass, he just cryptically replied "Pulled a hamstring." Seamus wasn't even sure what a hamstring was, but he had heard it referred to on a football game broadcast. It seemed to satisfy his inquisitors nicely. Never one to forget a valuable lesson, he decided to cut his first name in half and call himself Shea. "Shea?" people would ask. "Yeah, like the stadium," he'd reply, and sure enough the magic of sports seemed to short-circuit any more potentially embarrassing questions about the matter.

The vindictive relentlessness of the guys in the back of the bus, however, had quickly convinced Seamus that such protective coloration was next to useless. High school, his teachers kept reminding him, would open up new worlds for him. He had to agree. The afternoon rides home on the bus opened up a whole new world of fear. There was no sense in fighting back. These guys were seniors. They were big. They were strong. Some of them even shaved. Seamus still had the smooth, round skin of childhood and a voice which cracked under strain. He longed for puberty to transform him into something else but suspected he would die of embarrassment before his hormones kicked in. He and the other freshmen were helpless. Only the end of the bus ride offered relief. Intervention by the bus driver, an exceedingly rare occurrence, was just as humiliating as the abuse itself. What thirteen-year-old boy wants a bus load of thirteen-year-old girls to know that he needs a blue-haired lady in a Budweiser hat to fight his battles for him? No, something else had to be done. Seamus had decided he needed a secret weapon.

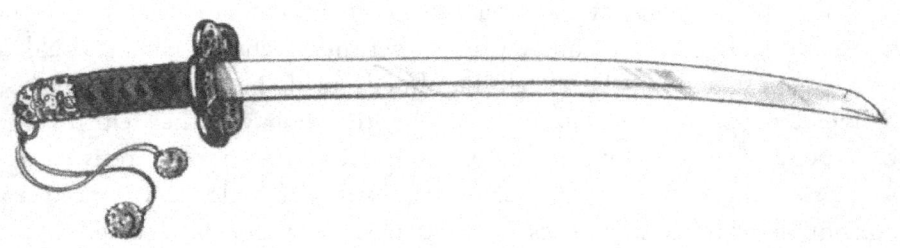

He had a strong interest in history. A relentless parade of *National Geographic* magazines had filled the rainy Saturdays of his youth. An article on Japan had piqued his interest. There, in glossy color, he had found the agent of his deliverance. The samurai sword. It was beautiful and dangerous at the same time. There was a history and philosophy behind it that appealed to him. Even better, you didn't need strength or size to wield it. It was the Oriental version of the Great Equalizer. He had pursued his readings on the samurai with an obsessive intensity, devouring tales of the great swordsmen, solitary men who wandered the land and faced their opponents alone. The themes of competence, freedom and violence were what attracted him (they were the same things that, the year before, had convinced him he should become a cowboy). For Seamus the samurai sword exerted a mysterious attraction and the promise of deliverance.

He continued his readings. He tried meditating on the floor of his bedroom (his feet fell asleep). He yearned for a Toshiro Mifune film festival on Public Television. He discovered karate magazines, just the visible tip of a whole industry designed to inflame the passions of martial arts fanatics across the country. He found, to his joy and amazement, that it was possible to buy samurai swords (not real ones, of course, but replicas—and they were sharp!) through the mail. They were priced well beyond his means, of course, but some day. . . .

His fantasies were fed by the daily ordeal on the bus. In the semi-coherent moments before sleep, he could picture a stormy, dark dawn. His tormentors, uncharacteristically active on the morning trip, howl and yip like dogs as they watch him make the long walk down the aisle to the back of the bus. They don't notice the black lacquered sheath which juts out just below his J.C. Penney raincoat. Hogan, the gang's ringleader, moves to grab him. The whirring, silver arc of the sword flashes in the gloom of the bus. Seamus whirls and slashes, driving his enemies back in terror and confusion. Humbled by his display of skill, they cower in their seats. He glances at them contemptuously. He sheathes his sword smoothly, the handguard making a faint click in the silence which reigns after the pandemonium of the fight. He is the savior of his friends and the object of adulation for every girl on that bus.

Seamus savors that fantasy as he rides to school that Monday. He smiles faintly with a sense of anticipation. Chris Koenig, who's on the freshman wrestling team but still talks to Seamus because they went to grammar school together, takes judo lessons from a Japanese teacher. And, he said, the teacher has a samurai sword hanging on the wall of his office. Seamus smiles because tonight he is going to meet this man. He is one step closer to becoming the swordsman he dreams about. He has found a master.

The judo school had a narrow storefront of plate glass windows which were completely fogged up. Later on, Seamus would be able to remember very few nights when those windows were not clouded with the heat and humidity of effort. He walked through the door with Chris and was immediately assailed by the aroma of sweat and athletic performance. An acrid odor, not unfamiliar, but alien. It was the smell of the school gym, the locker room, which was another arena of humiliation. The smell of enemy territory. Inside, the training hall was lit by banks of fluorescent light. The walls are inexpertly covered with cheap grey panelling which, Seamus thought, was supposed to look like weathered, sun-bleached oak. The relentless glare of the lights, however, revealed it as merely cheap panelling. Most of the floor was covered by a canvas mat.

Chris introduced him to the middle-aged Japanese man sitting at a desk on the small part of the room not covered by the canvas. "This is the guy I was telling you about," Chris said, and gave him a little nudge toward the desk. The Japanese man rose out of his seat to take Seamus' hand. That night the judo instructor was not an awe-inspiring sight: he had on some sort of baggy pajama-like pants and a grey sweatshirt that read, "The MOOSE is Loose!"

"I am Mori," the MOOSE said, and he bowed slightly. His face was smooth and round with crinkly eyes that looked like they got that way from laughing a lot. His lips were liver colored and his hair was a spiky black crew cut with silver tips showing here and there.

Seamus looked up over the desk where Mori sat and asked questions about him. And saw the sword. It hung in lethal repose over the master's head. Seamus' mouth answered the questions put to him, but his brain was not really fully engaged in the process. His eyes stayed locked on the weapon.

"You like sword?" Mori asked. "But why? Sword is old-time weapon. Not for boys." "Yeah, but . . . ," Seamus breathed,". . . it's so . . ." He was struck completely incoherent by the propinquity of the blade. What words could sum it up? So beautiful? It was, but that really wasn't what he was thinking. So deadly? That was more like it. So lethal. So effective in cleaving a shimmering swath of razor-sharp terror which would leave his tormentors powerless to oppose him. It was both weapon and shield, a magical talisman which would work an irrevocable change on him. It would make him more and his enemies less. But you couldn't tell an adult that stuff. You couldn't look Mr. Mori in the eye and say, "What I'm really hoping, sir, is that you'll teach me the art of swordsmanship so that I can hack and chop and dismember a crew of obnoxious seventeen-year-olds who harass me on the school bus to pieces. I'm also interested in its utility in impressing chicks." Adults, many of whom according to the 11 o'clock news, spent a lot of their time bludgeoning estranged spouses to death, shooting each other during gas station robberies, and hurtling into one another in automobiles, had a strong aversion to hearing about the relatively tame violent fantasies of teenagers.

"Sword no good to carry now," Mori said. "You cannot. Police would come." Seamus had a momentary image of himself running through dark, wet side streets, clutching his precious blade to his side, hounded by the modern constellation of forces (bus drivers, teachers, parents, police) set in array against his aspirations to greatness.

"Much better you do judo," Mori concluded. He must have seen the look on Seamus' face, for he added, "To be sword-man, judo-man, all the same. Technique does not matter. Only spirit. You play judo with me, you learn about being sword-man too."

So Seamus signed the papers for judo lessons. He was that kind of kid. A lifetime of Catholic conditioning (and a paucity of experience) had taught him that adults and those in power were invariably right. He silently accepted the printed material Mori gave him ("All About Judo") and sat quietly on a battered blue bench that faced the mat.

Mr. Mori looked immensely pleased as he stepped onto the training floor. He had changed his sweatshirt for a judo uniform top and a red and white belt. "Hey Mr. Mori," Seamus called. The teacher's smiling moon face swiveled around to look at Seamus. "Can you really use that sword?" The smile disappeared. And very rapidly, so flickering a change that it almost seemed an illusion, Seamus glimpsed the phenomenon he called Adult Face: Mori's features grew rigid, skin so taut it appeared mask-like, flat and two-dimensional. His eyes narrowed and seemed to focus on Seamus with a beam-like concentration. For a moment, it communicated to the boy all the intensity, the seriousness, the weird combination of terror, rage and power that lay hidden behind the buffoon-like exterior of adults. Then the face surface rippled and it was gone. Mr. Mori smiled his sappy smile once again and said quietly, "Oh, yes. You will see."

All Seamus saw that night was Mr. Mori prowl the mat like some good-natured dwarf bear, suddenly attacking his students and launching them through the air with judo flips. The crash and bang of students as they were propelled into the mat made Seamus flinch. "Judo is a Japanese martial art," he read in his little booklet (Thud! Another body hit the mat.), "which means" (Crash! An overenthusiastic student apparently attempted to put his partner through the wall.) "Gentle Way or" (A senior student stopped to briefly rewind the ace bandage which was wound around his arm from hand to elbow.) "the Way of Flexibility." By the end of the lesson, most of the students were soaked in sweat. Many finished their last matches by collapsing into panting heaps on the floor.

Mr. Mori was inordinately pleased, it seemed to Seamus, that the bulk of his students were perilously near heat prostration. "Yes, yes," he kept repeating, "gooooood." He smiled that stupid smile. When Seamus left that night, clutching his pamphlet and membership card, stunned by the ferocity of the training session, he was on the brink of never returning. Then he saw the sword and remembered the slam and crunch as smiley Mr. Mori wiped the floor with all comers. Seamus concluded that maybe he should come back. If he could do that much damage to people, he'd smile all the time too.

So his apprenticeship began. He came faithfully through the dark winter evenings three times a week to the steamy room with the mat. His new judo uniform was so stiff with starch that it gave him a rash. The repeated falls he took made him feel like he had been in a massive car crash, and he felt that way for the better part of a month. He had never been particularly good in sports, and exertion in general made him feel nauseous. They made him buy an athletic supporter and a cup, which were not only weird feeling to wear but also struck him (for reasons he couldn't fathom) as vaguely obscene. Nonetheless, he kept at it with that peculiar intensity which kids have. He staggered home night after night and sat stupefied in the bathtub as he watched his legs turn slowly yellow as that session's bruises began to come out.

There was, however, something happening. Although Seamus hit the mat the average of about one hundred thousand times (it seemed to him) every lesson, he no longer woke in the morning feeling like he had been pounded with mallets. Occasionally, he even got lucky and knocked his partner down. The satisfaction Seamus began to feel was eclipsed, however, by the thrill of something even more wonderful. The Transformation had begun.

His voice began to squeak and bottom out and sounded like he had a continual cold. He stared in the mirror every morning at a face that had begun to look like Lon Chaney Jr.'s halfway through his transition to a werewolf: it looked sort of lumpy and his eyebrows were darker, thicker. You could practically hear the creak and moan as the bones in Seamus' face grew, stretched and reshaped themselves into something which would some day approximate an adult visage. There was even hair (yes! hair!) growing on his legs. Seamus, in an unarticulated way, was convinced that all the slam and crunch of the judo hall had shaken something loose inside him, had kicked his glands into the hyperactivity which resulted in The Transformation.

The hormonal riot of adolescence combined with the relentless physical activity of judo wreaked a dramatic change in him. That Christmas, most of the clothes he got had to be returned; Seamus the Irish Butterball had been stretched and pared down to a form quite different from the one in his relatives' memories. He no longer could be the recipient of an endless (and humiliating) parade of trousers bought in the HUSKY BOYS department.

Mr. Mori, too, saw the change. He began to treat Seamus with a little more seriousness during training. The lessons got harder, the punishment and exertion more intense. It began to get scary. Seamus now got to train with the older guys. In the heat of contest, he glimpsed the terrifying apparition of Adult Face with greater frequency. Even more frightening, Seamus had caught a glimpse of the Dreaded Visage flickering on his own face in the mirror which hung on one wall of the training hall.

In some ways, the challenge of the judo hall began to exert a greater hold on Seamus' imagination than did his bus fantasies. It was much more common now for Seamus to see in his mind's eye, not the beefy menace of Hogan, but the smiling terror of a match with Mr. Mori. In the half-dreaming state just before real sleep took over, Seamus' arms and legs would jerk spasmodically, not in fear, but in judo move and counter-move.

Things were coming to a head, however, on the bus. As the boys got bigger over the course of the school year, the harassment grew more intense, the punishment more severe. The freshmen began to resist in brief moments of unthinking bravery. They were ultimately overwhelmed by the still-superior size of Hogan and his cronies, but something (Seamus' Inner Voice told him) had to give.

Mr. Mori had told him that all life could be interpreted as an exercise in judo (or was it the other way around?). You observe your opponent, you sense his strengths, you find the point at which his balance can be broken. You knock him down. It wasn't an exercise in strength, but of intelligence, of skill, of insight. Seamus began to observe Hogan carefully.

The revelation came (like most revelations) unexpectedly, while Seamus was concentrating on something considerably removed from his twin obsessions of either judo or Hogan. The lunch room at Our Lady Light of Pagans High School was a yellow-painted neutral zone where the inmates of that institution ate in uneasy harmony under the watchful eyes of patrolling teachers. It was a place redolent of teenage sweat, half-eaten tuna sandwiches, and the milk which seeped out of the bottom of waxed cardboard containers like some sort of glandular secretion. It was also a place, Seamus had learned, where you could watch people. He was shuffling along the milk line with his gaze locked on a figure on another line.

Anne Marie Abatino. A junior. A rounded, blonde, perfumed presence who sat in regal beauty in the front of Seamus' bus. He was gazing at the well-filled rear of her pleated uniform skirt not so much with lustful intent as with a sort of inchoate longing and fascination. The physical sensation was similar to taking a sudden plunge in an elevator: butterflies in the stomach and the feeling that something mysterious was stirring deep in the core of his torso and rearranging his internal organs. It was both pleasurable and alarming at the same time.

His attention was momentarily distracted by the woman behind the cash register. She was one of those Cafeteria Ladies. She had all the characteristics: hair net, grossly swollen ankles, and a goatee. Seamus paid for his milk, tore his eyes from the hideous apparition, and locked them once more on Anne Marie. So intent was he on plumbing the wool-clad mystery of her form, that he bumped into someone.

"Sorry," he mumbled, barely even glancing at the guy, who also seemed distracted. Seamus walked on, then stopped and stood rooted to the spot. That was Hogan!

Seamus' brain went into overdrive. He was sweating slightly, both with the closeness of his call and with the mental effort he was bending toward trying to figure out why his sworn enemy, the terror of bus riders, had let Seamus careen off him without retribution. Seamus watched Hogan closely. His face, never overly intelligent looking at the best of times, was fixed into the immobility of intense concentration (an unfamiliar activity for Hogan). His gaze was tracking someone, a gorilla-like laser beam focused on . . . Anne Marie! He was looking at Anne Marie! Hogan and Seamus had been doing the same thing: taking their stomachs on the elevator ride of sexual titillation.

Continued observation throughout the week confirmed the initial discovery. Hogan and Anne Marie danced in the elaborate courtship ritual of high school: sly glances, whispers among friends, chance meetings, both saying little, but hoping that, like planets on parallel orbits, the sheer power of the gravitational pull of desire would join them together. Seamus noticed that Hogan's Neanderthal behavior was considerably toned down when Anne Marie was present. Like some primitive hominid coaxed from the cave, Hogan was mesmerized, soothed (tamed!) by Anne Marie's charms. Whatever chagrin and aesthetic distaste he felt, Seamus had to admit that there was something going on between beauty and the bus beast and that here was Hogan's weak point, the point of critical balance.

It all flowed together on a hot spring Friday, the potent blend of freshman fear and suppressed rage and senior cruelty mixing like unstable chemicals which were heated to dangerous levels through hormonal agitation and libidinal energy.

The harassment on the bus had been growing in intensity to almost unbearable levels. The blasts of cruelty had even begun to surge out from the chromium yellow shell casing of the bus. Seamus and the others were no longer safe in the halls or the lunch rooms. All corridors at Our Lady Light of Pagans took on the menacing, grainy look of jittery hand-held camera scenes in cheap horror flicks. The play area outside the cafeteria had a sun-blasted, dusty aspect. Dodge City before the big gunfight. Even so, the showdown came unexpectedly. It had to really, because Seamus, although a dreamer, had a pretty good lock on reality. His search for Hogan's weak point was really just an intellectual exercise. He never would have seriously planned anything like what happened.

At lunch, Seamus was lingering outside, feeling the spring sun bring out beads of perspiration which made the grit on his neck feel like it was being ground into his skin by his tie. It was one of the drawbacks of giving up clip-ons, but no high school kid in his right mind wore the clip-on ties of parochial grammar school. After the dim light of cinder block classrooms, it was almost too bright to see, but Seamus squinted carefully around, his vigilance fueled by freshman paranoia.

He heard a vague commotion off to his left, and knew with an icy certainty which came quicker than the process of thought that a freshman was in trouble. The faint sounds of terror, like a rabbit screaming, were overlaid with the thick guffaws of teenaged sadists. Hogan had found a victim.

Seamus experienced a brief feeling of relief that it wasn't him. But he was also drawn to the cluster of boys with a morbid curiosity and some strange feeling of freshman solidarity. Executions, like weddings, required witnesses.

He saw with a sick feeling that Hogan's victim was Koslowski, a diminutive kid with elf-like features and a large mole on his face. His size, his name, his mole (mark of Cain!) made him a natural victim. Hogan had stolen Koz's book and was torturing him with the tried and true techniques big kids everywhere and in all ages have used to taunt smaller ones. The book is held out, the kid grabs for it, it is yanked out of reach. The smaller kid dances and leaps around the larger one, whose sheer height and bulk make him unassailable.

Something snapped inside Seamus. Without really thinking, he broke out of the circle of spectators, walked up behind Hogan, and plucked the book out

of his hand. Seamus gave it to Kozlowski and expected him to take off like a rocket. Koz stood there staring at him. Seamus looked around. Everyone gawked in a kind of fearful incredulity. Even Hogan seemed momentarily taken aback by the inconceivable turn of events. Deep inside Seamus' head, a little voice said, "Uuuhhhh oooooh."

Hogan's piggy little blue eyes narrowed in rage. Soundlessly, he shoved Seamus. The crowd sighed. The die was cast. The outcome of this unexpected turn of events was now a foregone conclusion. It was the Shove. The ritual precursor to every teenage fight. For reasons lost deep in the past, all teenagers feel the primeval urge to soup themselves up for fisticuffs by exchanging a series of shoves which increase in speed and intensity until the internal pressure cause an explosion in which the combatants leap at one another, arms windmilling, breath whistling and spit flying. Seamus knew that he was in a very dangerous situation. If he wasn't careful, Hogan would see to it that nothing remained of Seamus except a grease spot and maybe his non-clip-on tie.

Seamus shoved back. (What are you doing! his Inner Voice raged.) Hogan shoved Seamus with two hands. Seamus shoved him again, actually making Hogan step backward a step or two. Hogan came at him then. Seamus grabbed him by the collar with both hands, leaned back, planted one foot in Hogan's stomach, and executed a perfect judo sacrifice throw. Seamus threw himself onto his back, and the momentum of his movement and the placement of his leg launched Hogan completely over him. At the last possible moment, Seamus pulled in with his hands a little bit. It was a neat little trick Mr. Mori had shown him which shortened the arc of the fall and accelerated the speed of Hogan's fall. He slammed into the ground with the same sickening smack a dead flounder makes when it's dropped on a pier. Seamus heard Hogan's teeth click together on impact with the ground. Hogan the two hundred pound flounder lay motionless on his back, momentarily stunned.

Seamus sprang to his feet. "I should jump on him and choke the life out of him," he thought. (You should run for your life, his Inner Voice told him.)

Hogan began to stir. The movement snapped Seamus out of his dazed interior dialogue. He looked at Kozlowski, who stood there with his mouth open, his little raspberry lips bright against a face grown pale with the enormity of recent events. "Run, Koz!" Seamus shouted, and gave himself over to his instincts.

Hogan raged after them, plowing through crowds of students like a rabid gorilla trampling through the dense vegetation of a rain forest. Seamus could hear the meaty thud of Hogan's size twelve feet gaining on him. They had the relentless quality of pistons in a machine. Seamus was too terrified to look behind him as the engine of death drew closer. He knew that even the slightest wasted motion could spell doom. He had only one hope. He had to reach sanctuary. The point of critical balance.

Anne Marie. She and her friends stood, blissfully unaware that they were the terminal end of a series of events which had served as a kind of adolescent particle accelerator. Now the excited elements in that accelerator plowed into the girls in a sliding, sweating, grunting mass. Hogan caught Seamus just as he reached Anne Marie and knocked him off his feet. The momentum of his run pitched Seamus face-forward, and he felt the burn as his nose and forehead scraped along the pavement. The girls squealed and began to scatter but were drawn back in morbid interest by the sheer intensity of Hogan's rage. So strong are the twin instincts which drive teenage boys (aggression and sex) that Seamus, in pain and on the ground, briefly wondered if any of the girls would get close enough for him to look up their dresses.

It was a fleeting thought, quickly eclipsed by Hogan. Seamus knew that death was upon him. He huddled on the ground, tucked in the defensive posture used in judo mat work, while Hogan swarmed over him like some psycho Neanderthal. "I'm—gonna—kill—YOU," Hogan grunted, his broken delivery a stylistic effect of the systematic activity he was engaged in: beating Seamus to death.

"Now!" Seamus' Inner Voice prompted, "Now!" The timing was perfect. The moment was right. The critical point had been reached.

"You shouldn't take little kids' books," Seamus said, just loud enough for Anne Marie to hear. It produced no apparent reaction, and for a moment, Seamus felt a stab of panic. "You shouldn't take little kid's books!" he shouted at the top of his lungs.

The voice of deliverance spoke: "Michael!" (Anne Marie was one of the few people to actually use Hogan's first name. Seamus supposed that Hogan's parents had named him in the same way that divers at Sea World give killer whales cute little names that end in vowels: it helps disguise the fact you're dealing with unpredictable, feral creatures.)

Hogan kept slugging away. "Michael!" she said again in that half-exasperated, half outraged tone that teenage girls have elevated to a minor art form. Seamus knew then that he had them. He lay on the ground like some pathetic victim (she hadn't seen him toss Hogan through the air) and bleated at the top of his lungs about the fact that Hogan was picking on little kids. It was a finely calculated piece of work. Hogan was too big to beat. Hogan the Jock, Hogan the Warrior, Hogan the Bus Terror was invincible. Hogan the Big Man, Hogan the Suitor, Hogan the Guy with the Hots for Anne Marie, however, could be defeated by his very desire to look good in front of her.

Eventually, Hogan stopped his attack. It was partly the result of Anne Marie's entreaties, but Seamus also suspected that Hogan's arms were getting tired. Seamus unfolded himself and stood up to stare directly into Hogan's face. Seamus was shaking so hard that he was afraid to speak. Hogan's nostrils were flaring spasmodically: when you got a primitive engine of mindless muscle going it took awhile to shut it all down completely. They stood there panting at each other until Anne Marie eventually succeeded in pulling Hogan away. Nothing was said, but both boys knew something significant had happened.

Seamus tottered weakly away, Kozlowski in tow. Finally, he felt strong enough to speak.

"Koz," Seamus said, "do me a favor. Don't bring your books to lunch period anymore."

The scratches on Seamus' face had begun to scab over by the time he arrived at the judo school for his evening lesson. Mr. Mori had already heard what happened from Chris Koenig, who had not been at the fight but had picked up a wealth of details from eyewitnesses. The story had gotten embellished as it sped through the Kid Grapevine. It was surpassed surreptitiously on sweat-stained looseleaf under the unsuspecting noses of teachers, rapidly related in hushed but excited tones in the dark cavernous halls till the facts ricocheted, collided, snowballed and eventually congealed into a true Kid Epic: freshman taunted to the breaking point snaps, runs amok, and attempts murder. By the end of that school day, kids were avoiding Seamus, watching him with the bug-eyed, rolling eyes of scared horses like they thought he would suddenly whip out a live chicken, bite its head off, and drink the blood while cackling madly.

Mr. Mori questioned Seamus briefly on the how and why of the fight. When Seamus told him how he had found Hogan's point of critical balance, Mr. Mori's lips bulged out and his eyes widened as if he were about to laugh, but he made no comment.

The practice session was an unremarkable one although Seamus felt a bit worn out and listless. When practice was about to end, Mr. Mori told his pupils to sit against one wall. He walked quietly to his office and returned. He held the sword.

Mori knelt in the middle of the room, performed the ritual bows, and placed the sword in his belt. The blade leapt free of the scabbard, a shimmering blue-grey blur, as Mr. Mori began a series of sword forms. In his hands, the sword whistled through the air, cutting horizontally, vertically, and on the diagonal with a speed and precision so great that you could almost hear it when the strikes

stopped at their imaginary targets. He crouched, whirled, thrust, cleaving phantom opponents with a technique so pure, so focused, that the awed boys felt that they were no longer watching Mori use a sword, but rather were witnessing some occult fusion of metal and flesh.

The display ended as the sword slid silently back into its scabbard. Seamus was aware that he had been holding his breath. Mr. Mori sat facing the students. "You see," he said. "Sword is just sword. Just a thing. Mind makes it a weapon."

He held up the weapon. "This not important." He set the sword down carefully. "Mind only is important. So. Sword, no-sword all the same. Sword-man, judo-man the same." He looked at Seamus. "Now you begin to be sword-man."

The lesson was over.

That night, as he lay in bed, feeling the ache in his back and not sure whether it was from Hogan or tonight's judo, Seamus knew that something had changed for him. He had passed some sort of significant marker, but like a passenger in a car speeding along out of control, he was moving too fast to know precisely what it was or what it meant. He felt relieved that he had stood up to Hogan, outsmarted him, and actually lived to tell the tale.

He was happy that judo, which had propelled him along the first unsure steps of adolescence had, in an odd way, helped him do what he had to do. Most of all, however, he felt an overwhelming sense of melancholy. A feeling of regret which was as poignant as it was vaguely defined. Was it because, like Alexander, he had conquered something and now was depressed at the loss of the challenge? He didn't think so. He still had his biology final to pass.

Seamus was tired. His head felt warm and fuzzy, like his brain was slowly being packed in cotton balls. It was the inevitable sign that he was falling asleep. Just before he slipped under the rim of consciousness, Seamus' regret crystallized and briefly took on shape: when he was down on the ground with Hogan, he really wished that he had been able to get a look up Anne Marie's dress.

His scabbed face settled into the rounded-cheek and pursed-lipped innocence of a sleeping boy. It held just a hint of a smirk.

chapter 4

Wang Wu Notices the Commotion on Music Hall Street

An Excerpt from the
Tales of Chivalrous and Altruistic Heros
Introduction and translation by Christopher Bates, M.A.

Foreground photo courtesy of the Government Information Office, Taiwan, ROC.
Background photo by M. DeMarco.

Introduction

Contrary to many people's impressions, China's literary tradition has not been limited to terse expositions on the "Way" and non-conformist love lyrics, but has also included a virile, active genre known as the *wu xia xiao shuo* or the military-chivalric novel. China's history of recording martial feats is a lengthy one going back to Sima Qian's "Tales of Roaming Heroes" included in his historical annals (circa 90 BCE). A later work which provided many a plot for Chinese opera tales is Shi Nai'an's *Tales from the Water Margin*.

The modern military-chivalric novel was fathered by Xiang Kairan. Known by the pen name "The Most Unworthy Man of Ping Jiang," Xiang is recognized as the first of many authors of this century to popularize this literature in the vernacular. He wrote during the 1920's and 1930's, a time when waves of nationalism were sweeping across China. The rise of this literature can perhaps be attributed to these strong patriotic emotions. Xiang's stories emphasize the strength and courage, both moral and physical, of some of China's great martial artists. The rousing stories served as a medicine for the melancholy of China's "weak man of Asia" image. The implication was that conscious and diligent training could produce in a man a supernormal level of ability which could make it possible to defeat Western strong men and wrestlers. The connection with broader national goals is self-evident.

The stories translated in this article are from Xiang Kairan's *Tales of Chivalrous and Altruistic Heroes*, published in a sixteen-volume series between the years 1926 and 1931. The central character is Huo Yuanjia, an actual person who lived from 1862 until 1909 when, as hearsay has it, he was poisoned by jealous Japanese boxers he had bested.* There are no recorded losses tarnishing his fighting name and he would still be one of the truly great boxers of modern times even if the tales surrounding him were scaled down by half! Today, the school he founded, the Jingwu Men Academy, has wealthy branches throughout Asia.

Several times in the story below the term *jiang hu pai* appears untranslated for the reason that it lacks any satisfactory English equivalent. It is defined by current dictionaries as "vagabond, itinerant, or wanderer," but this is a more current usage we feel and does not reflect the spirit of the expression as used in the wuxia genre. Here it implies men usually possessed of martial ability, who travelled about as free-lancers for the cause of justice as they saw it. Thus the term is close in meaning to *xia*, people dedicated to helping the poor and weak. The Jiang Hu Pai is that group of men and women in society who shared this lifestyle.

In the excerpt below, we are told of Huo Yuanjia's youth. But, moreover, we are told about the kind of life led by some boxing families in China and the general climate of the martial arts in China at the time. In telling his tales Xiang Kairan includes long discussions on facets of the martial arts and does not just narrate the story at hand. These diversions have been translated intact and included for the reader's enlightenment and enjoyment.

* This was the basis of the story behind one of Bruce Lee's first hits, *Fists of Fury*.

• • •

Wang Wu Notices the Commotion on Music Hall Street

Wang Wu had come to Tianjin from Beijing as a part of his search for China's very best boxers. In his youth he had first mastered the teachings of such notables as Zhou Liang, "The Daytime Rat," and later the marvelous single-sword virtuosity of "Old Tung" of Shanxi province. He had since made a name for himself with that weapon, sometimes being called "Big Sword Wang."

It was November and for the past several days it had been snowing, so Wang Wu had stayed in his hostel and not gone out at all. On this day he rose early. The weather was bright and clear and Wang went downstairs to wash up. He immediately noticed a lot of people gathered outside who appeared to be watching some fight or spectacle. He hastily finished his washing and went out the gate to take a look. And what did he see? He walked to the front of the crowd, but first saw nothing out of the ordinary. Then he observed that in front of the Huai Brethren's Meeting House everything was all disordered and two immense curbstones lay strewn about. Each must have weighed eight or nine hundred pounds and everyone was gaping at the sight. Wang Wu looked first at the stones and then at the onlookers, yet was unable to perceive what it was about those rocks that was so startling or what had caused such a crowd to gather.

Now, Wang Wu was a very skeptical fellow and not given to asking others questions. Therefore, when he saw all these people absorbed in the sight of the curbstones, it made him examine the situation even more minutely. At this time the street was covered with snow. Though many people had already walked over it and the snow looked like trampled rice gruel, still two tracks could be discerned. What could these tracks be? They were the tracks of the stones tumbling, of course. Looking at the impressions in the road, Wang Wu saw that they came from the gate of the pharmacy at the Huai Brethren's Meeting House and that the two stones had been moved over ten feet each. He walked to the gate and took a look. On each side there were impressions two or three centimeters deep as if the rocks had fallen into place there.

While looking at these tracks, Wang Wu realized that it must have taken quite a strong man to move these two slabs. However, he suddenly had second thoughts: "I usually kick a three hundred pound sandbag. The bag is soft so I can kick it with all my might and not injure my foot. But if I were to kick the grinding stone like that, surely my bones would break and sinews separate. Even if this man possesses over a thousand pounds of strength, is it possible that his foot is living iron?! This certainly isn't the work of a foot." In his heart Wang Wu had difficulty squaring this sight with what he knew to be humanly possible. "No matter whether they were struck by a foot or not, only a man's physical strength could make these stones tumble so far. If a man could move them at all, then he must be extremely able." Then, without talking with any of the bystanders, he returned to the inn for breakfast.

When the waiter came in with tea, Wang called him over, "Do you know who runs the Huai Drug Shop around the corner on Music Hall Street and how long has it been open?"

The waiter replied with a chuckle, "Everyone in Tianjin knows that Huo the Fourth opened it not too long ago. His strength is really something; anyone who has seen it is simply overwhelmed. Why, only last night on this street there were twenty or thirty guys gathered together, shooting the bull, and talking about how strong Huo is. They couldn't decide just how strong so they talked over ways to test his strength and finally decided on one man's proposal.

"They pushed and pulled two large curbstones over to Huo's place and stood them up leaning against the door frame. I saw this and knew they must be trying to test Huo as so many had tried before. They had never seen how really strong he is!

"It wasn't yet dawn and the group hid on the side of the street and waited to see what Huo would do to those stones. I was inside waiting when the door opened. Through the open door I saw the head chef, who looked to be about fifty years old, preparing food. He saw the two stones and they really shook him up. He tried to move them but it was as if they had taken root. How could he possibly have budged them! He looked at them for a while and then went back inside. It wasn't long before the cook brought Huo out. I came out at this time and what should I see but Huo looking them over. He was wearing a long leather robe which he lifted up to afford movement. He then made a half turn and kicked out with his left foot. The stone on the right side fell and toppled over ten feet. This was enough to scare the shit out of us, but then he kicked again, this time with his right foot hitting the stone on the left. It tumbled end over end over ten feet and landed standing on end in the street! With this I don't know how many people were startled, but they all ran up for a closer look."

On hearing the waiter's story, Wang Wu could not help but be both frightened and ecstatic at the same time. He was frightened by the thought of so powerful a man, but ecstatic over having come to Tianjin and gained an opportunity to meet him, supposing the story to be true, that is. On inquiring further as to Huo the Fourth's family history, Wang discovered that the waiter was unable to elucidate the matter any further. Wang immediately changed his clothes and, name card in hand, went to the Huai Brethren's Drug Shop.

I will take this opportunity to introduce Huo's personal history. He was from the Tianjin area, Jing Hai county, a place called Little Henan Village. His personal name is Yuanjia and his cognomen is Chunching, his father being Huo Endi. When his father was young, he was famous for his bodyguard service. He was a friend of Zhou Liang, "The Daytime Rat," and his ability was not inferior to Zhou's. Huo Endi's family's style of boxing was famous throughout the five northern provinces and was known as Mizong Yi. The art, by decree of a family grandmaster long ago, had been handed down through the generations only to the male heirs. Daughters could not be taught the art for it was feared they would pass it on to their spouses' clans when they married.

According to members of the Huo family, the name Mizong Yi has two meanings. One interpretation is that the movements of this boxing style, when used against an adversary, so confound him as to render him unable to discern what has occurred. Therefore, it is called Mizong, "Deceptive Stepping," and the name denotes a method. According to the second interpretation, the art is so old that the originator is unknown, and so the name Mizong, "Lost Traces," describes the origin. To this day I have not determined which is the correct interpretation. However, no matter which interpretation one chooses, this Mizong boxing style is the exclusive technique of the Huo Family. It is an uncommon method.

In the Huo family group of uncles and sons, altogether ten in number, Huo Yuanjia was the fourth in line. His father, Endi, was in his middle years. In his youth Endi had acquired no small number of possessions. Having always been frugal, Endi upon entering middle age decided he had enough finances to retire to a small country town for the rest of his life. No longer willing to suffer more adventures and endure the wind and frost, he gave up the bodyguard service to spend his remaining years enjoying his fortune.

He moved into Little Henan Village, on the one hand farming for small but safe profits and on the other hand training his nephews and sons in their boxing legacy. As the son of a laborer should persevere at labor and a farmer's son should continue to work the land, so the son of a martial artist certainly must train in the art of his father. How much more so should this be the case in the Huo family with its long tradition of boxing!

As rural land was not expensive, houses were always spacious. The houses of Huo's family and Wang Wu's family were about the same in this respect. A practice hall was built on a special piece of the Huo's land. Because mirrors were hard to come by, the Huo hall did not have one, but the practice hall of Wang Wu's family did. However, the size of the hall was larger than the Wang's, with enough room for over ten men to train together, and of course, it was well stocked with all manner of weapons. On the wall was hung a scroll with the advice, "Let the Altruistic Spirit Fill And Cleanse Your Body."

When Huo Yuanjia became seven or eight, his father planned to teach him in the group along with the others. Each day from morning to night they would be at the gymnasium training their fists and feet. However, Yuanjia's body was too lean. Although he was now seven or eight, he was unspeakably short, and his height gave him the appearance of a four year old. He was even unable to walk correctly. Huo Endi told Yuanjia that he was too weak and that he had to wait several years until his body could develop more strength. As it was, he was so weak he could barely stand, much less train in boxing.

When the boy turned twelve he had grown a little but still could not pass for more than seven or eight. When arguing over playthings with seven year olds from town, he would sometimes fight and would invariably be beaten into the ground. Crying and wailing he would return home a bloodied mess. There he would tell his father what had happened and Endi would become so angry he would not utter a word. My son," he thought, "has been beaten by children all eight years old or younger, yet he is twelve. If he had been trounced by an older bully, I could still walk tall and go to the parents' homes and caution them against a next time, telling the boys not to pick on kids. But now he is trampled by tykes with no boxing experience whatsoever whereas he is an heir to our family's famous fist art. How can I go to their homes and talk it out?"

On several more occasions Yuanjia was naughty, somewhat enjoying these scraps, and his father was furious. He immediately forbade Yuanjia to go beyond the farm and further forbade him to enter the training hall. He explained, "It seems that with your body so weak and useless we may as well not teach you martial art. Huo's have never displayed weakness outside of the family. Now Yuanjia is twelve and he can't whip eight year olds. If his actions lose face for anyone, it will be us. By all means we must avoid tarnishing our family name." For generations past, all of the sons had trained in Mizong Yi, and this was to be the first exception. All the relatives were stunned to hear the news and pleaded with Endi to let Yuanjia practice, but Endi was adamant.

Not only was Yuanjia not allowed to enter the training hall; moreover, he was not even permitted to bring up the subject of boxing. Fortunately, his small body provided him with an opportunity to hide just outside the gymnasium and watch the others exercise. Each day from morning to night he would watch unnoticed by anyone. Behind the Huo's house was a dense date grove. After watching all day, Yuanjia would go back into the grove to practice what he had seen. He continued this regimen for twelve years until he was twenty-four years of age. In all this time he never had a chance to compare his skills with anyone.

One day a travelling boxer came carrying a sack on his back. He said he was a Henanese surnamed Tu and named Yuchuan, and had trained in the martial arts since childhood. Because of the notoriety of the Huo family art, he had especially come to pay his respects. Huo Endi saw that the man had travelled far to visit a stranger on rumor alone and so was an attentive host.

Tu stayed the night and the next day was invited by Endi to view the training of his nine sons and nephews. Tu stood and watched closely, clapping now and then, but never saying a word. When all nine students had performed Tu turned and bowed, saying, "Hmm, well, that answers my questions all right. Thanks a lot."

Endi perceived that Tu was not particularly impressed. Because Endi felt himself to be already past his prime and he did not know how talented Tu was, he feared to come to blows with the man and risk losing face. Tu had viewed the students' demonstrations and had not praised them, seeming to place himself above them all. Huo could not but stifle his anger, return the bow, and reply, "It must all seem very amusing. None of them have practiced very long, and they are all a little rusty. To an expert, this must all seem rather clumsy."

Tu Yuchuan laughed and said, "For years now I've heard tales about Mizong Yi, an art matchless under heaven, I was told. Even seven-year-old members of your family were reputed to be terrific, even though they had not practiced long. It is evident that the rumors I've heard outside are to be turned about here. What

I have seen today really does not live up to the reputation."

Huo Endi's face turned red and he was unable to reply, but Huo the Sixth, whose ability was highest among the nine students, could no longer contain himself. He walked out striking his chest, challenging, "Our clan's boxing has always been without rival. Who dares to disagree? If you don't believe it, we can take a walk, all right?"

Before he could finish, Huo Endi was bellowing, "In our art, etiquette is first. Tu came here as a guest. How can we be disrespectful?"

Tu rejoined, chuckling, "How can determining martial ability in the ring be deemed rude? To think I walked a thousand *li* to see what you showed me. If you're not too stingy about your techniques, let's have a go at it!" As he spoke, he advanced forward several steps.

Immediately the situation in the school became more volatile, and though Endi feared that Huo the Sixth could not beat Tu, he knew none of the others had a hope. Since Huo the Sixth had challenged and Tu had stepped into the arena, the Huos could not but fight. All Endi could do was fearfully watch his son and Tu cross hands and begin to probe each other's defenses. At the end of only one round, Huo's left shoulder had already been injured. How could he wish to continue the fight? Taking advantage of the fact that he had not been totally defeated, he retired from the ring, and though suffering from his wound made no mention of it.

On seeing Huo withdraw from the arena, Tu bowed and said, "I'm sorry." Then, he too, left the fighting area.

So angry was Huo Endi that he was even willing to risk his own life to save the family reputation from destruction. He took off the long robe he was wearing, but just then Huo Yuanjia dashed in and challenged, "Our clan's boxing has always been without peer. Who dares to disagree, then come with me, Huo the Fourth, for a try."

As soon as Yuanjia ran in, Huo Endi became incensed and shouted, "You unfilial animal! How dare you come here? Are you seeking death?!"

Tu Yuchuan sneered with amused contempt at Yuanjia, "Everyone here sure likes to talk big, but I certainly hope you won't be as useless as the last," and so saying he jumped back into the fighting area.

How could Endi possibly have stopped this match, for within the wink of an eye the two men had already joined in combat. Endi was, of course, very anxious, but at the same time he wondered where Huo the Fourth had learned to fight. The two continued their struggle for ten rounds when suddenly Yuanjia kicked out with his right foot. Tu Yuchuan flew up and back over ten feet and then lay crumpled on the ground, motionless for some time.

Huo Endi walked over to where Tu lay and supported him. He examined Tu's left leg which had been broken by Yuanjia's kick. Owing to Endi's highly skilled medical abilities, a balm was quickly prepared and the wound tied up with the bark of the Cryptomeria tree. Tu stayed at the Huo's for two weeks before recovering enough to walk. Then he bade the Huos farewell, paying homage to Endi's medicine and the family Mizong art, and left almost as he had come, with his pack on his back ... yet far wiser.

Huo Endi asked his son what kind of training had resulted in such wonderful gongfu. Yuanjia told him the story of his quiet listening and quiet training. The father said with a sigh, "Without incentive, the young are enthusiastic about nothing. If you had trained together with your nine brothers, you might have lost interest in seeking mastery. Then you could not have attained this ability." Right then and there, Endi had Yuanjia show them all of his skills, and they were a wonder to behold. The father was so happy he could not but hug his son and commend him.

• • •

Now at this time in Tiger's Head Village in Shandong Province, there lived the Chao clan. They were like the Huo family in that a former master of the family's boxing style had decreed that the art be kept within the family. Likewise, their skill was renowned throughout the five northern provinces.

Formerly in China, martial artists had several distinctive traits. Foremost among these traits were their extreme jealousy and envy. In this kind of climate, if two men are equally famous, they will vow to strike the other down. They can always find some pretext or grudge with which to risk their lives for the other's death. Therefore, martial artists generally did not associate face to face with other martial artists. As soon as they would see each other, it would not be one or two words before they were at each other's throats.

Sometimes the two parties would work through an intermediary who would arrange for them to sign a waiver and buy a suit of burial clothes. These were placed near the chosen field of honor and the two boxers would begin their fight. Whoever was killed received the suit of clothes and the body was given back to the family who had to bury the corpse. There could be no further legal recourse on their part.

This type of fighting is called "trial by combat." Trials by combat are divided into several classes. The Northern Chinese have the "Single" and "Double Pan," and the Southerners have the "Hard" and "Weak Chop" varieties. Though different in name, the idea is the same. The "Single Pan" of the North is the "Hard Chop" of the South. Both North and South also make distinctions between a "cultured" or a "martial" fight.

These trials by combat are really blood-chilling to speak of. For instance, if two people employ the "single pan," one of them must stand and allow his opponent an agreed upon number of blows of the fist or foot. Sometimes the man being hit is permitted to bob, weave, and sidestep. After the first man has given his best strikes, he must stand fast while his opponent returns the blows. If the two men are equally matched, they will often repeat this sequence ten times without determining the winner.

Within the "single pan/hard chop" category are three further distinctions: the opponents must decide whether to strike the head, chest, or leg targets; they cannot just wantonly pummel the adversary. Furthermore, there is the "cultured pan," which allows only the use of the empty hands whereas the "martial pan" allows the use of weapons. So long as both opponents choose the same weapon, even the cruelest ones can be employed. One's whole body can be split apart by a sword or spear, with the blood turning the earth red, and yet there will still be no compunction on the winner's part.

In the "double pan" or the "soft chop," the two fighters must stand and simultaneously make their strikes and must not try to block. This is done with and without weapons.

The "cultured fight" is actually a viewing of the opponent's abilities: jumping, sidestepping, and such. It consists of fighting with pulled punches and kicks, poison-hand techniques are not allowed, and there is no need to take off one's long robes for the performance. This type of trial by combat is most common between those who are friends. It is a chance to gauge one's level of ability and there is no thought of a death match. In the "martial fight," the contestants first sign a waiver releasing the victor from any responsibility for the loser's death. Martial fights are fatal matches between mortal enemies.

During the period in which Huo Yuanjia was practicing martial arts, the Northern schools had just made popular these trials by combat. Ordinarily there were no truly able fighters, so on hearing of the Huo family, who would dare to come forth for a test of skill? Only the Chao clan of Tiger's Head Village, whose art and name ranked almost equally with the Huos', harbored such bold ideas. As the Chao family became more famous, they could no longer endure standing in the Huo family's shadow. For the purpose of discrediting Mizong Yi, several Chao members had secretly been sent to have it out with the Huos. This happened not once or twice but several times and each time the Chaos were defeated.

This year Huo Yuanjia was twenty-four, and like most men his age, he had big ambitions and certainly was not willing to live and die in a hick town. Therefore, he requested that his father allow him to go to Tianjin to do business. Huo Endi, seeing that Yuanjia was more determined than the general run of Huo sons and nephews, gave him his blessings and a sum of money to be used as capital, confident that his son would not let it burn a hole in his pocket.

Huo the Fourth went to Tianjin, rented a shop at the Huai Brethren's

Meeting House, and set up a pharmacy. It had not been open a year when the news spread to the Chao family. They had heard tale that Yuanjia was the only Huo who had gotten the family secrets. They assumed that this was just a cover on the Huo family's part, that indeed Yuanjia had trained, but was the worst boxer in the family. The front, the Chaos assumed, was put up in order to prevent losing face, but if Yuanjia had trained in boxing at all, then defeating him would make the family lose face anyway. With this in mind, they thought to take advantage of him when he moved away by himself to Tianjin. From the boxers of the Chao family, four youthful and strong members were chosen especially to be sent there.

On meeting with Huo, they said they had come from afar having heard his name praised high and low and were requesting to receive some of the Huo family teaching.

Yuanjia laughed at this and said, "Of the Huo family progeny, all but I are martial artists. Although we are not famous, yet the name is still passed around here and there. I, myself, am twenty-five, yet not even an hour have I spent in my family's gymnasium. My father chose not to pass the family teachings on to me, and here you come asking for instruction. Where did you hear my name lauded? What shall I teach you?"

"The son of a Huo cannot box?! Who can believe such talk?" the Chaos exclaimed. "If you aren't a martial artist, can you really call yourself a member of the Huo family? Those in the Jiang Hu Pai all say 'Huo Endi doesn't have sons who can't fight.' You aren't Huo Endi's son if you haven't entered the training hall. Aren't you Huo Endi's son?"

Huo Yuanjia was a full-spirited, young man. How could he easily endure such groundless talk? He knit his brows, his eyes fairly glowed, from his throat came the roar of a tiger, and his palm slammed down on the table.

"You ignorant bastards. You dare to disturb me with this insolence. Whether I have trained in boxing or not is my family's business. What's it to you? So I have trained in boxing. What of it?"

The Chaos angrily replied, "Since you do box, we sought you out to see how good you are. We only came to see who's best. Who cares about the rest?"

Huo heard this and stood up. "That suits me fine! But I don't have to use the Huo art on scum like you. Are you coming as a group or one at a time?"

"If we four attack as a group, it means nothing. Let it be your choice whom you fight first."

Huo and the four Chaos entered the large room of the meeting house, and when Huo had removed his long coat, he said, "Since you all came as a group and it is unavoidable not to fight each of you, you just suit yourselves and attack as you will."

The four decided on the order of attack. When the first one advanced, it was not seven or eight passes before Huo, with his "Single Hua Shan Palm" technique, struck him in the spine. He collapsed to the floor, breaking his nose in the fall and then rolled away unable to get up. Fresh blood came from his mouth and continued flowing out. The second Chao saw this and his eyes burned with fire as he lunged with all his might to strike Huo dead.

These fights were out of the ordinary and one couldn't treat them lightly. When Huo had crossed hands with the first of them he did not know how able they were, so he looked out only for himself. After the eighth pass he had knocked the first Chao down and then had a better idea of just how good they were. Even if the second Chao used all his ability, how could he face up to Huo?

Huo did not steel himself for the coming attack, but moved in directly, his two arms opening then closing onto the second Chao's arms. He flanked him and then shot one arm up. Up toward the ceiling the opponent flew. That room's central beam was almost thirty feet high, but with the throw the opponent's body missed the beam by less than a foot!

The onlookers were left speechless and petrified by the sight of this high throw. If the hapless opponent were to fall onto the brick floor, he would surely die. The other Chaos thought of trying to catch him, but in the first place, they feared the falling body would be too heavy to catch and that they themselves would be injured. In the second place, they had to guard against Huo taking such an opportunity to attack them. So their eyes followed the body's flight up and then down, helplessly staring. The thrown man yelled a loud "Aiya!" and then began to tumble down through the air. Huo leisurely waited until the Chao was only three or four feet from the floor, then extended his arm and caught him just as if he had thrown and caught a man made of paper.

Huo held up the man's trembling body and shook it. "Now do you think I am Huo Endi's son? Now what do you think of the Huo family's martial art? Will you ever again dare to speak so rudely? I could have killed you all and it would have been easier than stepping on so many ants. However, before today I harbored no ill will toward you, and I am still without enmity. If you hadn't been so cocky, I would not have wasted my ability on riffraff such as you. Get out of here and go back where you came from." Saying this, he threw the man he held, but his technique was truly marvelous. Not only was the miscreant uninjured, but he landed on his feet as if he had jumped from a table to the floor. Huo pointed at the three remaining Chaos and threatened, "If you want to look ugly, then attack now. I don't have spare time to fool with, and if you're afraid, then attack together."

The three saw Huo's fierce spirit and cowered under it, not daring to come forward. Then, one choked out some face-saving words: "All right, we've already had a taste of your Huo family skills. But after three years we'll come again to face you, and at that time teach you a lesson or two." This phrase is a cliched expression of the Jiang Hu Pai. All martial artists, when they have a trial by combat and survive a defeat, always say this. What they mean to say is, "This time my ability was not enough to beat you. Next time I'll return to defeat you. I'll remember this enmity and train bitterly until I can come back and settle this score." There are cases in which after three years fighters have truly trained themselves into a superb state and have gotten revenge. However, those who use these words just to save face are by far in the majority.

When Huo heard the declaration, he laughed. "You can wait thirty years if you like. It makes no difference to me. There's no hurry. Go home and work hard."

It was several months after the Chaos had ignominiously left that Wang Wu came to town. He had come to the door of Huo Yuanjia's drug shop carrying his name card. There were still many gawkers milling around who wanted to catch a glimpse of Huo by waiting at his doorstep. Wang Wu went straight inside. Huo's servant came and received Wang's name card. The servant himself had heard of Wang's great work with the sword and went right in to inform his master of the visitor.

As they were both men of chivalrous and altruistic spirit, they felt friendship toward each other at first sight. They talked for long hours of their first love, the martial arts. Wang Wu viewed and admired Huo's fistic ability. Likewise, Huo admired Wang's work with the single sword.

For several years, Wang had already been famous with the double hook swords, and in the five northern provinces no one could best him. Since he had received the teachings of "Old Tong" of Shanxi province in the single sword, he had diligently trained in it. At this time, Wang had already made quite a name for himself, yet toward Huo he still only felt praise, no condescension. He perhaps felt even a little shame because his own fistic skills were deficient. Wang's experience was great. Conversely, Huo felt he could bow to Wang and, furthermore, praised him in front of others.

With young, relatively unknown boxers, Wang would always include in his praise some encouraging words. If the person would humbly ask to be taught, then he would, in all cases, with a benevolent countenance and a kind voice teach and instruct him. As long as the other fellow never thought of a trial by combat, he himself never did. So, though Wang stayed at Huo's drug shop for over two weeks, because they had this mutual admiration and politeness, they never had a single bout. According to an evaluation by a person at that time who knew the capabilities of the two, in boxing Wang Wu could not defeat Huo, and with swords Huo could not stand up to Wang Wu. In the final analysis, as far as fame and capabilities are concerned, there was no one who could beat them.

chapter 5

Inside Interview with Curtis Wong:
Extraordinary Contributions to Martial Arts Popularization
by Michael Maliszewski, Ph.D.

Curtis Wong's Chinese name in Mandarin is Huang Fulin, beautifully brushed by Chou Yueh-Yun, a noted calligraphy teacher in Taiwan. The photo of Wong was taken in his early days as he started to blend his martial art training with entrepreneurship. All photos courtesy of Curtis & Douglas Wong.

Introduction

Curtis Wong is not a name which most readers will quickly identify or recognize. However, the name is familiar to many well-known martial arts champions, practitioners, celebrities and writers. Mr. Wong has published some of the best-known martial arts magazines (*Inside Kung Fu*, *Inside Karate*, *Martial Arts and Combat Sports*, etc.), plus many books and videos (Unique Publications) over the past thirty years. His impact on martial arts "behind the scenes" is indisputable.

Mr. Wong is a humble, self-effacing and polite gentleman, and when I approached him some two years ago to tell his remarkable story in print, he was characteristically shy and reticent. However, I am pleased that he finally consented to share his experiences with us in the following interview.

Several themes in Mr. Wong's story are worthy of note. His involvement in the martial arts began at a time when its popularity was developing and spreading throughout North America and around the world through exposure in the visual media and a variety of publications. Given his roles as martial artist, performer and creative entrepreneur, his experience deserves our attention.

Mr. Wong believes that all martial art styles have merit. His observations of the salient events and experiences during his career deserve consideration, as does his role in bringing many aspects of the martial arts to public attention. In his career, it is possible to observe the influential role played by the martial arts in a broader sense when the philosophy associated with those arts is applied to life in general.

The reader will find that this fascinating story provides a different perspective on the evolution of martial arts and its impact on society today. I will let the interview speak for itself and hope that the reader finds it as interesting as I did.

FAMILY BACKGROUND

Wong Family (L. to R.): brothers Douglas and Frank,
parents Bing and Mary, and Curtis.

- MR. WONG, I'D LIKE TO BEGIN BY ASKING YOU TO GIVE ME SOME GENERAL INFORMATION ABOUT YOUR BACKGROUND, INCLUDING SOMETHING ABOUT YOUR FAMILY AND EDUCATION.

My parents were born in Canton, China. I was born in Los Angeles in 1949. I have two brothers: one younger (Frank) and one older (Douglas). I'm married and have two daughters and one son.

I went to school in the Los Angeles area, but I did not learn to speak English until the third grade. I went to an all black school.

My parents had a grocery store in Watts. It was the first one to burn down during the Los Angeles riots in 1965. Our whole family worked at this store. It was a family owned store. We worked from 7:30 in the morning until midnight. We spent most of our life at that store.

- WHAT HAPPENED AFTER THE STORE BURNED DOWN?

My parent's entire savings were involved in this store. Afterwards, my father had difficulty finding a job. My mother learned how to sew. She would sew a lot of clothes at home. My brother and I went out to get work as well. I worked as a janitor from midnight until seven o'clock in the morning, and then I would go to school.

I graduated high school... barely. Then I went to Los Angeles Community College for a couple of years and then went on to Woodbury College for another two or three years to study interior design.

MARTIAL ARTS BACKGROUND

- OBVIOUSLY YOU ARE INTERESTED IN THE MARTIAL ARTS. COULD YOU GIVE A LITTLE INFORMATION REGARDING YOUR BACKGROUND IN THE MARTIAL ARTS?

I used to get into a lot of fights at the store, of course. Mainly, you walk down the street and the guys want your money (laughter). I remember picking up an issue of *Black Belt* magazine that had a picture of a man on the cover who was breaking all kinds of blocks of ice. I was about twelve years old at the time. Around that time, I started to study martial arts with my cousins. There was a lot of backyard training at that time. I started with Ark Wong (Shaolin style). I also studied taekwondo.

- DID YOU PRACTICE TAEKWONDO FIRST?

Yes, for about a year and a half or so with Mr. Cho. I never really ranked in it... Then I switched to gongfu.

- WHAT WAS YOUR REASON FOR THAT?

I liked the instructor's daughter (laughter).

- How long did you practice gongfu? Any belt ranking?

I studied gongfu for about two and a half years when I was about fifteen years old, but have no official ranking. At this time I was practicing martial arts off and on.

- Who were the noted people teaching gongfu publicly or privately in the early 1970's? Were there any names that really stood out at that time?

In Los Angeles, there was Ark Wong; and in San Francisco, Y.C. Wong. Of course there are a lot of prominent people, but as far as I'm concerned, these people come to my mind.

Ark Y. Wong, a pioneer in bringing Chinese martial arts to the United States, poses in front of the Dragon Inn. Curtis Wong was one of his students.

- Was Ark Wong the only one in the Los Angles area at that time —in the early 70's when you were first getting started—that was teaching Chinese martial arts?

No. Jimmy Woo was also teaching. There was one man named Jimmy Woo who taught in Hollywood, and there's another Jimmy H. Woo who taught Sansoo, a southern Chinese style, and Shaolin Five-Animal Style.

- What style of gongfu did you actually study? What did you particularly enjoy about that style?

Shaolin Five Animals was what I studied, but I had no special interest in that particular style. I just took it because of the teacher's daughter and it was convenient.

- How did you feel about Ark Wong as a teacher? Did you have a good relationship with him?

Yeah… a real good relationship with him. He was a traditionalist with strong traditional values. He had his students practice many exercises before learning much of the authentic forms.

- What about your brother, Douglas. Did he study the same style or a different style?

He also studied with Ark Wong, but he studied a lot of other styles. He studied Mok-Gar, a Choi-Li-Fut style, with a guy named Haumea "Tiny" Lefiti.

Right: Ark Wong striking a pose.

Below: Practicing with double-edge sword in his studio. Note the training devices and weaponry.

Curtis Wong and his brother Douglas put long hours in to their martial arts study. They caught some history of their training in these backyard photos: **1-2)** taekwondo days. **3-4)** Chinese martial arts, defending against weapons attack.

Chinese martial arts: **5)** standing side-kick (*1968 photo by James Lew*); **6)** inward crescent kick at a demonstration; **7)** demonstrating the nine-sectional chain; **8)** jumping roundhouse kick; **9)** blocking a heal kick.

MARTIAL ARTS BUSINESS

Here Curtis frolics with David Chow,
technical advisor for the *Kung Fu* television series.

- YOU HAD MENTIONED TO ME AT ONE TIME THAT YOUR MOTHER WAS INVOLVED WITH MAKING GONGFU UNIFORMS. CAN YOU TELL ME A LITTLE BIT ABOUT THAT?

When I was in martial arts schools in 1972, there really weren't any martial arts uniforms around, especially "kung fu" uniforms. So I designed a uniform. I had my mother sew up a few and they looked pretty good. So we ended up making two hundred uniforms. They ended up selling really well. We sent out a flier for the uniforms and that's how I got my idea for starting the magazine. I found out that you could put ads in the magazine for uniforms, but they were $600 per page for each ad. I didn't have the $600 to do this. So I thought I could start my own magazine and advertise the uniforms for free. I did that before I realized how much it would cost to start a magazine.

- BLACK BELT MAGAZINE WAS ALREADY IN CIRCULATION AT THE TIME...

I think *Black Belt* magazine was already out there for twelve or fourteen years... something like that.

There was no real competition for them, other than *Official Karate*. At that time I actually started working on the *Kung Fu* television series in August of 1972.

- TELL ME HOW THAT ALL DEVELOPED.

I was working in a pharmacy for the last four or five years. My brother [Douglas Wong] was asked at that time to work on the TV pilot series. Now, the reason that they asked him was kind of interesting. Our insurance agent, David Chow, was the technical advisor to the series. David was looking for a good martial artist and there was no one in Los Angeles that knew martial arts at that time. He knew that my brother was involved in the martial arts so he asked him if he would be interested in working on a television series. So my brother said "yeah." So he got to work on the pilot film. At that time they were having a party, and my brother asked me if I wanted to go to the party, and I said "yeah, I'll come by" and that's where I met David Chow. He asked me if I knew any martial arts, and I said "yes, of course!" (laughter) and then he asked me if I could get a photograph taken. So the next day I met with him and I brought a whole pile of photographs. At that time I could do splits as well as jump up high and kick. So they hired me for the first twenty-one episodes.

- WHAT PARTS DID YOU PLAY?

I played all different parts. I played the disciple too… you name it. I spent every weekend with David Chow. He was involved in showing people how to get involved in martial arts movies. He was mainly a judo man. I taught him a lot of things he didn't know before. By the time it got back to David Carradine it was all diluted.

- DID YOU DO ANY FORMAL TEACHING OR CHOREOGRAPHY WITH CARRADINE?
Not really. Very, very little.

On the *Kung Fu* set, Curtis Wong poses with actor David Carradine.

- SO THAT WAS YOUR FIRST ACTING DEBUT?
Yeah.

- IN ADDITION TO THE KUNG FU TV SERIES, WHAT OTHER ACTING PARTS DID YOU PLAY? I THINK YOU MENTIONED A NUMBER OF DIFFERENT ROLES.

I did a lot of TV shows like Police Story, The Quest, Night Rider, The Hardy Boys, Different Strokes...

- AND AT THE SAME TIME YOU WERE DOING THAT, AT WHAT STAGE WAS THE DEVELOPMENT OF YOUR COMPANY AND THE MAGAZINE?

At that time in August of 1972, I worked in the Kung Fu series. I think by October of 1972, I opened a school in Panorama City, California, in the valley. Within three months we had over two hundred students. So I quit my daytime job in the pharmacy and I took off from school for awhile because it was a full-time job. I was concentrating on the martial arts school. Everything took place pretty fast.

- WHAT WAS THE NAME OF THE MARTIAL ARTS SCHOOL THAT YOU OPENED UP IN PANORAMA CITY? HOW DID YOU GET SO MANY STUDENTS IN THREE MONTHS?

The school was called Sillum Kung Fu. Most of the students heard of the school just by word of mouth, plus I had a picture of David Carradine and myself in the front window.

A dapper Curtis Wong
gets some acting direction on the Kung Fu set.

- I'M SURE THAT HELPED... (LAUGHTER).

It helped a lot! My brother was also quite a good teacher... I wasn't much of a teacher. We were all teaching Shaolin gongfu. There were five instructors including myself. At that time, we took every single event across the country, in weapons forms, in fighting... first, second, and third places. This was in 1972, 1973, and 1974. They won trophies everywhere.

- AND HOW LONG WAS THAT SCHOOL IN OPERATION?

It started in December 1972, and is still there today. My brother, Douglas, owns the school.

- MANY HAVE THE IMPRESSION THAT GONGFU WAS VERY WIDE SPREAD... THAT IT WAS PRACTICED THROUGHOUT THE ENTIRE LOS ANGELES AREA DURING THE 1970'S. BUT YOU'RE SAYING THAT THERE WERE NOT ALL THAT MANY PEOPLE WELL VERSED IN GONGFU?

There weren't that many martial arts schools... at least not gongfu schools. At the time that we started our school, James Lew and Albert Leong were teaching, along with my brother, Douglas.

- WHAT ABOUT JAMES AND ALBERT'S BACKGROUND. WHAT PARTICULAR STYLES DID THEY STUDY?

I know Albert and James both studied Shaolin Five Animals with Ark Wong. They taught just a year, or a year and a half, then my brother took over.

- WHO WERE SOME OF THE BETTER-KNOWN STUDENTS AT THAT TIME? ANYBODY THAT HAS GONE ON TO ESTABLISH THEMSELVES?

At that time... I know my brother's taught Kevin Sorbel, who does the Hercules series and Jason Scott Lee, who played Bruce Lee in a recent movie. Actually, there were quite a few celebrities.

- WHEN YOU WERE AT YOUR SILLUM KUNG FU SCHOOL, YOU WERE DOING A NUMBER OF DIFFERENT THINGS. WERE YOU INVOLVED WITH TEACHING, ADVERTISING, ACCOUNTING... WHAT KIND OF ROLES DID YOU PLAY THERE?

I did everything, but I originally taught a little bit, did some advertising and the promotion aspects of the business, but then eventually I started dropping everything. I got pretty busy doing other projects.

- ARE YOU STILL INVOLVED WITH THE PRACTICE OF THE MARTIAL ARTS?

Not at all... not since 1974. I became too busy with the magazines, gathering articles, editing, marketing...

- CAN YOU TELL ME ABOUT HOW THE MAGAZINE DEVELOPED?

During the daytime there were no classes so I started sketching the cover of *Inside Kung Fu* because I just happened to be on the cover of *Black Belt* magazine along with the other forty disciples of the *Kung Fu* series. I just put *Inside Kung Fu* at the top of the sketch and said "this could be a magazine." I really didn't really know how much it would cost at that time to do this. So I think around January or February of 1973, I saved up about $4,000, and I went to the bank and borrowed an additional $6,000 to get $10,000 cash. This was quite a bit of money back then. So in March I started looking for an office and by May I had hired an art director, a photographer and an editor. The first issue came out in August, dated December, 1973. So it happened pretty fast. With the money that I had, I made a brochure and copied *Black Belt's* formula, and it is the same thing basically.

- HOW MANY ISSUES DID YOU PRINT AND THEN SELL?

We sold 25,000 copies. What happened was that we didn't have newsstand distribution back then. We didn't have 600,000 copies for a newsstand, but the best thing to do with limited funds was to develop a four-color page brochure and send it to 6,000 martial arts schools in the United States saying that they could make 6% profit off of the cover price. The main thing was that they could get their school listed free in the back of the magazine, every single issue, as long as they subscribed. That was part of the hook. We had over a thousand schools subscribe. We sold 25,000 copies.

- WHAT WERE THE CIRCULATION NUMBERS FOR *BLACK BELT* AT THAT TIME?

Black Belt was producing 200,000 copies… sold copies. If I had the capital at the time we could have printed between a hundred to two-hundred thousand copies and they would have all been sold out. I spoke at that time to the distributor for Kable News and they said they wouldn't take us because they already had *Black Belt* magazine. So I asked at the time how I could get a national distributor. In 1977, there was a turning point. In order to get a national distributor, to carry a martial arts title, we had to come up with other magazines. Once you had a non-competing title, they had to take whatever else you had. So in 1977, I came out with *Racquetball Illustrated*. It is the number one racquet ball magazine today. After that, they picked-up *Inside Kung Fu*. And then my company went national.

- SO THEY TOOK *RACQUETBALL ILLUSTRATED* AND THEY HAD TO TAKE *INSIDE KUNG FU* (LAUGHTER).

That's how we got in. And then we were definitely competing with *Black Belt* at that time. *Black Belt* had already made a lot of money over the past ten or fifteen years. They were there when Bruce Lee was alive and they wrote a lot of books then.

- MITO UYEHARA [OWNER OF BLACK BELT] HAD SOME KIND OF CONNECTION WITH BRUCE LEE?

Oh, yes… he had a very close connection with Bruce Lee. So that's why they were so very successful.

- SO, YOUR MAGAZINE HAS CONTINUED TO GROW. WHAT WAS THE RELATIONSHIP OF YOUR MAGAZINE TO THE MANTIS SUPPLY COMPANY. DID YOU OWN THAT COMPANY?

Yes. Once I first started the magazine company I didn't have that many advertisers. So I figured, well, if I don't have any advertisers, I would need to have some kind of cash flow coming in, so I decided to start a mail order company and sell some products. So we called it Mantis.

- BESIDES THE GONGFU UNIFORMS, WAS THERE ANYTHING ELSE THAT YOU SOLD?

Oh yeah, we sold a total of about 1,400 different items. It sounds like a lot, but for instance you have many different color belts. There could be ten different belts for karate and ten different color sashes for gongfu. We sold shoes, nunchakus, every single type of weapon, and different equipment.

- IS THE MANTIS SUPPLY COMPANY STILL IN BUSINESS?

No. Actually what happened is that we started to get a lot of advertisers to advertise in the magazine, and they started to complain that we were competing with them. And then I decided to stop Mantis because it was too much work… so much overhead. Many times when we ordered from Asia, they would always "short" us, so we always had a lot of backorders. It became a big headache, and I decided to cut the mail order out…and to take in advertising revenue, and actually there was more profit in that. At that time that's what I thought. So we just killed Mantis. Then we started the book division.

- WHAT WAS THE RELATIONSHIP OF CLOSING MANTIS DOWN TO OTHER PROJECTS YOU WERE DOING? WAS THERE ANYTHING YOU WERE STARTING UP AT THAT TIME?

In 1974 we started the book division. We also had a Las Vegas show called Orient '75 in production. I didn't have to do that much with this. I basically got the talent for the martial arts together and that went through Tadashi Yamashita, James Lew, Harry Wong and Todd Taguchi. They're the main four guys that did the martial arts.

- So it was like a troupe that went around and gave demonstrations?

A demo troupe that played at the Sahara Hotel and at the Landmark Hotel—a regular Las Vegas variety show. And the show was on twice a day, seven days a week.

- And how long did that run for?

It ran for about a year. The troupe went different places too. The main place was Las Vegas. It was a variety show. They had magic shows, topless girls, singing, and part of it was martial arts.

- You started with *Inside Kung Fu* in 1972, and then you started publishing books under the Unique Publication logo in 1974. What made you decide to do other titles such as *Kick Illustrated* or *Inside Karate*?

Mainly because we didn't want anyone else to compete with us… although we like competition. At that time, I think *Black Belt* had four magazines in the martial arts field. We had one. What we were trying to do was to come out with two or three other titles so that we would have a whole martial arts section on the news stand. So that way when people came over they could see there's six, seven, eight, nine titles, so they can pick and choose, rather than have only two titles that get lost in the shuffle. There were so many magazines out there. We wanted to create a whole section just for our little martial arts group.

- What made you decide to do the books as well?

Basically, I just copied the *Black Belt* formula (laughter). They were so successful at that time, I figured books were selling well for them… it was just another avenue.

- You had told me at one time that you had sixteen different magazine titles and now the numbers are not so high. Is there any reason that you downsized? Has anything changed in the business?

Well, like they said… never fall in love with a title. At that time we had five comic books as well as magazines outside of the martial arts, for instance, *Skate Boarding*, *Back Packing*, *Golf Magazine*, and so forth. And you know in the golf magazine area, it's really hard to compete with *Golf Digest* and *Golf Lifestyle*. That kind of distribution you have to have a lot of money to launch that title and we didn't, so that title lasted about a year. And then *Skate Boarding* lasted like six or seven years, but that's not a fad but it just went up and down every two or three years. It's all numbers. When the newsstand sales start going down, of course you have to kill the title. Most of the magazines out there, like the ones we started, are faddish, so they last a year to two years. You have to give a big discount, by the time you give a big discount there's no profit. We had to kill those titles.

- IS THERE A PERCENTAGE CUT-OFF BY WHICH YOU DECIDE THAT YOU'RE GOING TO KILL A TITLE?

There's no right formula because some magazines you strictly go by newsstand sales. In other words, there's no advertising so you have to hit a certain breaking point in order to keep that magazine afloat. There are other magazines that don't sell well on the newsstand but you have a lot of advertising revenue which makes up for the loss at the newsstand. And then there are magazines that are eighty percent subscription, and you don't really rely on the newsstand or advertising. It's really hard to say.

- SO WE GOT A PUBLIC OUT THERE THAT REALLY DOESN'T STICK WITH ANYTHING FOR VERY LONG?

Yeah, there's a big turn over. That's true of every magazine. We only have eight titles right now. We had up to sixteen different titles.

- DOES MARTIAL ARTS HAVE THE BIGGEST INTEREST?

No, no. *Paintball* is a big interest. It is a really big sport.

- YOU WERE TELLING ME AT ONE TIME THERE WAS AN INCREASE IN PAPER COSTS.

Yes, in 1991, we hit that little recession and the paper cost went up, everything was going crazy. People didn't have the money to buy magazines. The paper was literally double in price. So that put a lot of publishers out of business, and it put a lot of printers out of business.

- HOW DO YOU SEE THE BUSINESS AS HAVING CHANGED?

Business as of right now is changing because the distribution is starting to cost the publisher more money. The publisher has to pay additional money to get the magazine out, and additional money for all the returns on unsold copies. So that's going to hurt the publishers. The reason for that is because distribution is getting tougher with over four thousand magazine titles out there. And they claim that 1,600 of the top titles make up ninety-five percent of the total magazine revenue. So the other 2,400 titles, such as ours, only represents five percent of the revenue. So, if we want our magazine to be distributed, we have to pay. The top 1,600 titles don't have to pay anything. That's unfair in a way, but we understand where they're coming from too.

- WHERE DOES THE ROLE OF VIDEOS COME IN? WHAT TIME DID YOU DECIDE TO

START DOING VIDEOS AND HOW DO YOU LOOK AT THAT IN RELATIONSHIP TO THE BOOKS AND THE MAGAZINES?

We were approached over twenty years ago to come out with videos, but at that time there weren't that many VCR's. And the videos were so expensive, I didn't think there was a market for it.... And meanwhile, Panther Productions came out and they proved us wrong and they did real well. In 1991 we decided to come out with our own line of videos. Since we're in the publishing business, everyone approaches us with all these different video ideas. So we decided to start our own production company, and we produced a hundred videos the first year. Then, we slowed down production once we had a pretty good size library. We have a total of three hundred right now, and we have one hundred and twenty ready to go. We've been really cranking out a lot of videos this year.

- IS THERE ANY TREND OR DIFFERENCE IN TERMS OF WHAT PEOPLE WERE LOOKING AT IN VIDEOS WHEN THEY FIRST CAME OUT VERSUS WHAT THEY'RE LOOKING AT NOW... EITHER A PARTICULAR STYLE OR A TRAINING FORMAT, OR ANYTHING DIFFERENT, OR IS IT PRETTY MUCH THE SAME?

It's trendy too. I think grappling was really, really popular like a year or two years ago those videos were selling really well. Wing Chun was hot a few years ago and is selling well. Right now, everything is selling pretty steady across the board. There's no one area that's really hot right now.

- ARE BOOKS NOW AS POPULAR AS VIDEOS?

Books are more popular at this time. We have better distribution with books than videos. The average video store does not want to carry "how to" videos.

- YOU HAD MENTIONED ALSO THAT YOU WERE LAUNCHING A NEW PUBLISHING COMPANY CALLED MULTI MEDIA. HOW DOES MULTI MEDIA RELATE TO UNIQUE PUBLICATIONS AND INSIDE KUNG FU? IS THERE A NEW DIRECTION YOU'RE TAKING?

Multi Media... we're putting that on the sideline right now. We still have a lot of magazines we still want to do, but we just haven't gotten to it because of the distribution problems. It really is a big, big problem. Before, we could put out a new magazine just by calling the distributor up and telling them we want to put out 150 or 200 thousand copies in the next three or four months. Now it takes over a year to get authorization. A year ago it took six months. Now they're telling us they don't want any new publications. They can't handle it.

- SO WHAT'S GOING TO HAPPEN TO THE ONES YOU SAY ARE ENTRENCHED THERE that are picking up the big percentage? They are always going to be there, right?

That's right, and that's the thing where every publisher is concerned right now. A lot of them will pay the extra fee but that could break them and I don't know how they can make that kind of money back up. You can't charge advertisers more money, and you can't raise the subscription price too much because otherwise people won't subscribe, so we're stuck. I think the bottom line is that we are lucky because we can sell products which are the books, videos, and so forth. We have pretty good distribution for our books throughout all the stores in the world. So there's different kinds of distribution than magazine distribution, but that's getting tough too.

- You also started extending into the idea of fitness supplements, such as the nutrition bar you were talking about. How is that going, and how did you get into that?

Nitrokick is one of our brand names and we're still trying to launch it. That's a very difficult market to break into also, because the chainstores requires "X" amount of dollars to get in and you have to buy shelf space. So that's very hard. It's really all about money, but then again, once you get into the grocery store chains it doesn't guarantee that it is going to sell your products. So, it's a big, big gamble. And right now that's where we're at there, where we're still trying.

- What made you decide to go into that area? Was there any kind of focus that you had, or was it just another idea, a spin-off of the martial arts?

We know that there's no supplement for martial artists. We thought maybe it would be a good idea to give the martial arts their own supplement. . . We tried marketing it directly to the martial artists and the schools. The response was pretty bad. Now we're just gonna go for the general public.

- Obviously, with the developments you've had with these projects you became more directly involved with media and television. Could you tell us a little bit more about how that all developed?

Just by parties and meeting people… just good timing. For instance, like the first time I met Elvis Presley. Ed [Parker] invited me to a gathering. We were on Sunset Boulevard at that time and Ed invited me to watch Elvis rehearse. This was a Saturday evening. So at ten o'clock at night, I left my own party to go visit Elvis Presley. He was my idol. And at that meeting Elvis invited me to his house. In turn, I invited Elvis Presley to a one-year anniversary party that we were having for the magazine…. And you meet people like that all the time. Elvis loved the martial arts. And you really meet a lot of interesting people who love the marital arts.

- **IS THERE ANYTHING YOU HAVE DONE WITH YOUR COMPANY THAT'S A "FIRST"?**

Yes. We produced *Racquetball Illustrated*, and also *Paintball*. There was a small paintball magazine at the time; but when we came out, we made it into a bigger industry.

- **WHAT DO YOU SEE THAT CFW ENTERPRISES HAS DONE TO ASSIST THE MARTIAL ARTS? WHY DID YOU DECIDE TO PROMOTE THEM?**

Because I love the martial arts. I had the school to begin with, and I figured out a way to get the message across on a larger scale—from two hundred students to thousands of people.

- **IS THERE ANYTHING THAT YOU WOULD HAVE DONE DIFFERENTLY IF YOU HAD A CHANCE TO DO IT OVER AGAIN?**

Perhaps I would have made an attempt to raise more money and then produce more copies of the magazine when I first got started. Otherwise, I wouldn't have done anything different.

- **WHERE DO YOU SEE YOUR COMPANY, CFW ENTERPRISES, AND YOUR MARTIAL ARTS MAGAZINES GOING FROM HERE?**

Hopefully it will continue to grow. We're also trying to do something on the Internet, but I don't know how that's all going to take place. Basically we're trying to do a better job on *Inside Kung Fu*. In the last four or five issues the layouts are better. We hired a top-notch art director from *Muscle Fitness* magazine to do the layout. We're printing on better paper with heavier stock.

PEOPLE

- **PEOPLE THAT YOU HAVE BEEN INVOLVED WITH—CONTEMPORARY MARTIAL ARTISTS, WELL-KNOWN MOVIE STARS—CAN YOU PROVIDE ME WITH SOME NAMES OF INDIVIDUALS YOU ARE INVOLVED WITH DIRECTLY OR INDIRECTLY AT THIS TIME?**

Jackie Chan has been really good friend of mine for the last twenty years. Tadashi Yamashita is a really good friend… I know most of them… martial artists throughout the country as well as throughout the world. They often come in and out of the office [CFW Enterprises].

- **IS THERE ANYTHING THAT STOOD OUT IN A PHENOMENAL WAY ABOUT PEOPLE THAT YOU MET WITH OVER THE YEARS?**

Yeah, Ron Sarchanowski. His group use to write to us at the office. They would claim that he could take a full hit to the throat with a baseball bat.... you know, punches and kicks to the temple. "You can kick him directly in the groin." I said "this guy's gotta be a wacko." We never responded. Then one day three guys showed up in my office on a Saturday. Nice guys, dressed up in suits. One guy says his name is Dr. Ron Sarchanowski, and said he's the one that has been writing to us and we never wrote back. I said "Oh, man, this guy's a nut case here!" But he's a real gentleman. All the guys there were really, really nice people.

- WHERE ARE THEY FROM? WHAT'S THEIR BACKGROUND?

He was a chief of police back east somewhere. I can't remember the state. They may be jujitsu people. And they started doing little demos in my office. Sarchanowski asked one of the guys to wack him right in the temple. I told him "Don't do that here." I'm thinking lawsuit. I said "I'll tell you what. Tomorrow I'll get some of the top black belts here to witness all this." So they said "OK, fine." So I got Tadashi Yamashita, Ed Parker, I think Mike Stone, Tino Tuliosega... some of the key guys. I tried to get a lot more but it was last minute notice. Everyone witnessed the whole demonstration and Ed Parker's black belt, Tino, had a big Samoan guy that was a black belt. These are the guys that hit their guys in the temple and kicked them in the groin. It didn't even faze them. I remember afterwards, Ed Parker took off and he called me later at the office and he said "Who are these guys?" It scared the heck out of him. He'd never seen anything like that before.

At the *Broken Arrow* premiere, left to right: Curtis Wong, Davis Fung, Jackie Chan, John Woo, Willie Chan, Stanley Tong.

Above Bruce Li flanked by Douglas and Curtis. Below: Gathering of friends: Jackie Chan (middle) at his surprise birthday party given by Curtis Wong. Chan's former side-kick Sammo Hung was there too.

- DID THEY GIVE YOU ANY INDICATION OF HOW THEY LEARNED TO DO THIS?

Well, they tried to explain it, but we couldn't grasp it. That was one of the most amazing things I've ever seen! It would be different if their students hit their own masters. They could fake it. But it was our guys, as a matter of fact, even James was one of the guys that hit Sarchanowski. There were four guys hitting him in the throat at the same time. One guy was hitting in the front of the throat, the other guy was hitting the guy in the back of the neck, another two guys were hitting him in the side of the neck at the same time… full-blast. The guy just stood there. It was unreal.

- THEY COULDN'T EVEN KNOCK SARCHANOWSKI OFF BALANCE?

Oh, you could knock him off balance, but that's what I asked him, I said "OK, if you hit a guy and the guy takes a punch and goes back a little bit, you know from the punch…" and he said, "oh, no, put the guys head against the wall." And the guy started kicking him on the head. That was a scary thing. I mean the guy got on his knees and put his head against the wall and this guy side kicked him on the temple. There's no place to go! We all had chills (laughter). It's unbelieveable! Then one guy got in the horse stance, a wide horse stance, and kicked him straight up on the balls until he lifted the guy up, and that's amazing. It wasn't a trick. That's probably one of the best demos I've ever seen.

- DID YOU EVER DO AN ARTICLE ON THESE GUYS?

Oh, yeah, quite a few articles and people didn't believe it. They were even featured on the *Wide World of Sports* on television when they had this big tournament coverage. I think it was aired in a big tournament in New York. They did a demo there and people wrote in saying it's fake, but it wasn't.

Curtis with another martial artist/actor Jean Claude Van Damme.

- WHAT ABOUT IN TERMS OF SPECIFIC PEOPLE THAT YOU'VE SEEN, ANY IMPRESSIONS AS TO WHO HAD THE FASTEST OR STRONGEST KICK AND THE FASTEST HAND MOVEMENTS?

I think Joe Lewis had the absolute strongest punch and even kicks; Tadashi Yamashita had the fastest movements. I was always impressed with Steve Sanders hand-to-hand… he was really fast. And, Danny Inosanto is extremely good.

- WHAT SPECIFICALLY DID DANNY DO THAT IMPRESSED YOU?

He had an answer… For every punch or kick that's thrown at Danny, he had an answer for it. If he slipped and missed, he would still have an answer. Unbelievable counters.

- WHERE DO YOU SEE YOURSELF GOING IN THE FUTURE WITH THE EQUIPMENT, ACTING, MAGAZINES, BOOKS, VIDEOS AND SUPPLEMENTS?

Well, the supplements—we're going to continue to try to put a catalog together soon of the different supplements. With the books and magazines we will continue, of course trying to make it grow. We have a lot of books that we are publishing now. Our goal is to come out with thirty new martial arts books a year. As for the magazine, we will try to make it better. We've done that so far. We changed the layout, better paper, more pages.

- BLACK BELT WAS SOLD. HOW DOES THAT AFFECT YOU IN TERMS OF ANY COMPETITION?

Yeah, they were sold. They're trying to grow and we are too. I think they just came out and launched a new magazine that was on hold for quite awhile. So they're trying. We're all trying. I think competition is always good.

- ANY PARTICULAR VIEWPOINTS THAT YOU HAVE ON ANY DIFFERENT STYLES OF MARTIAL ARTS… ARE YOU THE KIND OF PERSON THAT LIKES ALL STYLES, OR DO YOU HAVE ANY SPECIFIC PREFERENCES?

I like all styles.

> Dr. Michael Maliszewski met with Curtis Wong
> at the offices of CFW Enterprises where this interview
> was taped on September 27, 1999, and on February 18, 2000.

- ANY IMPRESSIONS ON THE VALUE OF STUDYING THE MARTIAL ARTS?

It definitely has an impact. Even just from a self-confidence point of view. Not just from a fighting point of view. It definitely helped me out. My son right now is studying the martial arts. Martial arts and business are definitely similar. They help you understand strategy.

- DO YOU HAVE ANY COMMENTS TO MAKE ON MARTIAL ARTS, AS IT IS USED IN THE ENTERTAINMENT INDUSTRY?

Martial arts have become very big. There is less mystique about the martial arts at this time. You have full contact karate, ultimate fighting championships... A lot of guys are out there now just kicking and fighting. Martial arts are common. Years ago people use to think that if you touched a guy with *dim mak* he would be gone. And that's what sold a lot of magazines. At that time they wanted to know more and more about these types of things. Now, there is nothing mysterious anymore.

- ANY IMPRESSIONS THAT YOU HAVE ABOUT THE CLASSICAL TRADITIONS AND POINT CONTACT FIGHTING?

I actually wish they didn't have full-contact fighting or ultimate fighting championships. I just don't think it's a sport. I don't know... I kind of like it back in the old days with point tournaments, demonstrations and all that. It was more fun at that time. Now the kids all watch ultimate fighting championships. I think it's too violent... now they ask: "What is martial arts?" It's just not such a big deal anymore.

- THANK YOU VERY MUCH FOR PROVIDING US WITH THIS INTERVIEW AND AN INSIDER'S VIEW INTO THE PUBLISHING AND MARTIAL ARTS AREA.

Thank you.

chapter 6

Don Wilson: Kickboxing Champion and Film Star Gives His Perspectives on Training

by Michael Maliszewski, Ph.D.

All photos courtesy of Don Wilson.

Introduction

Don Wilson is a well-known performer to many followers of the martial arts. Some will recognize his name through the twenty-five films he has starred in and/or produced. Others will know of his accomplishments in the sport of kickboxing, where his distinguished career included some eleven championship titles (in different weight classes).

The focus of this interview was to try and get a true picture of the man behind the role of actor and fighter. Additionally, I hoped to glean some insight into the influences that chronicled his development and shaped his life. His views on training and fighting offer the reader the opportunity to apply these perspectives to his or her own personal development.

This initial interview took place on May 14, 1999, in Lowell, Massachusetts, following Don's championship fight against Dick Kimber for the International Kickboxing Federation (full-contact rules, heavyweight division) and a follow-up interview in Hollywood on March 2, 2000.

FAMILY BACKGROUND

- I WOULD LIKE TO DISCUSS A LITTLE BIT OF YOUR BACKGROUND. COULD YOU PROVIDE ME WITH PLACE AND DATE OF BIRTH? AND WHERE YOU GREW UP?

Alton, Illinois, September 10, 1954. At four years old, I moved to Florida. I grew up in Florida and lived there until 1985. Then I moved to Los Angeles.

- INTERESTS AS A CHILD/ADOLESCENT; ANY PARTICULAR ATHLETIC INTERESTS?

I played basketball. I think that was the first thing I was interested in, then football. I ran track. I wrestled in college. I did a little in many different sports. I was captain and most valuable player on my basketball and football team in high school. I played football and basketball for the Coast Guard Academy. I wrestled two years in junior college. In my second year, I took fourth in the state at 177 pounds.

- WHAT HIGH SCHOOL DID YOU GRADUATE FROM? AND, WHAT DID YOU DO AFTER GRADUATION?

I graduated from St. Andrew Prep School of Boca Raton, Florida. From there I went to the United States Coast Guard Academy for one year, and then, transferred to junior college and graduated from Brevard Community College in Florida.

- AND YOUR PARENTS? FAMILY?

My mother, Toshie Wilson, is still alive, but my father, James T. Wilson, is deceased. I'm married with two children. I have one eleven-year-old and one eight-month-old. I've been married to Kathleen Karadine Wilson for over four years, but we've been together since 1990. Going on eleven years we've been together. This is my second marriage.

- YOUR CHILDREN'S NAMES? DO THEY STUDY MARTIAL ARTS AT ALL?

Jonathan Hoshino Wilson and Drayden Alexander Wilson. Drayden is the youngest; Jonathan is the oldest. They haven't really studied martial arts. Off and on Jonathan has studied but he's more into computers.

MARTIAL ARTS BACKGROUND

- WHY DID YOU START TRAINING IN THE MARTIAL ARTS?

My brother started me. I weighed about two hundred pounds. He was at one-sixty, and he totally controlled me. But, as you know, it would happen if you get a trained martial artist sparring a guy who had never done martial arts. He could kick or punch me at will. So I realized there is something to this. You can't just get in shape, lift weights, and be a tough guy. You may think you're tough, but fighting is a specific thing just like playing tennis. You can be in great shape, be a great basketball player, but you get a tennis racket and you can't even return a serve. So every activity is specific to training. And I had done no training as a fighter and about 17 or 18, that's when I started.

- I'D LIKE TO HEAR MORE ABOUT YOUR BACKGROUND IN THE MARTIAL ARTS.

My older brother, James Wilson, was my manager. He was the one that got me into martial arts. He started out in gongfu before I had an interest in martial arts. I sparred and worked out with him when I was in high school. When I went to the Coast Guard Academy, they didn't have gongfu, but they had karate. And there was a man named Chuck Merriman who was teaching Goju-ryu. I studied under Chuck Merriman my first year of martial arts. That's where I got the hard style that I was able to adapt into the gongfu style that I did … a different kind of gongfu: part hard style, part soft style.

In Goju-ryu, more than anything, I learned about the value of force … force on force. Chuck was a very traditional hard stylist. I think I learned movement after that. I learned gongfu's fluidity after I learned about force, which is a good combination. You don't want to be dancing around the ring because you don't have the power. You develop power first and then learn to move so that you can use your power. For example, people say I had forty-seven knockouts. However, I never really go for knockouts. If a knockout comes to me, I take it. That was because of starting out with a hard style, learning from Chuck the value of having power when you need it. Then learning gongfu from Daniel K. Pai. How you can beat somebody? … by having the opponent think that everything is going their way, and then you pull the rug out from under them. This is also considered counter fighting.

- HOW MANY YEARS DID YOU PRACTICE GOJU-RYU?

One year. And then I went to Florida to study Pai Lum Kung Fu with Daniel K. Pai. That was his own system.

- HOW WOULD YOU DESCRIBE IT, BESIDES BEING SOFT AND CIRCULAR?

Soft style with undertones of hard style within it. You know he's related to

Ed Parker. They both came from Hawaii and they're like cousins or something. And so they recognized our style, we recognized theirs, and they cross trained. As of right now, Glenn Wilson—he's not related to me—is the grandmaster. He lives in Orlando, Florida. He took over after Daniel K. Pai passed away. They teach equally kenpo and gongfu. He's a black belt and teacher of both. Pai and Parker exchanged techniques: hard style mixed with the Chinese flavor. That was right when grandmasters were starting to... when Bruce was saying "study everything", "take what's best" ... and that was just starting to happen. And Daniel K. Pai believed in that philosophy: studying as much as you can, using what works, and disregarding what doesn't for you individually. Now it's common practice.

Cross training... Nobody studies one art, especially those involved in the UFC [Ultimate Fighting Championship]. They learned you can't do it with just one system of fighting. Basically, it's an amalgamation of systems. As much as you can absorb, you should try to absorb: grappling, striking, kicking. Pretty much it's the new wave of martial arts I would say. But the beginnings of it were in the early sixties; right when Pai was coming over to this country and Ed Parker and Bruce Lee—and they were good friends by the way—Bruce Lee and Daniel K. Pai. They knew each other. I practiced that style for about six years but it wasn't consistent.

In 1974, I started kickboxing. You know, gongfu is not kickboxing. Kickboxing is a sport. I spent most of my time doing kickboxing. I did receive a black belt rank there and then I heard they're giving me some honorary degree, seventh degree—I'm going up in degrees. But really, the belts don't really mean anything to me. I'm happy that my style recognizes me as a higher degree, but I'm not pursuing any degrees seriously.

- WHAT PROMPTED YOU TO GET INVOLVED WITH KICKBOXING?

Actually, my brother was teaching gongfu and it was free. First, I went into point fighting. It was enjoyable, fun, but it was a little bit frustrating. It didn't have as much realism as I would have liked. I wanted something a little bit closer to what a real self-defense situation would be like. We called it full-contact karate in those days. In 1977, when I first fought, I loved it. I fought the first full-contact karate fight in the state of Florida. This was around September or October of 1974, in Orlando, Florida. I lost my first fight, broke my hand, and I loved it! So I figured, well, if it's this much fun when you lose and get injured, it must really be good when you win [laughter]! I just like the whole style of competition and the atmosphere.

- WHAT WERE SOME OF THE MAJOR INFLUENCES AT THIS POINT IN TIME IN YOUR CAREER? ANY PARTICULAR PERSON THAT STOOD OUT BEFORE MERRIMAN WHILE IN HIGH SCHOOL ... EARLY COLLEGE?

Well in martial arts, of course, Bruce Lee. He popularized it. And then I'd say in the film business, Chuck Norris. Actually I'd like to pattern myself after Chuck—a sports stand out, to film star, to television star. Chuck produces his show. I produce most of my films. I produced eighteen of the twenty-four films that I've done. So I pattern myself after Chuck in a way.

Arnold Schwartzenager is another one. He came from sports and had a lot of setbacks. He didn't speak English ... had a freakish body for those days when he came out here, yet he became the highest paid actor at one time, in the world. So from Chuck came probably one of the most successful Saturday night shows. He has the number one action show award. I think only Tom Selleck outdid him for the first two years of syndication with Magnum P.I. But he's a phenomenon in the TV industry and also became a phenomenon in film. I'm hoping to do the same in my own slow methodical way. The way of the Dragon is not the quick way; notice I'm still fighting 25 years later. It's just really becoming ... it's the biggest thing I've been involved with. My biggest thing happened at 45 not 25. So I'm looking forward to my bigger films and my bigger opportunities coming later on in life.

KICKBOXING, TRAINING AND PERSPECTIVES

- CAN YOU GIVE ME AN OUTLINE OF WHAT WAS DIFFERENT WITH YOUR TRAINING FROM TRADITIONAL MARTIAL ARTS AS COMPARED TO KICKBOXING?

Traditional training focuses on a lot of different things. Doing forms of kata is just a form of exercise to me. It is not really correctly useable for actual fighting, although I value it. You want to be in condition, have coordination and speed and balance, and you could develop this with kata. If people were just doing boxing katas, and they step in the ring to fight, they would get knocked out. To learn to swim, you need to get into the water. To learn to fight, you need to have a human being in front of you punching and kicking back while you're punching and kicking at them.

- WHAT IS IT THAT YOU REALLY HAD TO LEARN THAT WAS DIFFERENT?

Combinations, combinations. In point fighting, which was the only type of fighting that existed early on, if it looked liked you landed, they stopped everything. How many fights last night went one punch and the fight was over? It doesn't happen. So combinations are the main thing.

- CAN YOU ELABORATE A LITTLE BIT FURTHER ON THIS?

Any kind of combinations of hands or feet. They just did not do it. In the 60's and 70's, it was he who hit first as opposed to he who hit best in those days.

- IN TERMS OF YOUR TRADITIONAL TRAINING IN MARTIAL ARTS, WHAT DID YOU HAVE TO MODIFY WITH TECHNIQUES, STRATEGIES OR WHATEVER IN ORDER TO BE EFFECTIVE AS A KICKBOXER?

Mainly keeping my hands up. You don't develop that habit in point fighting. The chin is the main target where you really can't get hit. You can take a lot of punishment in main areas of your body—arms, the legs, the stomach, sides of the head—but the chin you really can't take much punishment. I don't care even if you're Mike Tyson. If you get hit on the chin, you go down. That was the main thing in my defense and my fighting that was different from anything that I had done before ... fighting with my hands around my chin.

- IN TERMS OF THE POINT FIGHTING, FULL-CONTACT KICKBOXING, ARE THERE ANY IMPORTANT FIGURES AND DATES WHICH COME TO MIND?

The important information would be the first time I entered the Battle of Atlanta, the heavyweight white belt division. Larry Reinhart was the head referee. I didn't win, but I did experience a good tournament. The 1973 Battle of Atlanta, as it turns out, was a good tournament to start with because really, that set the standard for many years as one of the tournaments. It's now "the" tournament. It's gone on for over thirty years now. So it wasn't just some local high school gym I went to for my first tournament. I got to see tournament competition at some of the better competitions.

So, that was the beginning of tournament competition. I got to watch Bill Wallace fight in, I believe, a Chattanooga, Tennessee, tournament. He fought Larry Reinhart again for the finals and won. He was one of the best guys of that era. That was what was important. I won the overall white belt. Bill won the black belt. We're ten years apart. He was the kickboxing champion when I was the number one contender.

- ANYBODY ELSE THAT STANDS OUT IN TERMS OF MENTORS OR SIGNIFICANT OTHER PEOPLE?

I really didn't know any of the big names. They were names for me, but they were not people that anyone would know. When I was a white belt, I looked up to the green belts … from green belts to brown belts … more locally, in the Florida area, because that's where I competed mostly. There was a guy named Mike Foster, who I thought was pretty impressive. Joe Corley was one of the first ones I saw using the safety equipment, which revolutionized everything. He was a top point fighter in his days. In kickboxing, it was Bill Wallace. He was my mentor. He was the champion of my weight division and probably one of the most prolific champions … Benny Urquidez for the lighter

weight classes. They were mentors and people I looked up to and still do.

- You were very influential in developing the kickboxing organization and rules involved in this type of fighting. Can you tell me where you think the movement is going?

Actually it was a trial and error kind of an era. We fought with safety equipment, boxing gloves, and ring ropes. My first fight we fought on a concrete floor. There were no mats. If anybody got knocked out, they would have been dead. Nobody knew enough at that time about how to punch or kick to knock anybody out. It's now a regulated sport by the athletic commission. Again, it was all trial and error. We made mistakes and then the kickboxing community would rehash the rules and come out with a new set.

- Are there people now going into kickboxing that have no formal martial arts training?

Many now, but they are limited, in my opinion. But I'm cut from the old mold. I came from martial arts. Bill Wallace, Benny Urquidez … we all came from martial arts backgrounds. But now you have guys who are rough guys, they know how to box, they know how to kick, and they get involved in the sport of kickboxing. But they don't have the repertoire or technique that we have. For example, a lot of them have only two kicks. I have every kick that you can see … in my movies [laughter].

- Kickboxing now has a finite set of rules that apply to the sport itself. How do you view this in relationship to some other forms of fighting in organizations such as grappling, the Ultimate Fighting Championships and other similar events?

Oh, I think it's great! There's nothing better for the whole fighting sport than to allow grappling. First of all, it's safer for the fighters. They're going through their own growth period too. They used to have no gloves and now they're using gloves. I was in Moscow. They now have an amateur division where they wear headgear and where there's no strikes on the ground. When they're on the ground, it's a grappling match; when they're on their feet, it's a kickboxing match. So it's much more realistic fighting. The athletes who have twenty years of that style of fighting are much better prepared than the martial artist that does not. Those guys are learning the true way to subdue an opponent. I deal with my strikes, but I was a wrestler in college. Perhaps the only thing I can do naturally is grapple. And even though there were no submissions for fighting in my day, I would be better at that than I have been at kickboxing. Grappling would be the sport I was born to do. I just never got the opportunity to do it.

- **Do you ever see grappling becoming a component of kickboxing?**

No, I do not. People like to see fights. When you go to watch a boxing match, you're allowed to kick and punch. You're not allowed to grab because it stops the action. I don't see it being integrated into kickboxing.

- **I was wondering if you could describe to me what your workout regimen is like in preparation for a fight? Can you break it down for me in detail?**

I used to spend three hours a day in the gym, with one hour for aerobics. Stairmaster, running, cycling—whatever I do for aerobics—the whole thing is actually a three-hour day.

You know what? That's my twenty-year-old workout. That's not what I'm doing now. I'm not in the gym for three hours. Right now because of the championship fight, I'm doing exactly ten rounds a day, because that's what I'm going to fight. Of course I'm doing three-minute rounds with fourteen ounce or sixteen-ounce gloves, as opposed to two-minute rounds with ten-ounce gloves. So I'm getting more of a physical workout than the actual fight, which is the way you should train. When you're starting, what I would do is get an hour of aerobics and two hours in the gym.

- **What did you do in the two hours in the gym?**

Bag work, shadow boxing—a lot of shadow boxing—probably thirty minutes of shadow boxing, which most people don't do. I do the sit-ups. I do the stretching. I do at least two days a week of weights. I did weights even when I was competing, but I actually did more when I retired because I wanted to gain the weight. I moved up in weight division. So I had to do it by lifting weights. Standard workout, sparing before the fight, mainly pad work… hand pads, heavy bag for power. Pretty typical, there's nothing there that would distinguish me from other fighters other than the fact that I may do more aerobics than most fighters. I use to run six to nine miles, which is a lot for a fighter. Now I'm running three to four a day. Nine miles is a lot for a fighter.

- **In terms of dietary concerns, is there any particular kind of food that you avoid?**

I ate everything when I was young, now I don't. Now I stay away from high fat, high sugars. I got a fight coming up. I can't have all that bad stuff in my system. Of course, no alcohol. I haven't had a drink since I came out of retirement, which I did do when I was young. I would drink when I didn't have a fight schedule. I think I'm doing things more right now … taking vitamins, supplements. I can feel when my legs are cramping up or my calves start getting a little tight, then I take potassium, magnesium, calcium tablets and I can feel them go right away. I'm a firm believer in those because I get sweaty. When you sweat so much, you need electrolytes or you'll get cramps. I think I'm a smarter athlete at 45 than 25, out of necessity. I didn't have to be maybe so smart when I was 25.

- I WAS WONDERING IF YOU HAD SOME SPECIFIC TYPE OF STRATEGY, MOVEMENT, OR TECHNIQUE FOR WHICH YOU ARE WELL KNOWN?

I would have to say that it would be my sidekick that would illustrate that point. It's actually pretty basic. It would probably be difficult to see it in a sequence set of photographs. However, it would basically begin by looking like a beginner's sidekick. There are little idiosyncrasies that I do, the way I use it, where it is used for many different angles ... the same kick. You use different areas of the foot against different areas of the body depending upon the situation, and, you know, the difficult thing about it is that if you have to begin to think about it how you're going to use the foot, then it's too late.

Basically, once I get into the ring, my mind goes into subliminal mode. It becomes a "feel" thing. I feel the direction that he's coming from. I think that's the best way to be a fighter. You do everything with proper form consciously and then you train your conscious mind to train your subliminal mind because that is the mind that instantaneously reacts. For example, when a guy throws a three-punch combination, you don't consciously think, oh, here comes a left hook, and I bob down and slip under that and come back up and watch for the right cross. You can't think of any of that. You can in the gym when you're working and watching yourself in the mirror. In the ring, you have to be operating subliminally beyond the conscious mind. If not, it's too late.

- IS THERE ANY SPECIAL TYPE OF MENTAL EXERCISE THAT YOU DO IN PREPARATION FOR A FIGHT OR AS PART OF YOUR TRAINING?

It sounds like a cliché, but I think positively. I imagine the many different ways I will beat my opponent. I never imagine the ways that he can beat me. If I hear for example that he has a good left hook, I imagine ways of blocking it, slipping it, and avoiding it. I never think about that left hook landing on my chin. Before something physical happens, the thought ... you think it and then maybe you say it and you write it ... there are varying levels of making a reality. The first thing is that you think it and, if you don't think about getting knocked out, it's just a little bit further away from reality. It's not in denial... I wasn't trying to think I didn't have the ability to throw a right hand knock out. I was just thinking of all the ways I would avoid it ... my hands out, my chin down, slipping, sliding, getting ready for the sidekick. I went over it in my mind over and over and over. I never really considered it [the knock out] to be a threat ever. You know when I was a middleweight and a light heavyweight, with most of the guys in my weight division, I never got touched. I was kicking them. It was all a matter of them getting inside. I really didn't think about it very much.

- WHEN YOU THINK OF APPLYING A PARTICULAR MOVEMENT OR TECHNIQUE, OR STRATEGY IN A FIGHT, DO YOU VISUALLY SEE THIS IN YOUR MIND?

Visually, totally, one hundred percent! It's almost like I'm daydreaming. When I'm jogging or I'm on the treadmill, it's actually a form of meditation. There's no other thought going on. If you do that over and over again ... you know. If I lose a fight, I'm the most surprised guy in the auditorium! I never go into a fight thinking anybody's going to kick my butt and then at the end of the fight think I guess he did. I have always felt that even if I felt I was going to win, it doesn't always mean that you are going to win. Sometimes you bobbed when you should have weaved.

- HAVE YOU HAD ANY CHANGES IN ATTITUDE SINCE MARRIAGE TOWARD FIGHTING LIFE IN GENERAL. ANY SORT OF PHILOSOPHICAL, PRACTICAL COMMENTS?

Marriage and family make it more of a risk. Before, when I was a single guy, there was just me. If I got hurt or injured, hopefully nothing really bad was going to happen to me. If something did happen, it affected only me. Now it affects three other people in a drastic, major way. So, I'm taking a very calculated risk here. You only have a certain number of punches your brain can take before there's major damage, and no one knows what that number is. You can imagine, I've taken 10,000 solid shots to my head minimum over twenty-five years ... all the sparring ... all the fights. Who knows how many shots. The average guy walking here probably has never taken one. So we didn't evolve to be constantly having your brain shook up. So it's a risk and, because of that, I'm a different kind of fighter. I'm much more conservative ... much more.

If I was in my youth at the Kimber fight, I would have come out banging from the first round, but you noticed I was more or less just thinking about not getting hit. People thought I was carrying him. People thought he took a dive. There were all kinds of rumors going on. I took a conservative approach to the game. I know I had twelve rounds. That's a lot of time to make something happen. I wasn't rushing anything. He was forcing me to mix it up, but I wasn't. I don't go out there like I used to. I used to go out there, throw flashy kicks—they look good—it had nothing to do with winning the fight. I just wanted to impress the audience. That's how crazy I was. But now, I'm not there to impress anybody really. I want to conservatively win and get out unharmed.

- WHAT PHILOSOPHICAL PERSPECTIVE DO YOU HAVE ON YOUR DEVELOPMENT AS A RESULT OF YOUR FIGHTING EXPERIENCE OR EXPERIENCES IN THE MARTIAL ARTS?

When it comes to life in general, you shouldn't think negatively about anything you set your mind out to do. A lot of people who think negatively eliminate the possibility of positive things happening in their life. When I started out with kickboxing I thought to myself, "I want to be world champion." And I believed I could do it and I did it.

When I decided that I wanted to become an actor, I got into my car and said to myself, "I want to be a star in action films." I knew nothing about it. I knew no one. I got in my car and I drove to Los Angeles. I bought a bunch of books, which told you what to do and I did it. Three years later, I'm starring in those kinds of pictures. It wasn't easy and it wasn't fast, but I set my mind to it. If I had allowed any negativity in the picture, it would have made it much more difficult. Also my friends were concerned about me because they didn't want to see me disappointed. But I think if you have a goal, you should pursue it. The alternative is that you're defeated without starting.

MARTIAL ARTS AND THE MEDIA

- IN WHAT DIRECTIONS DO YOU SEE THE MARTIAL ARTS AND MEDIA GOING?

I think it's at an all-time high right now. Jackie Chan has made 130 million dollars at the box office. I don't think anybody realizes what that means. Jean-Claude Van Damme hit 40 million in his films in the United States. Jackie's film was his first comeback since he did an earlier film known as *The Big Brawl*. That one didn't do very well, but since they have re-released his old films, he's extremely popular. Chuck Norris' TV show is the number one action show in the world. The TV show, *Martial Law*, is another example. Martial arts are really hot. Tae Bo is the new fitness craze. It's like the aerobics of Jane Fonda.

I think martial arts are at an all time-high. This is true not only in the United States but worldwide. Two years ago I was at the K-1 competitions, and there were 55,000 people in the audience, with a $140.00 average ticket price. I was in Russia where "Absolute Fighting" had a sold-out audience.

- IS THERE ANY WAY YOU WOULD LIKE TO SEE THE MARTIAL ARTS PORTRAYED IN FILMS THAT HAS NOT YET REALLY BEEN DONE?

I'd like to see some changes. There are a lot of martial arts action films with shooting, killing, and the use of guns. I want to do something more that's a cross between *Billy Jack* and *The Karate Kid*. I'm looking at more of something of the karate of today. I'm looking at inner city youth, gangs.

There's a theme of a guy coming out of nowhere and using his martial arts to clean up the town. Not that he stops drugs altogether, but he gets drugs to move out of the town. I kind of got the idea from Chuck Norris' program "kicking drugs out of America." His program is about turning peoples lives around and I thought the idea should be in the movies. Outcomes are not dependent upon car chases, blow-ups, explosions, and things like that. It's more a relationship of how the martial arts influences individual lives.

- How has fame as a kickboxer and actor changed your life?

Well the major change is acting: you become famous, you make more money. That's the major thing. Because that's why people want to become famous, I think, unless they just want their egos rubbed. But a certain amount of fame is translated into dollars and cents in the film industry. And in that respect, it's a good thing. But the flip side of that is, sure, you're sitting here eating and somebody comes up to you, you might be having a romantic dinner or something. It doesn't fit your schedule to be Don "The Dragon" Wilson. Sometimes I just want to be Don ... just be relaxed. But usually, because of the activities I'm involved in, I know when I'm gonna get mauled. If I'm not mauled, I'll know something's wrong. I better start driving a truck for a living. But if I'm sitting in a place like this, unless these people are watching late night cable, they're not going to know who I am. So I have the best of both worlds. I have the fame when I want it and I have the anonymity when I don't want it.

- What about your film career?

Well, I did sign for a film called *Redemption*, which I believe is one of the best stories I've worked with and now it's got a really good screenwriter who's going to rewrite it. Chris Penn is going to be in it with me, and I'm really thinking optimistically ... about selling very well at the film market last week. We did pre-sales. And that's a good indication of a movie even before it's made. Do the buyers want to see a movie with Don Wilson and Chris Penn ... in this action film? And they do. They're already buying it ... and we haven't even made it yet. But they just anticipate, of course, the quality will be up. I've done twenty-four movies now. This is my twenty-fifth, and they know that the quality's good on all of them. I keep a certain level of music score, sound, story, the technical flow.

- Are you involved in the production on this film?

Yeah. This is the first one I actually put my own money into. I had a monetary investment, and when Chris signed on, I doubled it. The fight career is doing good, film business is doing good. I'm on the Universal lot like

I said. We were able to get on the lot. Now we have access to all their sets, equipment, post-production facilities, and all the in-house guys there.

- WITH RESPECT TO YOUR FUTURE PLANS, IT APPEARS THAT YOU INTEND TO CONTINUE WORKING AS AN ACTOR AS WELL AS BEING INVOLVED IN KICKBOXING?

In all honesty, I will continue with the kickboxing for the money. I have nothing against the sport of kickboxing, as you know, but I have done it for seventeen years now. That is a long time. You know, I have eleven titles now. You know I don't even know where my belts are now. They're somewhere in my closet and in my garage. I don't need my belts and I don't need my ego rubbed at this time. I really don't want to beat anybody up. I don't have anything against anybody. If my participation serves to stimulate a revitalized kickboxing, then that's good. I am not so giving a person that I would sacrifice my film career in order to promote kickboxing. I did it for the money in order to make money for pay-per-view and to see what the numbers are.

- THANKS VERY MUCH. WE APPRECIATED THE INTERVIEW.
Thank you.

Don Wilson and Michael Maliszewski following
the interview in Lowell, Massachusetts, May 14, 1999.

chapter 7

Dianxue
A Genre-Specific Form of Attack in Martial Arts Fiction
by Olivia Mok, Ph.D.

In martial arts fiction, there is an abundance of references to superior skills which require the knowledge of dianxue.
All illustrations courtesy of The Chinese University Press.

A genre-specific manner of attacking one's enemy, known as dianxue, recurs in martial arts fiction. This is rendered "pique" throughout the translation of *Fox Volant of the Snowy Mountain*, penned originally in Chinese by Jin Yong, a contemporary master writer of martial arts fiction. The present chapter attempts to introduce this genre-specific form of attack to martial artists in the West and to help readers understand pique by underpinning their assumptions with examples drawn from *Fox Volant of the Snowy Mountain* (Jin, 1993).

The first example of this mode of attack is found in Chapter 1, where the monk known as Tree tries to force Hawk into accepting his invitation to go to the snowy mountain. The monk resorts to a vile trick. The passage reads:

> Before Hawk could find words, the monk, describing a circle with his left hand, twisted it round suddenly and grabbed Hawk's right wrist.
> Half of Hawk's side was numbed and aching. The next thing, which happened before Hawk could collect himself, was that the monk had already pinched his wrist, at the Pulse Gate, the point where blood vessels were located and the pulses felt.
> – Jin, 1993: 36

The translation can be considered a faithful but extended rendition of the Chinese original. The passage does mean what it says yet an informed reader also would know immediately that Hawk has been "piqued" in the process. Piquing is a genre-specific cultural practice found in martial arts fiction. It is the act of applying pressure, by jabbing with a finger or attacking with a weapon possessing a sharp point or edge, to certain paralytic points on the body to effect an imbalance of the life force (*qi*) that circulates through the body's energy meridians. Pique will inflict upon a victim any of five effects, namely, soreness or aches, a limp, numbness, paralyzation, or death. There are supposedly 360 paralytic points in the human body and each one has been named. Thirty-six of these are major ones.

Explaining piquing skills across linguistic boundaries is difficult because no target language will contain matching features of universal discourse for concepts of human anatomy and the internal circulation of gaseous fluids as conceived by traditional Chinese medicine. It is unrealistic to expect a target audience devoid of genre-specific assumptions and holding divergent cultural ideas to infer the logical consequences of, or to salvage any implied information from, such an attack. Would the reader know that, when "half of Hawk's side was numbed and aching," Hawk was experiencing sensations typical of one suffering from pique? Here, the implied act to be salvaged mentally by the reader is that the monk had already jabbed a finger at a paralytic point on Hawk's wrist on the sly, thus piquing him in the process. Also, would the target reader know what is being signified by the literal translation "Pulse Gate" if the explanatory phrase "the point where blood vessels were located and the pulses felt" was not inserted after the term?

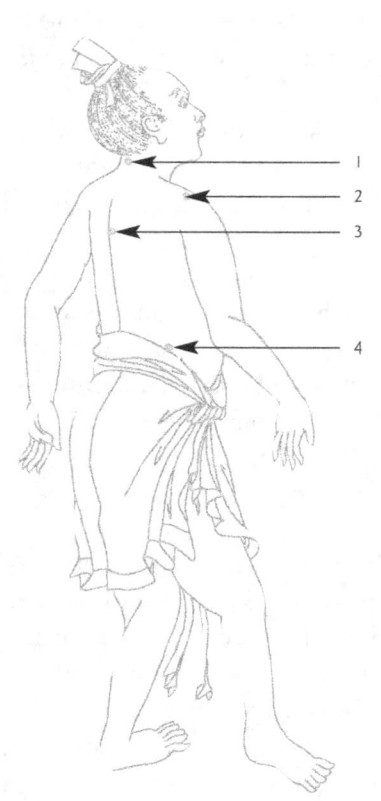
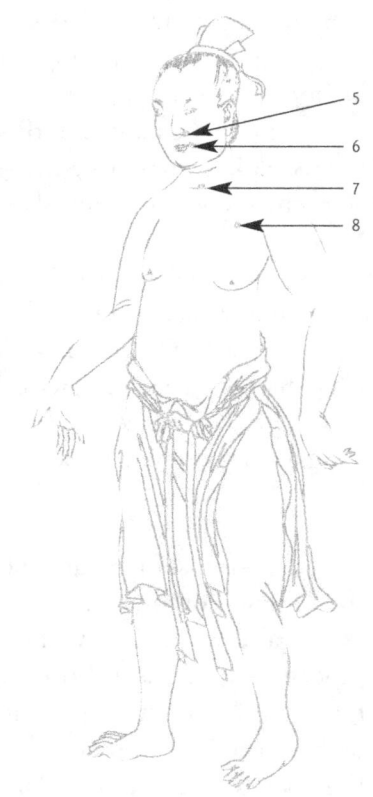

PARALYTIC POINTS

1) Gusty Mere   5) Fragrant Sac
2) Large Bone   6) Terrestrial Crypt
3) Celestial Tract 7) Heavenly Butte
4) Imperial Gate   8) Celestial Abode

點穴

dianxue

Contrast the example cited above, in which the act of piquing is not expressly described and has to be inferred by the sensations suffered, with other acts of piquing that are openly portrayed, such as:

In one leap, he found himself alongside to the younger twin, almost touching him. Valour hit the lad on the shoulder with his left finger, piquing the paralytic point Large Bone and snatched the sword straight with his right hand, practicing the pugilistic skills of the Grappling Hand. – Jin, 1993: 62

Although the act of jabbing a finger at the paralytic point Large Bone on the shoulder is clearly spelled out, the unpleasant sensations suffered, be they mild or severe, are left to the imagination of the reader. At least one thing being implied here is that the lad would suffer a disadvantage after being piqued, making him more vulnerable. Both examples of jabbing with a finger bespeak the distinctive martial prowess of individual fighters. Chapter 4 describes what befalls Gully's enemies when he arrives at an inn in a stage coach:

Presently an answer came from behind the blind of the coach, "Paupers awaiting their alms, eh? Fine: some money, then, for whoever is present." In no time, their eyes were dazzled by the glittering and glistening of gold and all dropped to the ground in a second, letting out cries. Fan and Tian, being proficient in martial arts, were the only two who survived the ordeal. They managed to maintain themselves in an upright position, even though each had caught one of the dispatched arhat quoits* in the wrist, forcing them to slacken their grip on their weapons, so that they dropped to the ground. Tian reacted quickly, "Big Brother Fan, move to the side quickly!" – Jin, 1993: 124-125

* NOTE: *Arhat quoits are metal bracelet-like rings, which Buddhists sometimes wear.*

Readers claiming shared knowledge will have no difficulty in identifying those who dropped to the ground as being less martially endowed; therefore, they fall prey to Gully, who piques them with arhat quoits dispatched from a distance. The presumption that Gully has piqued his enemies is soon confirmed when he immediately restores the afflicted back to normal with coppers again dispatched from a distance:

Fan the Ringleader proved himself exceptionally alert and agile. He bent down to retrieve his iron shaft and whipped around in a trice, planting himself upright beside those lying on the ground, intending to revivify their piqued points. When I received my training in osteopathic arts, my Master gave me a few lessons on the thirty-six major paralytic points of the body. When Fan the Ringleader set to revivifying the piqued points of his people, I knew a little about what he was doing. Though he applied himself with vigor to massaging and applying pressure onto the vital parts of the bodies of those attacked, he failed to get the expected response. Those piqued remained lying on the ground, completely paralyzed.

Presently the man inside the carriage broke out into loud laughter, "Very well. One lot of cash is not good enough for the job? Here comes more." All at once, ten or more coppers sprang out in quick succession, flying in every direction, each aiming at a paralytic point. There and then the victims previously inflicted by the coins thrown at them now recovered their senses in their limbs, all raising themselves to their full height. – Jin, 1993: 125

This scene seems to suggest that the damage done to the victims can perhaps be alleviated by massaging the vital paralytic points, which will hopefully restore the circulation of the life force back to normal. Judging from how Fan and Tian survived the ordeal yet failed to restore the wounded on the spot, informed readers would conclude that Gully inside the coach is a paragon of a fighter because his long-range piquing turns out to be so stunning that fighters less endowed, such as Fan and Tian, can never succeed in undoing its harm, try as they might. Unless the pique is intended to be fatal, victims can normally recover after a certain lapse of time, even without help. This is what is expected to happen to Orchid:

> I have taken off all her clothes. Even if she manages to recover when the time is up, she still will not be able to move about.
> – Jin, 1993: 287

If the pique proves to be too stunning, it will take the victim quite some time to recover, even with outside help. That is precisely what happens to Wish and Profundity after they receive a stunning pique from Fox:

> Heralding his own triumph, Fox doubled the power in his blows. Wish and Profundity passed out without even the time to let out a sound. Fox's pique proved stunning. The recovery of the two injured would take at least two weeks, even in the hands of adepts.
> – Jin, 1993: 336

Readers might also expect to find that the less martially endowed, such as Orchid and Lute, will suffer greater injuries even from minor piquing at the hands of a martial fiddler like Tree the monk:

Tree advanced two paces, wreathed in smiles. No sooner had he waved his sleeve than he had piqued two of Orchid's paralytic points, the Heavenly Butte at her nape and the Celestial Tract on her back. Orchid was afflicted immediately: her body ached, and she was paralyzed, lying back full length in the chair. Abashed and indignant, Orchid could not utter a sound. Seeing that the monk had wrought harm to her mistress, Lute again braced herself and reached for his arm, meaning to bite deep into his flesh. Tree allowed her to pull his right hand until it was almost touching her lips. Then he turned his fingers and piqued two of Lute's paralytic points also: the Fragrant Sac near her nose and the Terrestrial Crypt at the corner of her mouth. Lute trembled and fell to the ground.
– Jin, 1993: 286

Readers' assumed knowledge of piquing tells them that even adept fighters such as Gully and Phoenix, although they themselves possess dexterous hands in piquing, can also be rendered powerless if their major paralytic points are piqued. Gully has the misfortune to receive a pique from Phoenix, who is wielding a sword on their fifth day of dueling:

In a trice, the sword retracted with a spurt, darting the tang off the blade and placing itself right on Gully's chest, on the paralytic point Celestial Abode.

The Celestial Abode is a governing vital point of the human body system. On being piqued, Gully instantaneously dropped limp to the ground, like a rag.
– Jin, 1993: 164-165

The predicament of Phoenix is no better than Gully's when he is attacked by Fan the Ringleader, who has stolen behind his back:

> Suddenly terrible sensations crept over the paralytic points of the Gusty Mere behind his ear and of the Celestial Tract behind his back. Matters had suddenly gone wrong. Alerted, Phoenix swiftly thrust out his left arm, striking a blow. Alas, it was too late. His two principal paralytic points having been piqued by Fan the Ringleader practicing the Grappling Claws of the Dragon. Phoenix immediately felt sore and numbed all over. Even were he a divine incarnation, or a necromancer incarnate, Phoenix would have found himself completely unable to expedite any moves. – Jin, 1993: 327

Seasoned readers also expect to find adept martial artists who have dexterous hands not only at piquing but who also are skilled at surviving this mode of attack. Witness how Phoenix manages to extricate himself from another pique in the end:

> Commissioner Sai was the one who had piqued Phoenix on his paralytic points. The two guardsmen were at a loss as to how to revivify him. Just as Fox was reaching out his hand to invigorate him, Phoenix channeled energy appropriately within his internal system, thus taking the lead in resuscitating his own body. His limbs having been set free, Phoenix drew in a deep breath. By tucking in his midriff slightly, he had his paralytic points reinstated in a moment. Suddenly, without warning, his left foot swept up from the floor towards Spirituality the Buddhist Devotee and sent him soaring like a rocket. Thrusting out his fist at the same instant, he threw a straight punch at an opponent, propelling him forward.
> – Jin, 1993: 337

After going through numerous incidents involving the martial feat of piquing in earlier chapters, readers, initially uninformed though they may have been, by now should not have much trouble in recognizing the following scene from the last chapter as an act of piquing.

The incident described takes place some twenty years later. Fox turns out to be just as proficient as Gully, his father, in piquing with snowballs dispatched from a distance:

> At length, he bent down and scooped up some ice flakes. Using the strength in his fingers, he kneaded the granular snow into hard spheres. Then his arm twirled and sent the snowball flying headlong, catching the more distant escapee on the back at the waist. The victim immediately fell sprawling and lay upon his face, unable to pick himself up again. Fear gripped the heart of the less distant fugitive. He turned about. Another snowball came whirling at him, catching him on the chest and sending him sprawling upon his back. Though the two wretched preys differed in the way they had dropped to the ground, they resembled each other in having lost the ability to scramble to their feet again.
> – Jin, 1993: 359

Fox proves no less proficient, again like his father, at restoring sense to his enemies a short while later, also from a respectable distance:

> Fox twirled his arms and both snowballs which he was gripping in his hands went shooting ahead, catching again the two boorish fighters lying on the ground. Unlike the previous attack in which the victims were piqued by the ice weapons, Fox intended the second attack only to revivify their afflicted points. The two victims writhed a little, struggled to their feet and fled, making good speed.
> – Jin, 1993: 361

References

Jin, Yong (1993). *Fox Volant of the snowy mountain.* (O. Mok, Trans.). Hong Kong: Chinese University Press.

Mok, O. (1997). The 'reader' factor in martial arts fiction in English translation: With special reference to the 'yellow knapsack' in Jin Yong's *Fox Volant of the Snowy Mountain. Tamkang Review* 28(1), 77-89.

chapter 8

Film Producer Andre Morgan & the Evolution of Asian Martial Arts in Movies

by Michael Maliszewski, Ph.D.

Bruce Lee and Andre Morgan (on far left) watching as the camera records scenes for *Enter the Dragon*. Photographs courtesy of Andre Morgan, except where noted.

Introduction

Andre Morgan is a name which may not strike a chord of recognition among people in the martial arts. However, his life has unfolded in a most unusual way where, as a Westerner, he unexpectedly played an early, central role in bridging eastern and western sensibilities in the martial arts film industry.

Beginning his career with Golden Harvest in Hong Kong and playing an interesting role in the production of Bruce Lee's films, his work has continued to expand internationally, including such recent television shows as *Walker, Texas Ranger* (with Chuck Norris) and *Martial Law* (with Sammo Hung), among other projects. He currently works at the Ruddy-Morgan Organization in Beverly Hills, California.

INTERVIEW

- I'D LIKE TO BEGIN BY ASKING YOUR PLACE AND DATE OF BIRTH AND SOME GENERAL INFORMATION ABOUT YOUR FAMILY BACKGROUND.

March 4, 1952. I was born in a French military hospital in Morocco [Casablanca]. No brothers, no sisters. My wife's name is Maria; we have no children.

- HOW DID YOU END UP BEING BORN IN MOROCCO?

My father was stationed in North Africa. He was in the US Navy. My mother emigrated to America after WWII where they married. In the heyday of the Cold War, the American defense establishment allowed you to rotate between places in Europe and places in the United States.

Bruce Lee, Raymond Chow, Andre Morgan, and others on location during the making of *Enter the Dragon*.

- IT SOUNDS LIKE YOU DID A LOT OF TRAVELING. WHERE DID YOU GROW UP?

I spent half of my time in Europe. In the United States, my family did tours of duty in Puget Sound just north of Seattle; Virginia Beach, Virginia; and Kansas City. I lived on both the east and west coast as well as the Midwest. I was also in England. By the time I was sixteen, I had been to twelve elementary and junior high schools.

- AS YOU WERE GROWING UP AS A YOUNGSTER, DID YOU HAVE ANY INTEREST IN PHYSICAL ACTIVITIES, SPORTS OR THE LIKE?

I was a typical 1950's kid—Cub Scouts, Boy Scouts. I was on the swim team; I was on the diving team. Because we also lived in England, I played as goalie on a soccer team, and also played on a cricket team. I also played American football.

- ANY OTHER FORMAL EDUCATION? WHAT ABOUT YOUR ACADEMIC BACKGROUND?

I graduated from high school in Kansas City in 1969. I then went to the University of Kansas, Lawrence campus. I left in May of 1972. I didn't graduate. I'm a dropout. I had five years of Chinese.

- CAN YOU TELL ME A LITTLE BIT ABOUT YOUR COLLEGE EDUCATION?

I had a triple major. I had a declared major in Oriental languages and literature with a specialization in modern Chinese. I had a second major in history. For the History Department, I majored in Chinese history with a minor in Russian history and Korean history. I also had a third major in Asian studies. For the Asian Studies Department I had a major in Chinese culture, a minor in Korean culture, and also a minor in Japanese culture. I was training to become, what was called in those days, a "China watcher." This was someone who could be involved with diplomatic relations. At that time, we were at the height of the Vietnam War (1969). There was a civil war going on in China at that time too. Nobody in America was able to explain at the time what was going on behind the "bamboo wall." I needed a scholarship to stay in the university.

- WERE YOU AN AMERICAN CITIZEN AT THIS TIME?

At that time I had triple citizenship. I was eligible for British citizenship and also for French citizenship by virtue of being born in a French hospital. I wanted to stay in the university at that time. I had taken French and German in high school—five years of French and four years of German. I had planned to major in these areas when I got to the university; however, there were some 20,000 students majoring in this area. It was pretty clear that I would not be able to qualify for a scholarship. I then inquired as to how many undergrads there were by department. You didn't have to be a rocket scientist to then discover that there were fifty-odd scholarships available in Oriental languages and literature. There were three students at that time with declared specialty in Chinese. So I enrolled in first-year Chinese. In the process of getting involved with that, I took some classes in Oriental philosophy. I also took two semesters of Asian studies. It was taught by the head of the Oriental languages/Asian studies program. This person was actually trained as a "China watcher." He was the first person able to explain what was actually going on in China. I found all this very interesting, so at that time I said "I want to be a China watcher." I then found myself on scholarship on the second semester of my stay at the university.

- YOU HAD NEVER ACTUALLY VISITED ANY ASIAN COUNTRIES UP UNTIL THIS POINT IN TIME. WHAT WAS YOUR INTEREST IN GETTING INVOLVED IN ALL OF THIS?

Truthfully, I've always had an interest in history and an interest in culture. And I think the benefit of growing up as a Navy brat, going back and forth... going to so many schools, you learn to make friends very quickly. You tend to be resilient. I think it also led to an inquisitive mind. I actually skipped two grades in school. I was 17-1/2 by the time I was in the university. I had had enough training in medieval history, Italian history, French history... China and Asia were blank pages for me.

What did we as Americans really know about China at that time? That was a whole new world being opened up to me. The world focus was turning towards Asia at that time because of the Vietnam War. It was the right time for me. I enjoyed being one of three undergraduates to major in Chinese.

For me, however, the problem was very fundamental; in three years, I had taken five years of Chinese, I had taken all of my courses for the major in Asian studies. All I needed to graduate from the university was requisite courses in math and sciences, which I had absolutely no interest in. The problem was very fundamental; I had a high draft number (327). I had been classified 4H with a military deferment. Then I woke up one day and asked myself what was I going to do with this degree? If I stay on for two more semesters to finish the requisite science and math courses, what was I going to do next? Was I going to go to grad school? There was not much more that you could do in this area unless it was to teach. There was no actual application of this field unless you wanted to become a spy or work for the State Department. I was not a good security risk for the State Department as I had been a member of SDS [Students for Democratic Society] and a few other groups. I decided that I did not want to go to graduate school. I did not want to sit around studying Chinese characters.

One of my professors and the head of the Chinese department used to sit around proving to one another what were the more obscure Chinese characters. I remember one drawing a character suggesting that the other did not know what he had drawn ... 32 strokes ... the other professor looks at it, and he looks at it again, and he says "I've seen this before!" The first guy looks at him and says "It is the hair from the underarm of a mole [laughter]!" I said to myself "That's it! I'm outta here! Graduate school is not for me [laughter]!" But I also wanted to get on to Asia. I was also concerned that I was going to be graduating but that I did not speak Chinese. I realized that I could identify the 32 strokes needed to identify the hair under the armpit of a mole, but that I could not carry on a practical conversation in Mandarin.

- So, what did you do next?

At this time, I met by accident or maybe by luck, a graduate exchange student from Beijing—Peking National University. He actually gave a speech at the University of Kansas on his way back to Sweden. His topic dealt with what was going on behind the "bamboo curtain." This inspired me. So I wrote off letters to Peking National University; however, this did not work out due to difficulties with what would be my declared country of citizenship.

The professor who actually got me involved into Chinese studies—his name was Robert [Bob] Burton—he had started the Asian studies program at the University of Kansas. He's also a Ph.D. in herpetology, the study of frogs. He had spent a year in China and had learned to speak Chinese. His friend in China at that time had been a young man by the name of Raymond Chow, who had graduated from St. John's University in Shanghai. Raymond had come from a very wealthy family in China and had majored in English and became a reporter for the Associated Press. They had spent a lot of time together. Bob had been best man at Raymond's wedding. Bob Burton had been assigned by the State Department to set up the Voice of America in Hong Kong. The first person hired by Voice of America was Raymond Chow. Raymond, in turn, hired an entire team of people that eventually became the backbone of Shaw Brothers. This converted Shaw Brothers into the powerhouse of the Chinese film industry. He left in 1971, to form Golden Harvest.

Burton was actually away on sabbatical for a year working for the Rockefeller Foundation. Burton came back to Kansas City in the Christmas of 1971 for a visit and we got together for dinner. I told him that I wanted to go to Hong Kong because I could not go to Beijing. I did not want to go to Taipei at that time, as did most American students because then you would not get entry to Beijing. My goal was to try to figure out a way to get into China. I asked Bob to think of any way he could get me to Hong Kong. He informed me that he was going to be meeting in Washington with his old friend

Raymond Chow, who was traveling around the world with his wife at the time. He had just quit Shaw Brothers and had formed his own company. He then met with Raymond Chow and spoke to him about my interest. He called me shortly thereafter and told me "You have a job. Raymond wants to meet with you in a week."

I was told that Raymond would meet with me in Los Angeles, and if I passed the interview, I would be given a job for one year. But I had to agree that I would work for a Chinese salary not an expatriate's salary. If I paid my own way to Hong Kong, they would pay my way back. However, I would be living like a Chinese starting out as an office boy, not a wealthy expatriate.

I was then called back three days later by Bob who informed me that I did not need to go for the interview, and Raymond asked when I could be in Hong Kong. I agreed that I would be in Hong Kong by June 14, 1972. I got money from my grandmother to get a one-way ticket to Hong Kong and finished up my semester at the university. I then got on the plane to Hong Kong and arrived at the airport. I did not have a work permit. Raymond told me to come in on a tourist visa and not to worry about it. I remember looking around at the airport in the rain and looking at myself and saying "What have I done?"

This was the summer of 1972. Raymond had just come back from Rome at this time after filming the fighting sequence for *Return of the Dragon* with Chuck Norris and Bruce Lee. I had dinner with Raymond and met his family. We then took the ferry across to Hong Kong, and he asked me "Well, do you want to be involved with production or distribution?" Here I am, twenty years old, and I don't even know what production and distribution are! He said "In production we make them, and in distribution we sell them." I then boldly said that I would be interested in distribution because I could both read and write Chinese. I didn't speak Cantonese in those days.

- So you joined Golden Harvest. What was your official title?

Office boy. I was actually working for a translator and sent out to work with Chuck and Bruce on the set of *Return of the Dragon*. I was translating a lot of the subtitles. By that time, Bruce had made two of the biggest pictures in the film history of Hong Kong. These were *The Big Boss* and *Fists of Fury*. At that time, they were trying to figure out how they would sell these movies to the rest of the world. There were only three of us who were bilingual: Raymond, his secretary, and myself.

- At this point in time, did you have any exposure to the martial arts? Did you have any personal interest or practice of the martial arts?

No. I had seen the film, *Billy Jack*. I had not even seen *Kung Fu* the TV series. The first Chinese kung fu movie I saw was *The Big Boss*. On my first day of work, I was taken out to the screening room and I watched *The Big Boss*. This was the first time I had been in a screening room my entire life. I had the whole theater to myself, which was pretty cool. They also ran *Fists of Fury* for me. Then they took me back to my hotel.

- WHAT WERE YOUR IMPRESSIONS WATCHING THE MOVIES?

They needed a lot of help [laughter]. I remember the next day going into Raymond's office and he asked if I thought we could sell them to America. And I told him "No, I don't thing so." He then asked why and I told him that the stories were too simple. You can't knock somebody through a wall and have a cardboard cut-out as a person. The acting is a little over the top. He then asked me how I liked the kung fu. I commented that it was all very good, but that they had to get past this other stuff. He then stated that he wanted me to have dinner with him, and I did along with his partner, Leonard Ho. Raymond then told me to tell his partner what I had told him. As I told him, Raymond translated it. So, I was then told I would work with them on future pictures. I then spent the rest of that summer working on sets of different movies. Raymond had gone with Bruce to the United States to make a deal which involved the first co-production between Warner Brothers and Golden Harvest.

- WHAT YEAR WAS THIS?

1972. The script had been called *Blood and Steel*. They sent me a copy of the script by freight to Hong Kong and Raymond called and told me that I was being promoted to producer. So I went from office boy to producer.

- HOW MANY MONTHS HAD YOU WORKED THERE AT THAT POINT IN TIME?

Three months. They then told me to prepare a budget and that Warner Brothers was coming out to Hong Kong to produce *Enter the Dragon*. I had a director friend with me at the time, King Hu. He was part of the original Voice of America group. He had actually become my other guardian in Hong Kong. I informed him that I had become a producer. He said, "Congratulations." And then I asked him, "What do I do?" He told me, "If you're smart, you'd hire a good production manager." That was the most important lesson I learned!

So, he gave me his production manager and we did the budget and the schedule together. We realized later that strategically this was probably the smartest thing that Raymond Chow could have done. It was my job to look at "foreign devils" who came into work with the company. We were in an unusual position of not being told what to do by the Americans. This was not a Hong Kong film industry being cast by people in Hollywood. It was a Hong

Kong production. This was a first—the first time this had ever been done. There is a lot of pride derived by the Hong Kong film industry knowing that they could do anything that Hollywood asked them to do and even do it more efficiently than expected. That became a touchstone for Golden Harvest after the next five or six years following Bruce's death.

How do we bounce back after Bruce died? We had successfully done the co-production and had successfully completed the picture, and the film had been very successful and made a lot of money.

Discussions between John Saxon, Andre Morgan, Raymond Chow, and Bruce Lee during the filming of *Enter the Dragon*.

- IN RETROSPECT NOW, HOW DO YOU LOOK AT THIS CONVERGENCE OF THE HOLLYWOOD AND CHINESE FILM INDUSTRIES AT THAT TIME?

In terms of matching the Chinese abilities and learning, and how Hong Kong interprets and takes some of the American techniques and applies them to the Hong Kong industry, of course, Bruce was instrumental because he had worked in Hollywood and was obviously in control of the films he was producing.

- DID YOU HAVE A PERSONAL RELATIONSHIP WITH BRUCE LEE?

Yes. I was the only other American in the company. Even though there was a twelve year difference, I think there was a certain simpatico. I was just starting out and he was starting his career as a star, and he had become a major star in Hong Kong. But Bruce's aspirations were much greater. He was a great martial artist and teacher; but he also wanted to be the first international movie star of Chinese descent. In those days his dream was to be a bigger star than Steve McQueen. And yet at the same time Lee did not want to let go of what he had in Asia. He wanted to be able to make a movie in Hollywood, return to make a movie in Asia that had Chinese values and was inspirational to get the Chinese people, and then come back and make a movie in America. That is what he was really striving for. It's very hard to understand in hindsight.

We worked very hard to make *Enter the Dragon* the very best movie we could make. We did not expect it to be the defining movie of Lee's life. We were hard at work on a movie called *Game of Death*. We had been working on it for two months before we stopped in order to start work on *Enter the Dragon*. And the idea was that we would finish *Enter the Dragon*. Bruce was very tired. Bruce would get a rest and get back in shape and work on the script of *Game of Death*. So that we would finish *Game of Death* as soon as *Enter the Dragon* opened. I went off to Korea to do a taekwondo movie with Jhoon Rhee. Bruce got sick and went back to the US, had a physical done, and came back to Hong Kong. He was dead in two weeks. Nobody expected *Enter the Dragon* to be the defining movie.

- DO YOU HAVE ANY IMPRESSIONS OF WATCHING BRUCE PERFORM COMPARED TO SOME OF THE OTHER MARTIAL ARTISTS IN THE MOVIE?

It's not really fair to give impressions. You'd have to look at it in the context at that time. The kind of films that were being made and the kind of heroes were different than what you see today. And your heroes are people like John Wayne and Steve McQueen. *Bonnie and Clyde* was a movie that appeared three years before. So our frame of reference and vocabulary was very different than it is to day.

Bruce's goal was to make movies where he and the underdog were to triumph. He also hoped to impart some of the wisdom and philosophy at the same time. But Bruce was also an actor as opposed to a martial artist who strives to be an actor. Bruce had been an actor as a young kid and came from a family of performers. He then went on to study martial arts and to evolve his own style of martial arts. He founded Jeet Kune Do. So the two parts of the man grew ... he was a martial artist, and he was a teacher. He was an actor who believed in doing things in a theatrical way. Bruce Lee did not walk into a room. Bruce Lee entered the room. He is a bigger-than-life person, and he had that kind of charisma about him. Most of the other actors/marital artists were either actors who just learned martial arts to get by in a film, or they were martial artists who had not yet really perfected their acting skills. I think Lee's uniqueness is clearly very evident when you see his much more flamboyant style of acting. He understood the importance of doing a theatrical thing in his films. You see very clearly that an actor is at work.

Steve McQueen told a story at Bruce's funeral in Seattle. Bruce called up Steve and told him he was going to be doing his first international film and asked, "Do you have any advice?" Steve said, "I'll tell you what I've learned. The camera either loves you or it don't." And that's the truth of it. People either have that special charisma that appears on camera or they don't. You can't give them a magic potion to drink. They either have it or they don't... The way he walked, the way he talked, his energy level... it was all there. That is the major contributing factor to his success. But his fame or the legendary status that he has achieved some twenty-odd years plus since his death... twenty seven years later... if you look at where Jimmy Dean was at twenty-seven years after his death, and that is an analogy that people make, Bruce is still a much bigger presence. And I attribute that to the energy he brought to the screen.

- YOU ARE ALSO INFLUENTIAL IN GETTING HIS FILMS EXPORTED OUTSIDE OF ASIA.

We came up with a strategy for selling them in Europe, South America and ultimately into North America. It was a lot of trial and error.

- WHAT YEAR OR YEARS ARE WE TALKING ABOUT?

1972, 1973 and 1974. We hired a salesman to come out to the Cannes Film Festival and got his lengthy reports of what was wrong with our film. And at the same time he was able to make deals to distribute the films throughout other countries such as Lebanon and Italy. And, to see how world's cross, my current partner, Al Ruddy, produced the original *Godfather*. The *Godfather* opened in 1972, at Easter time. I was here at UCLA visiting my girlfriend the opening night of *The Godfather*. She wanted to see it, so we went to the Village Theatre. The following spring, we were working on *Enter the Dragon*, and we had gotten our first report when *The Big Boss* opened in Beirut, Lebanon. We had out grossed *The Godfather*. We then knew we were onto something. The problem was that Bruce did not want the Hong Kong movies to be shown to the rest of the world. He wanted *Enter the Dragon*, *Return of the Dragon*, and *Game of Death* to be shown to the western world. In those movies he had control of the director and the writers. But Golden Harvest wanted to exploit his earlier movies too. So we developed a strategy to market them and slowly get them out there. Sales were made and deals were negotiated here in America... *Enter the Dragon* opened successfully right on the heels of his death. This established Golden Harvest as the preeminent company and producer of martial arts movies. And the income from Bruce's early movies is what allowed Golden Harvest to become as successful as they did.

Andre Morgan observes camera angles to help capture the proper mood for one of the more intense scenes found in the movie *Enter the Dragon*.

- WHAT WERE THE AMERICAN AND EUROPEAN FILM INDUSTRIES DOING COMPARABLY IN MARTIAL ARTS OR ACTION PICTURES?

The truth was that the American film industry was very much in the doldrums. The most successful American action movies at the time were the *Dirty Harry* series. Many of the studios were teetering on bankruptcy. There was no clear direction with the American film industry. In Europe, Dino DeLaurentis/Carlo Ponti was very prolific in Italy. They were also looking at a lot of the Japanese samurai movies because these stories were universal stories. The only other martial arts movie that could be seen that was made was *Billy Jack*! The Hong Kong film industry was also being put to the test. Shaw Brothers had also fallen into a slump. This was due to the advent of television in Asia. This is what gave impetus to the upstart company, Golden Harvest. Raymond Chow and his team did not believe that the industry had to end. That is when they started to follow the kung fu movies with Bruce Lee, with Jimmy Wang Yu, Sammo Hung, Jackie Chan… John Woo was a young, assistant director assigned to Golden Harvest. This was in 1972 and 1973.

- YOU HAVE MENTIONED THAT THERE ARE MANY PHASES OF THE EVOLUTION OF MARTIAL ARTS MOVIES. CAN YOU ELABORATE SOMEWHAT ON THIS?

This is a very subjective viewpoint. You have to look at the time flow of film. Just as you can refer back to silent movies and your first western in American film… when you list martial arts in the context of Chinese film, there have always been martial arts sequences. How martial arts were portrayed on film changes stylistically in time. Jimmy Wang Yu was the first martial arts star of Asia. The style of fighting at the time was much more theatrical as opposed to being reality-based. For example: the belief that one could fly over people, clearing their heads by ten feet. Just as you read in Chinese novels of great swordsmen of old, they could fight through the air and engage in battles twenty feet above the ground. A number of these movements are more difficult than real martial arts. This is a period that pre-dates Bruce Lee. Bruce's contribution was primarily his wanting to ground it in reality. His approach was no longer so simple as to wear a white hat. You know, *Dirty Harry* was slightly flawed; but it was a more gritty reality. Bruce did the same thing with martial arts films. He knew that I'm not going to hit someone twenty times before they fall down. I'm not going to get hit fifteen times. If you hit me, I get hurt. If I didn't get hurt, you didn't hit very hard. And if I kick you and you don't block it, you get hurt. It was still theatrical, but he brought a measure of reality to the martial arts.

- WHAT ABOUT SOME OF HIS EARLIER FILMS WHICH WERE MORE THEATRICAL?

The answer to that is to look at how the content of film progressed. Look at *The Big Boss*. Here we have some "flying through the air" stunts. We see Bruce leaping in the air for a flying kick. Unfortunately, he was not totally in control of the choreography at that time. This is Shanghai before the war. We see fighting against the Japanese in their dojo. Although directors brought down the number of "flying-through-air" kicks, they still showed one person fighting against twenty guys at once. The argument to this unrealistic portrayal was that we don't mind seeing one person fighting twenty guys at once, but we don't want them standing in the background waiting for the hero to fight them.

We can look at *Return of the Dragon* next. Here, Bruce kept the fighting much more *mano a mano* because he wanted to make it as if he was taking on a substantial opponent for a substantial fight. Whether it be one guy or three guys, it had to be serious, like watching a heavyweight boxing match. So he was much more into the spectacle of one-on-one. When we look at the fight between him and Chuck Norris, Lee pulls hair out of the guy's chest, and all kinds of things. This becomes the prototype of a choreographed Bruce Lee fight.

Now go to the next step. *Enter the Dragon* has a fight between Bruce and Bob Wall. There isn't an actual fight here, but he actually does the back flip somersault kick to give it a theatrical quality. But this was a one off. It wasn't to become the gimmick of the movie. In the big fight scenes where we have Bruce fighting against nine or ten guys, there's a legitimate context for their role. There's nobody just standing around waiting to be hit. There was an inherent logic to what was going on. Fight scenes were going with the reality. Bruce really grounded the whole concept of martial arts by portraying it in a world that was much more real. This was around 1973. Then you see people trying to emulate him, but not doing it too well, or else backsliding into more "flying kicks." But actually people got very tired of this.

The next phase is what I call the "Jackie Chan phase." This is where Jackie knows he cannot compete against Bruce Lee, knowing that he is not the same martial artist, but an actor. But the public needs heroes. Let us come up with a new kind of hero. Chan brought in the element of comedy… the *Drunken Monkey* movies… Sammo Hung and Jackie learned more acrobatics than martial arts, and you see that influence. They may be doing Wing Chun, taekwondo, or Hapkido, but they're adding in all of the juggling, acrobatics and tumbling that really comes from the world of Peking Opera.

Next, in the late 1970's or early 1980's, there was added a comedic "un-turn." What we get now are Western influences coming back. We get Chuck Norris, a black belt champion who says "I can do martial arts." It's from an American perspective. At this stage, we have the comedic element which is the underpinning of the Hong Kong martial arts film, colliding with the world of martial arts, which includes Chuck Norris, Michael Dudikoff, and a number of other individuals. We are now in the early 1980's.

- WHAT ABOUT VAN DAMME AND SEAGAL?

Van Damme and Seagal actually come later. We are now in the early 1980's and the genre is still going along strong. And now we get that next generation around 1987 or 1988. Here we find the American film studios looking for actors and seeing if they can make money. And that's where we get a Steven Seagal and John Claude Van Damme. But these are much further removed stylistically from the martial arts films that Bruce Lee made, or the martial arts films of Jackie Chan. Theatre is actually a dialogue. Nothing happens in isolation in the free world in film. There is a lot of borrowing going on. If I see something in a film that inspires me, I incorporate it. And I've seen films in Hong Kong reach a fork. In the mid 1980's, they had run out of gimmicks. They didn't know where to go. Jackie Chan does action films with stunts, cars, and fight scenes that are gimmicky... using a cup or whatever for blocking and striking. We get Western martial artists in more roles and films started taking on more of an American flavor.

And then "Sega" comes along—the game platform. Here you have the games and the programmers are running these games. They have all of these martial arts scenes, and they study angles and they study the kicks and everything else involved. And they now added this to the game war. Now we get the next set of possibilities, which takes the Chinese elements of flying through the air, applying it to cyber reality, Western sensibilities, and Chinese style action. This is exemplified by the film *The Matrix*. Look at *Mission Impossible II*... directed by John Woo, with Tom Cruise doing backward somersault kicks. I haven't seen that since *Enter the Dragon* in 1973! What happens is the real world of martial arts and the film world of martial arts rubbing off on each other.

- I'D LIKE TO RETURN TO THE DISCUSSION OF YOUR LIFE WHEN YOU RETURNED TO THE UNITED STATES. YOU WERE WITH GOLDEN HARVEST. WHAT WAS YOUR ROLE WITH THAT COMPANY?

I actually became a partner in 1976.

- WAS THAT A FIRST?

Oh yeah. The first non-Chinese partner in Golden Harvest [laughter]! I also became involved in Golden Communications as Chief Operating Officer. We packaged and produced English language films. Raymond Chow was also one of my partners here. He made a lot of money out of *Enter the Dragon*. I was sent to Australia to produce the first Australian/Hong Kong co-production in 1974. It was called *The Man from Hong Kong*.

It was a James Bond type movie. People who starred in it were Jimmy Wang Yu, and there was a young stuntman there named Sammo Hung, who now more recently starred in my program, *Martial Law*. This was the first movie about hang gliding. At that time we also began to believe that we could compete with Hollywood. We could compete in the international arena in marketing. We had the money and we had the expertise. So we setup Golden Communications in the spring of 1975. We were very successful. We developed Jackie Chan as an international star. In 1984 I sold out my interest in Golden Communications. I had been working very hard and was tired, and I was ready for a change. I thought I would go to Hollywood for awhile. I had been traveling from one city to the next constantly over the different years. I had so much jet lag, I was falling asleep in my soup on the plane.

- So what did you do next?

We then set up Ruddy-Morgan in 1984. Al Ruddy, my partner, had worked at Golden Harvest with me earlier. Al was a very successful producer here in Hollywood. He had created a very successful TV series known as *Hogan's Heroes*. He also produced *How the West Was Won*. He had produced *The Godfather*. I also had a company in Hong Kong with Dixon Poon and Sammo Hung called D & B Films. And then Dixon got out of the film business. We had been doing feature films and television series. We've had *Walker Texas Ranger* going through its seventh year, and *Martial Law* is in it second year. As they say, the rest of it is history.

- Given your experience here over time, any particular individuals that stand out in the entertainment industry... film stars, producers, directors, and significant associations you've had?

It depends on how you want to define being involved. If I look at that period at Golden Harvest between 1972 and 1984, literally it's the "who's who of action genre in Asia"—Jackie Chan and Sammo Hung, Jimmy Wang Yu, Angela Mao ... and all the action directors. At the same time, if you look at the world of action movies here in Hollywood, there are people I worked with earlier in Hong Kong. It's actually a very, very small world. There is a lot of cross-cultural pollination that goes on between those people in America that are aware of the older Chinese films and furthering the genre here. And then there are the young directors that have come over from Asia, such as John Woo.

- Where do you see martial arts going in the film industry? Do you have any projections into the future?

I think where martial arts goes depends upon the caliber of the practitioners both as martial artists and as actors. You need to find the right people. As with *Martial Law* for example, you need people with the right skill and humor. Otherwise the show cannot be defined as it has been defined. I think it's a function of finding that next generation of martial artist/actor and pushing the envelope. Interestingly enough, martial arts has opened the door—Americans and Europeans are much more knowledgeable and comfortable about Asia. Thirty years ago they would not have known what the word "kung fu" meant. They not only know Bruce Lee and Jackie Chan, but also now Jet Li and Michelle Yeoh, and people know Sammo Hung. And all these young kids that work on Sega know martial arts as well [laughter]. And I think they've learned a little bit about the culture too. People are now looking at other ways of seeing things: philosophical influences, medical interest in things such as acupuncture.... I know for a fact that twenty-five years ago people would not have taken it seriously.

Andre Morgan at his office in Beverly Hills, California. He is reading "Celluloid Katas: Martial Arts in the Movies," an article by James Grady (*Journal of Asian Martial Arts*, Volume 7 Number 2). *Photo courtesy of M. Maliszewski.*

- YOU MENTIONED A DISTINCTION BETWEEN THE LEVEL OF IN-DEPTH TRAINING IN MARTIAL ARTS AND ACROBATICS, A DISTINCTION BETWEEN CINEMAGRAPHIC MARTIAL ARTS AND MARTIAL ARTS AS PRACTICED IN AND OUT ON A DAILY BASIS—HOW IT COMES ACROSS ON THE SCREEN. COULD YOU ELABORATE A LITTLE BIT MORE ON THIS?

Martial arts practiced on a daily basis is done so for one of two reasons: as a form of exercise in which case it is stylized to teach people the different katas in order to get their bodies and their muscles trained to do those things reflexively, or it's done to tone up the body. That's the first set of reasons. The second set of reasons is done as a method of offense or defense for self-defense [unarmed combat]. The object of that is to take out the opponent as quickly as possible. Cinemagraphical martial arts is done to look visually the most exciting and to show off the acrobatic skills of the performer. Therefore, rather simply kicking somebody in the testicles, they may do a series of spinning roundhouse kicks. Arguably, a quick kick to the testicles is a more direct way of taking out an opponent than five spinning roundhouse kicks.

- HAVE YOU HAD ANY MARTIAL ARTS TRAINING?

No. I had no interest in martial arts until I got into the world of film. Once I got into the world of film, it became very apparent to me that this was something that required a great deal of time to study and perfect. That was something that I didn't have.

- HAS THERE BEEN ANY PHILOSOPHICAL IMPACT OR IMPRESSIONS THAT THE MARTIAL ARTS HAS HAD ON YOU BEING A NON-PRACTITIONER OF THESE DISCIPLINES?

I think there is a great deal of very valuable, personal philosophy or guidelines here for conducting oneself in society or with one's fellow man. You can apply this to everyday life without necessarily being a practitioner of martial arts skills. And I think that part of it is often overlooked in schools as they teach martial arts here in the United States.

- CAN YOU ELABORATE ON THIS FOR ME?

The philosophy. If you spend any time with a really good—at least with the Chinese martial arts instructors—they stress as much the concept of restraint and patience as they do aggressive use of martial arts to overcome an enemy. I think that part of it philosophically is very valuable and has been overlooked tremendously in the west. For me personally, I find that there is a great deal that can be learned from these people.

- DO YOU HAVE ANY ADVICE FOR ANYONE SEEKING TO PURSUE A CAREER IN TV OR FILM WITHIN THE MARTIAL ARTS GENRE?

My observation, what a lot of young martial artists don't realize, is that while they must hone their skills as martial artists, they also have to develop their skills as actors. It is simply not an issue of being the best martial artist. You also have to be an incredible actor. That requires as much due diligence as the time spent learning the martial arts. Those that succeed learn.

Dr. Michael Maliszewski shakes hands with Mr. Morgan at the conclusion of this interview. *Photo courtesy of M. Maliszewski.*

- ANY NEW PROJECTS THAT YOU ARE CURRENTLY WORKING ON AT THIS TIME?

We're producing a television series in Shanghai right now called *Flatland*. It stars Dennis Hopper, Michael Robinson, Francois Yip and Philip Rhys. The year is 2010. The battle continues—*St. Michael vs. the Devil*. We follow the story through the eyes of three young knight errants. Dennis Hopper plays St. Michael.... A lot of martial arts and wirework here.

chapter 9

Heiho: A Tale of Strategy

by John J. Donohue Ph.D.*

sensei

*"Heiho" is an excerpt from *Sensei*, a book published by Thomas Dunne for St. Martin's Minotaur.

You could usually hear a pin drop in that room. The slanting rays of the sun came in through the high windows. The angle was acute enough so that you never had to worry about being blinded (an important thing in a place where people hacked at each other with oak swords), but it showed the dust motes dancing around. Less wary students had been distracted by them. We had all been with Yamashita Sensei for a while, however, and that morning when he strode onto the floor, all eyes were riveted on him.

Yamashita was a small person: in street clothes he probably would have seemed surprisingly nondescript. In the martial arts dojo—the training hall—his presence was a palpable thing. It wasn't just the way he was dressed. Most of us had been banging around the martial arts world for years and so were pretty much used to the exotic uniforms. Yamashita was usually dressed like any other senior instructor in some of the more traditional arts: a heavy quilted top like the ones judo players wore and the pleated split skirt/pants known as *hakama*. The wide legs of his uniform swished quietly as he knelt in front of the class. Even in this small action, there was a decisive precision. He gazed at us, his round head swivelling slowly up and down the line.

Other than his head, nothing moved, but you could almost feel the energy pulsing off him and washing over you. He was the most demanding of taskmasters at the best of times, but today we were all tremendously apprehensive.

Yamashita was wearing white.

In Japan, white is the color of emptiness and humility. Many of us had started our training in arts like judo or karate, where the uniforms known as gi were traditionally white as a symbol of humility. Most mainline Japanese instructors I knew frowned on the American urge to branch out into personal color statements with their uniforms. The message was clear: a gi is not a an expression of individuality. People wanting to make statements should probably rent billboards and avoid Japanese martial arts instructors. They are not focused on your needs. They are concerned only with the pursuit of the Way. You are free to come along. But your presence is not necessary.

You have to get used to that sort of attitude. In the martial arts, nobody owes you anything, least of all your teacher. The assumption is that you are pretty much worthless and lucky to be in the same room with your sensei. You do what he says. You don't talk back. You don't ask rude questions. You don't cop an attitude—that's the sensei's prerogative.

In the sword arts Yamashita teaches, only the high ranking teachers are eligible to wear white. Yamashita could. He had done so in Japan for years. But he didn't do it much here. If he was wearing white today, it meant that he was symbolically adopting the attitude that he was the lowliest of students. Humility is nice, of course. The only drawback here was that, if Yamashita was being humble, it meant that, as his students, we were somewhere way down in the crud with other lower forms of life.

As we sat there eyeing him warily, I heard some very quiet sighs up and down the line: we were in for a rough workout.

You don't get in the door of this particular dojo without having considerable experience and martial aptitude. In the first place, it's hidden in Brooklyn among the warehouses down by the East River. We occasionally have trouble with our cars being broken into and stuff like that, but then a few us go out and spread the word that Mr. Yamashita is beginning to get annoyed. He's been in the same location for ten years and has had a number of "conversations" with the more felonious of his neighbors—there are people walking those streets whose joints will never work correctly again.

The neighborhood is dirty and smelly and loud. Once you get inside the dojo, however, the rest of the world disappears. The training hall is a cavernous space. The walls are unadorned grayish white and the floor is polished hardwood. There are no decorations on the walls, no posters of Bruce Lee or the Buddha. There's a small office area to one side with a battered green metal desk and two doors leading to the changing rooms. Other than the weapons racks, that's it. There is absolutely nothing to distract you from the task at hand. It also means, of course, that there is nowhere to hide, either.

The sounds of the passing traffic on the Gowanus Expressway are muted.

Half the time, the gasping and thudding and shouts would drown things out anyway. It's tough inside the building and out.

Yamashita doesn't accept beginning students—we've all got black belts in at least one art—and you have to have a letter of introduction even to get an interview. If he accepts you (and he's very picky, relying on some weird formula none of us really understand) you essentially get training that makes all the things you endured before pale in comparison. I've been doing judo for twenty years. I also have another dan ranking in karate. The first time Yamashita used me as a demonstration partner, the sheer force of his technique and spirit were overwhelming.

So when I say that the workout was going to be tough, I mean it.

We don't do a great deal of conditioning. What we do is basics.

Yamashita's idea of basics, of course, is bewildering. He thinks basics are essentially illustrated through application. This is where the bang and crunch comes in, but with a difference. Anybody can slam someone into submission—take a look at any tough guy competition or kick boxing match. Yamashita is after something different. He thinks that the essence of any particular technique should be demonstrated in its effectiveness. He doesn't separate form and practicality. He doesn't even admit they are two separate things. He likes us to destroy with elegance.

There are technical terms for this in Japanese. They can isolate *ji*—the mechanics of technique—and *ri*—the quality of mastery that allows you to violate the appearance of form yet still maintain true to its essence. It's hard to explain how they differ and how to separate them, since most of us have spent years in pursuit of ji and are pretty much conditioned to follow its dictates. Yamashita doesn't seem to have much of a problem, however. He prowls the floor like a predator correcting, encouraging, and demonstrating. And woe to the unlucky pupil whose focus slips during the exercise: Yamashita screams "*Mu ri!*"—*No ri!*—and slams you to the floor.

It's a unique pedagogical technique, but it works for him.

So, beyond the sighs of anticipation, once the lesson started, none of us spent much time worrying about how tough things were. In the dojo of Yamashita Sensei, the only way to be is to be fully present and engaged in the activity at hand. The unfocused are quickly weeded out and rarely return. The rest of us endure, in the suspicion that all this will lead to something approximating the fierce skill of our master.

The experience binds you to him in ways I can't even begin to explain. There's the conscious respect you have for his skills, of course—compared to him, we're in the infancy of skill development. But there are more subtle dynamics going on as well. Yamashita knows you. He knows your weaknesses and fears. He doesn't judge you for them, but he makes you confront them.

In this, he is without mercy. But, if you trust him enough and can stand the heat of his lessons, you come out changed. And when that happens, you see the faint ghost of a satisfied smile drift across his face. It doesn't last long, but in that subtle moment you feel a pride and a gratitude that keeps you coming back to him for more.

We were working that day on some tricky techniques that involved pressure on selected nerve centers in the forearm. At about the time when most of us were slowing down—shaking our arms out in an effort to get the nerves to stop jangling—Yamashita called that part of the lesson quits and picked up a *bokken*. We scurried to the lower end of the floor and sat down as he began his instructions.

The bokken is a hardwood replica of the *katana*—the two-handed long sword used by the samurai. It has the curve and heft of a real sword and so is used to train students of the various sword arts that have evolved over the centuries in Japan. Kendo players use something call the *shinai*—essentially a tube composed of bamboo strips—in most of their training. This is because they hit each other with them and don't want to get hurt. Bokken, on the other hand, tend to get used in situations where training is done solo. This is done because, in the right hands, a hardwood sword can be very dangerous. They have been known to shatter the shafts of katana and people like the famous Miyamoto Musashi, armed with a bokken, used to regularly go up against swordsmen armed with real swords. The results were never pretty, but Musashi used to walk away intact, bokken in hand.

Bokken are also used in set series of training techniques called *kata*. This is typically what Yamashita had us train in with bokken.

Kata means form: they are prearranged exercises. Don't be fooled. Kata practice in Yamashita's dojo was enough to make your hair stand on end.

When we perform kata, we do them in pairs of attacker and defender, and the movements flow and the blade of the bokken moans through the air as it blurs its way to the target.

There's nothing like the sight of an oak sword slashing at your head to focus your mind.

I was backpedaling furiously to dodge a slashing *kesa-giri*—the cut that with a real sword would cleave you diagonally from your shoulder to the opposite hip—when movement on the edge of the practice floor caught my eye.

The visitors filed swiftly in, bobbing their heads briefly in that really poor American version of bowing. There were three of them in street clothes and the fourth was dressed in a hakama and top. The outfit caught my eye: the top was crimson red and looked like it was made out of some silky sort of material; the hakama was a crisp jet black. Quite the costume, really, especially when its wearer had a shaved brown head the shape of a large bullet. He had come to make a statement, I guess. They sat quietly with their backs against the wall, watching the class with that hard-eyed, clenched jaw look that is supposed to intimidate you.

I suppose I should have been impressed, but my training partner would not let up. She was about as fierce and wiry as they come. And her sword work had a certain whip and quick snap to it, a slightly off-beat rapid rhythm that was hard to defend against, even though in kata you theoretically know what's happening. She wasn't at all impressed with the visitors. She was a relatively new student who was mostly intent on making one of Yamashita's senior pupils—me—look less than accomplished.

So even though I was pretty curious about these guys—Yamashita did not, as a rule, tolerate visitors and one of them was dressed like he came to play—I quickly got more interested in not making a fool out of myself during bokken practice.

It's a pride thing. There's a lot of talk in the martial arts about letting go of your ego and all that, and we try, we really do, but the fact is that, at this level, you have invested a tremendous amount of time and effort into developing your skills and creating a certain status position in the dojo, and you really get just a bit ticked off when something happens to threaten that. All the bowing and titles, the uniforms and colored belts, are all about status, your sense of worth. It's a closed little world with its own system for ranking you, but it's still a status system, and human beings respond to that.

This woman was good with her weapon. I could sense that and so could she. She was pressing me a bit—altering the tempo of the moves, delivering her cuts with something close to full force, shortening the time between parry and counter—delivering a type of challenge to see whether I could withstand it.

I could, of course, but that wasn't the real point. For me, the challenge was how to respond to her force with something more refined. It meant that instead of parrying her cuts with a force that would make our bokken bark out with the shock of impact, I needed to finesse it a bit.

I changed the angles slightly, moving my body just out of the line of attack, which served to place me out of the radius of her strikes. I tried to keep my hands supple as I parried, accepting the force of her blows and redirecting them slightly, but things were getting a bit sweaty and I didn't want the sword flying out of my hands and shooting across the room. It happens occasionally, and if nobody gets hit we all laugh and the one who let go gets ribbed unmercifully, but this was not a situation where I was willing to get laughed at.

I knew this woman was a relative beginner at the dojo, and I counted on her weapon fixation. It was an unfair advantage in a way, but it's also an example of what Yamashita calls *heiho*—strategy.

Between shifting a bit and redirecting a bit more through the next series of movements in the kata, I built up enough frustration in my partner for her to over commit in her next strike—a little too much shoulder in the technique, her head leading into it—and it was all over. I simply let go of my bokken with my left hand, entered into her blind side, led her around in a tight little circle and took the sword away. It wasn't a move that was in the kata, but Yamashita tells us any time you can do *tachi-dori* (sword taking) to your partner, you should, just to keep them on their toes.

The pivot took her around on her toes, all right. She knew what was happening about a split second after the spin began, but it was too late to get out of it. I handed her back the bokken; she smiled a bit ruefully and we bowed just as Yamashita called the class to order in preparation to bow out.

He glided to the head of the room and waited for us to line up. He was studiously avoiding looking at the gang of four in the back of the room, but you could tell from his body language that he was annoyed.

You don't come dressed to play unless you've been invited. Only the sensei can give permission for a student to train in the dojo. If you show up uninvited and suited up, it means that either you don't know anything about Japanese martial arts teachers and are in real risk of being beaten up, or that you are purposefully being insulting and wish to challenge the sensei to a match.

In which case, it is anyone's guess who gets beat up.

I've seen this happen before. Not often, but you don't tend to forget it once you've seen it. Especially if you're a student of the teacher being challenged. You get used as a type of cannon fodder for your teacher. He sends you or one of your pals out to fight the challenger; he watches the action; analyzes the skill level of the opponent. If the first student gets beaten, a more advanced pupil goes next, and so on up the line. By the time the challenger reaches the sensei (if he lasts that long), he has either revealed his strengths and weaknesses and so can be defeated, or is so tired that he's no longer much of a challenge to the sensei. It's not fair, of course. It's heiho.

We all knelt, a solid dark blue line stretching down the length of the dojo. Yamashita sat quietly for a minute then turned to one of his senior pupils, a mild-mannered Japanese-American guy named Ken who sat next to me at the end of the line reserved for higher ranks. He looked like he was dreading what was about to happen. Yamashita said to him, "I see we have visitors. Perhaps you would invite the colorful one to speak with me."

Ken bowed, got up and scurried to the back of the room to deliver the invitation. The guy in the red top nodded, exchanged a series of ritual handshakes with his companions and stepped onto the training floor. He struck a ready pose and let out a loud AUUUS! A few of us rolled our eyes. Some of the karate schools out there think that kind of thing makes you seem like a real hard charger.

Yamashita nodded slightly and Red Top moved forward.

"I regret that I was unable to welcome you properly to my dojo. I am equally distressed to say that I do not know who you are or what you want, since we have not been properly introduced." The words came out quickly, but were carefully pronounced. Sensei doesn't really have much of an accent, but when he gets annoyed his words get very precisely formed. I don't know if Red Top was picking it up or not, but there wasn't one of us who doubted that Yamashita Sensei was really ticked off.

"Mitchell Reilly, Sensei." He bowed, properly this time. Ken caught my eye. Mitch Reilly ran a notorious jujutsu school, pretty much specializing in combat arts of the one-hundred-ways-to-pluck-their eyeballs-out variety. He was a mainstay of the non-traditional Black martial arts community. He was built like a refrigerator and I could see his knuckles were enlarged from the damage too much board breaking creates. Mitch Reilly had the reputation of being a really savage competitor, a fair technician, and a guy staggering under the weight of a giant ego.

"So, Mr. Reilly. I must assume that there is a reason for your presence here. The school is hard to find and only a man in need of something would make a journey through such a dangerous neighborhood."

Reilly looked contemptuous. "No problem. I can take care of myself."

"And," Yamashita continued, "the obvious care with which you have selected your . . . charming costume tells me that you are, perhaps, interested in. . . ?" He let the question hang in the air.

I sat and watched the steam start to come out of Reilly's ears. I have to admit, he got it under control fairly well, which was a sign that he was probably a dangerous man. When the faint trembling stopped, Reilly finished Yamashita's sentence.

"A match," he said. "I'm challenging you."

You had to admire him. The guy pulled no punches. He was probably five years older than I was—in his early forties—and had been banging around the martial arts for at least two decades, and now felt he was ready to take on the closest thing the New York area had to a bona fide master. Most people don't even know Yamashita exists. He came to New York years ago from Japan for reasons none of us can fathom and hones our technique with a type of quiet brutality. The senior Japanese sensei send their most promising pupils to him, but he's never appeared in *Black Belt*, hasn't written a book divulging the ancient, secret techniques of the samurai elite, and doesn't have a listing in the Yellow Pages.

Which was why Reilly's presence—and his challenge—were so odd.

You could see Yamashita's quandary. Reilly was fairly dangerous in a savage, commonplace kind of way. Yamashita was a harsh teacher, but he never needlessly put any of us in danger of serious injury. It was beneath Sensei's dignity to accept the challenge, but you could almost hear the clicks in his brain as he weighed various other options. Would this match serve any type of purpose in terms of teaching his students? Who would be the most appropriate opponent? Ken was a senior student and could be a logical choice. We all knew—and Sensei did too—that his wife had just had a baby and that a great deal of Ken's mental energy was not totally focused on training at this time. He was good (even on his bad days) but a match like this was bound to be one where both parties limped away. Ken didn't need that right now and Yamashita knew it.

Yamashita's head swivelled along the line of students, weighing each one for potential, for flaws, like a diamond cutter rooting carefully around a draw of unfinished stones. The more experienced among us sat, trying to be totally numb about the situation, not really focusing on Reilly, listening to the hum of the fluorescents and the faint rumble of trucks. The newer students sat in various states: the smart ones were secretly appalled at the prospect; the really dense were excited.

When he called me, I tried to feel nothing. "Professor," Yamashita said. Ever since they found out I teach in college, the nickname stuck. It could have been worse. Early on I had worked out at a kendo school where the Japanese kids simply called me "Big Head."

I bowed and scooted up to the front. In this situation, you sit formally, facing the Sensei, which put me right next to Reilly.

"This is Dr. Burke," he told Reilly. "I am sure you will find him instructive."

Reilly jerked his head around to size me up. I looked back; flat eyes, sitting there like a blue lump with relaxed muscles, no energy given to the opponent.

"You think you want a piece of me, asshole?" Out of the side of his mouth, like he'd picked it up from old Bogart movies. I swung around—you could see a slight jerk before he realized what I was up to—and bowed, saying nothing. Silent. Passive. A shade. Heiho was keeping yourself in shadow.

Reilly looked back at Sensei. "You must be joking. I'm not fucking around with this piece of shit."

Yamashita is funny about foul language. He spends his days teaching people how to do serious harm to others, but he has this real thing about keeping conversation civil. Part of it's just Japanese politeness, but I think that the other part is that he is a man dedicated to an art that celebrates control of one sort or another, and foul language strikes him as either the result of a bad vocabulary and poor imagination or as a lack of mastery over your temper. In either case, this kind of language is forbidden in his dojo. Reilly may not have known it, but he had just committed a gross breach of etiquette.

"I am sorry, Mr. Reilly. I regret that we cannot accommodate you in your request for a lesson. You are clearly not ready for any serious training." With that, Yamashita looked right through him and stood up like he was preparing to leave the floor.

"Wait a minute . . ." Reilly shot up and looked like he was going to reach for the old man. Which was how I got to wondering about whether I could poleax him. I was targeting him for a knuckle strike right below the ear (I figured with any luck I could dislocate his jaw) but there was really no need. Yamashita had about reached the limits of his patience.

As Reilly came at him, Yamashita shot in, a smooth blur. There was an elbow strike in there somewhere before he whipped Reilly around to break his balance. Then Yamashita was behind him, clinging like a limpet and bringing Reilly slowly down to the floor. The choke was (as always) precisely executed: the flow of blood to the brain was disrupted as he brought pressure to bear on the arteries and Reilly was out cold.

Yamashita stood up and beckoned to Reilly's pals. "Remove him. Do not come back." Not even breathing hard. They dragged Reilly off the practice floor and trundled him away.

"What a foolish man. An arrogant and violent man." He looked around at us all, then turned to me. "I am surprised at you Burke. I would have tried for the jaw dislocation. Work on your reaction time, please."

He glided away and the lesson ended.

chapter 10

THE MASTER: CHINESE BOXING ACCOUNTS IN AN ENVELOPE

by John F. Gilbey, M.A.

All artwork by Oscar Ratti. © 2003 Courtesy of Futuro Designs & Publications.

Prelude

The following pages were given to me by an old friend, Colonel Zhou Yilai, many years ago in China. Zhou was a bright athletic fellow who coordinated economic and military matters with our staff in Tianjin City. For two years we played tennis together nearly every weekend. He invariably beat me but always by close scores. I later learned that he was a much better player than I—indeed, one of the best players in Tianjin—but one who contrived skillfully to spare my feelings by keeping the scores close.

He handed me the envelope containing these pages just before I returned to America, saying: "We are good friends at work and on the tennis courts. I want you to have an account of my years learning internal Chinese boxing and of the teacher who nurtured my skills. In our time discussing governmental affairs and playing tennis, I never mentioned this aspect of my life. Now that you are going from my ambit, I hope this little essay will extend our conversation and friendship for yet a little while. Farewell, good friend, and thank you."

Recently I learned that Zhou has passed on. Remembering him and rereading his fascinating words, I decided to publish his saga as a way to keep his memory warm. I believe his story may also have the happy effect of stirring students of the Chinese martial arts.

~ John F. Gilbey

"C" ~ The Culinary Warrior

When C was younger, my father hired him to teach his three rather unruly sons. But for the first six months he paid us no mind, contenting himself instead with culinary matters. He spent most of his time in the kitchen fixing exotic dishes and sampling our cook's triumphs. My father countered by delegating me—the oldest—to help the cook. Once I was ensconced in the galley, C made everything I did a challenge. If I chopped vegetables, an extra chopper would descend, missing my fingers by a fraction. If I was sweeping he'd seize another broom suddenly to attack me and, as I tried to counter with my broom, he'd disarm me with a flourish and a small cry, "Too slow."

That's all C ever said to me, "Too slow." Every day he'd slap me half a dozen times, catching me unawares, and would laughingly say, "Too slow." Well, I was a robust teenager and it irked me. So I decided to retaliate and watched for my chance. One day I got it. He had taken the lid off a pot of peas and was savoring the aroma. I had a wooden pestle and, catching him engrossed, I attacked. But my pestle never reached his head. He brought the cover up smartly, deflecting my weapon, and said with a smile, "Too slow."

This impressed me greatly, but I'm afraid I missed the real value of what he was trying to do there in the kitchen—to teach me awareness. My father missed the value of such training too, and it wasn't long before he let C go. Father had a more sanguinary view of boxing, and C's mastery completely escaped him.

The Labyrinthine and Sticking

There are those who claim to have seen C do something extraordinary. I actually felt him do it. When I first sought him out, years after he had tutored our family, I had been intensively trained in the "Labyrinthine Trace" method of boxing by its creator, the great Huo Yuanjia. I wasn't Huo's best student nor his worst.

Our art was called "Labyrinthine" because of its twisting, furiously changing, postures. The rapid and adroit forms we did were difficult for an observer to follow with the eye and even more difficult to neutralize.

People were astounded by how well we cavorted over rooftops and clambered up walls. What they didn't know was that we practiced on that kind of terrain, so we got very good at negotiating it. We tried never to fight in a new milieu: we always mastered the terrain first.

My army unit—I was a major by then—had been transferred to Beijing, and in off-hours I was teaching some cadre the Labyrinthine. But it was a poor life, dull and unsatisfying. One day I heard that our family's short-lived boxer of the kitchen, C, was still teaching. Curious, I went to see him.

He impressed me right off, not because he exuded great boxing skill, but because he didn't. He recalled laughingly our earlier training and was courteous without being unctuous. He laughed but wasn't a clown; he was serious but wasn't somber; and he talked a lot without being garrulous. A widower who had never remarried ("I'm like a mandarin duck who marries for life"), his grown children were in Beijing. He even disdained concubines.

So adroitly had he guided our conversation that I was back at my command before I realized we hadn't even discussed what had been uppermost in my mind: boxing. How he did it was to argue the Daoist side versus my

Confucian contentions through all the subject's ramifications. And he easily defeated me, I might add.

We next met sometime later in a tearoom in Chengdu City. I was having lunch with a pair of my aides when he came in and took a table near the kitchen. I dismissed my aides and joined him.

He greeted me warmly: "Does Confucius want another chance at Laozi?" he joked.

I responded, "No, seeing the dragon once in one's lifetime is sufficient." This, it turned out, was a salutary riposte as it led the ensuing conversation away from our previous topic. It wasn't long before I asked him about his boxing reputation. Was it true he boxed?

"Yes," he said quietly, "if you can call taijiquan boxing. Personally, I prefer to call it simply taiji; the only boxing one really does is against oneself. I also teach xingyiquan and baguazhang, though I prefer taiji. Are you a boxer?"

I told him then of Huo Yuanjia, whom he lauded to the skies, and of my training. He appeared genuinely impressed, and we continued talking as we strolled the streets of the old city.

After walking a while, we came to the house of a friend of his and were admitted to the courtyard by a servant who told C that her master was gone but would return shortly. We were to wait, she said, seating us in comfortable chairs and bringing tea.

Then it was that I asked him about taiji's sticking ability.

"True," he said, "our catchword is 'no resisting and no letting go.' We always want to keep our connection with our partner (or antagonist, as the case may be). In this way we intimately and immediately sense any changes."

"Even before they are thought of by your partner?" I asked.

He answered, "Perhaps; perhaps not. But the result is the same: the other can't escape."

Then he stood up. "Let me try to show you, though I'm not very good at it."

He put his light hand on my shoulder. I shrugged and wriggled but could not rid myself of it. I acknowledged this, but he knew I wasn't impressed: after all, sticking to a fairly static body isn't all that difficult.

So he said, "Perhaps you'd like to move?"

This was my metier! No one could keep contact with a Labyrinthine adept. No one could grasp a sleeve and stay with us. Here was a man who simply put his palm on my shoulder and urged me to get rid of it. He might have been a master, but on this skill, I thought, he was in over his head.

So I began, slowly at first, partly out of courtesy, partly to "tune in" on his hand so as to decide how to extricate.

Well, it was hard to become aware of that soft hand. It was there all right, but it held so little energy it was difficult to feel. Thinking that it was a function of the slowness, I increased my tempo. Around the courtyard we went at a good clip, me changing directions abruptly and alternating the tempo to throw him off. Not only did I fail at this, I couldn't even make his hand heavier.

Frustrated, I pulled out all the stops. I swung, crouched, twisted at lightning speed. He stuck. Then I jumped onto a small shed, thence to the roof, and whirling, squatting, circling, turning, and jumping we flew across many of the roofs in that section of the city. I dived under my armpit, swiveled my body, slowed, sped up, went under my legs, and then flipped into a chaos of circles to a higher roof, knowing now that I had won.

Standing a bit breathless on that rather high roof, I looked down for him. At what part of that careering chain had he disconnected? Then I felt that hand. From behind me he laughed and patted my shoulder gently with it. "Your Labyrinthine is very good. I'm glad you stopped; otherwise, you would have left me far behind!"

Can you wonder why I chose such a man as teacher?

Though the "sticking energy" of the "Labyrinthine" was first rate, it didn't approach taiji's vaunted excellence at it. It was said of Yang Jianhou, the taiji great, that he could put a bird on his palm and subtly neutralize it so that it couldn't fly off. I never saw C do this, but more than once I have seen a bird land on his shoulder and remain there while he did his stylish bagua circles. I grant that this was a cut under Yang's feat, but the fact that the bird would perch on only C's shoulder, not on ours, lent it some charm. When I asked him about it, he mischievously responded, "What bird?"

Youthful Ways

Some of us were young and wild in those days and caused all kinds of grief to our elders. A few of the foolish things we did then I wince at now. But our spirits were high and the blood thundered through our veins.

Some of our folly outed in violence. As we learned new skills in C's class, we tried them out in bars and tearooms. Usually they worked pretty well, especially against men disjointed by drink. It was a simple matter to scoop them up and flip them onto their backs. We didn't hurt them: we were only there to perfect our art. Occasionally though, we'd come a cropper and end up with our hands full.

It happened to me once. I was jostled by a slender man who looked to be tipsy. I turned away and he followed, upbraiding me for "pushing" him. I could have simply walked out of the place, but my friend was watching me and soon my ego stood up. So I squared off with the cursing man. He didn't look tough nor even stable. His weight shifted unsteadily from one leg to the other as he poked a finger at me and ranted.

Vexed, I put my hand on his chest and pushed. The next moment he neutralized my shove, and two of his fingers missed my eyes and drummed into my forehead. They felt like spikes; I felt the shock in my ankles. By this time my brain had flashed the panic signal and I swiveled away from his follow-up, another finger strike that missed my throat by less than an inch.

Now if an accomplished Shuai Jiao man gets hold of an antagonist, what follows is usually anti-climax (I had wrestled a bit as a boy). So I grabbed the man's arm. Or tried to. But the tipsy fellow fell away unsteadily, and I made the mistake of rushing him. He brought me up short with an open-hand jolt to my chin and then slapped me full on the cheek, knocking me against the wall and onto the floor. I made another mistake then: I got up and tore at him, tackling. He deflected my rush, scooped my right foot, and then side-kicked my left knee, putting me down again.

I tried to get up, all the while trying to stanch the flow of blood from my nose, but the leg wouldn't hold and I capsized. It was not considered ethical to hit a man when he was down, so my attacker stood over me, stared, then said: "Be careful of drunks, boy." And out the door he went, victorious.

It turned out that the man was Su Lancai, a famed Ti Tang (Drunken Style) boxer whose brother, authentically drunk, had been ill-served by one of our group the night before. Someone had mistakenly fingered me to Su as the culprit, and he had done the rest.

Occasionally, the gentle C would overdo when practicing pushing-hands with me. It was always gentle, but sometimes I sensed a lethal edge to the proceedings. I came to learn after a while that this was a corrective for some blatant street adventure of mine that he'd got wind of. I was not stupid. Soon this discipline had its effect, and I began to behave myself.

The Bite of a Dog

C always told us not to tell others what we were learning. Not because he was secretive—in fact, he was as open as the sun. No, the admonition was for our own sake. He knew that if we sought outside recognition and praise, it would impede our work in the internal—we would have been going out rather than in. And he knew it would create other troubles. This I found out.

After ten years of practice, I felt I had absorbed at least the rudiments of the art. In a euphoric moment induced by the good wine for which that area is famed, I told a cousin of my training. He must have passed the word, for shortly after that a local stalwart acclaimed for his *qinna* bone-locking prowess informed me through an intermediary that he proposed a "test" with the able representative of the C school—meaning me. This put me in an untenable position. We had been told by C not to broadcast the fact of the training and to avoid challenges. But I had already told, and the way this man had framed the challenge meant that, if I rejected it, it would have reflected on C. The "representative of the C school" had to accept. And I did.

On the appointed day I went to a small plot of ground adjacent to the magistrate's office where over a hundred people had gathered. My antagonist, a chunky chap named Wu, had preceded me and watched my approach with a dark, glowering mien. I walked up to him thinking we could discuss rules and the like. Without a word, Wu snared my right wrist in the damnedest, most excruciating vise imaginable. It not only stopped my blood; it literally cut my breath. But I didn't pause to analyze it. I relaxed and sank, transforming my surprised and rigid arm into a limp noodle, at the same time snapping it out of his grasp. I immediately used press, which propelled him back fifteen feet where he fell amidst a tangle of bystanders' arms and legs.

Wu got up unsteadily with something of a smile on his face, but he was through for the day. He bowed respectfully, muttering "No one ever escaped before."

"It was excellent technique," I answered, "It felt like a dog had my arm."

The crowd broke up then, and I swaggered to C's house intact except for a sleeve which had been ripped when I extricated. But where Wu hadn't defeated me, my ego had. For the quarter hour it took me to get to C's house, I was filled with self-as-warrior. No one in China, I was convinced, could hold me.

I entered C's house and approached him in his study. Without preliminaries, I told him what had occurred, all the while trying unsuccessfully to keep braggadocio out of my voice.

He listened patiently with a small smile. When I was done, he got up from his chair and came over to me. Taking my ripped sleeve in his light hand, he said: "You didn't lose, but you didn't win. Look at your shirt. This is obviously the result of a brawl. True taiji destroys nothing but the ego."

Our Class

We had a variety of men and women who trained under C. For the most part they came from middle-class homes. Although no poor person ever was excluded for lack of tuition, China was a poor country, and the poor often couldn't spare the time to work regularly at something that produced no income. So we had few really poor people. Students, of course, we had always, but they tended to leave us as they graduated and moved on.

But we did have military and police men, medical doctors, educators, tradesmen, salesmen, lawyers, and such. One international lawyer I remember for his beautiful form. His pushing-hands was of a fairly high level, though mitigated somewhat by his frequent recourse to force. Once he told a story occasioned by the International Disarmament Plan of 1935. The lack of trust among the delegates was reflected by a tale told by the Spanish delegate. He related how the animal kingdom had its own disarmament conference. The lion looked at the eagle and said talons must be abolished. The tiger eyed the elephant and said tusks must go. The elephant responded to the tiger that jaws and claws should be barred. Similarly, each animal proposed the abolition of weapons he didn't possess. Finally, the bear rose and sweetly said:

"Comrades, let's abolish everything—everything but the great universal embrace!" At this we all roared.

As gifted as he was, C avoided public display. In pushing-hands he completely managed our bodies but never showed off about it. Even in discussing general matters, he took the Daoist, non-competitive path. Liu, one of our circle, was a top philosopher and one of the leading Laozi scholars in the country. More than once I saw C best him on an arcane point of Laozi. But when we made too much of it, C would chide us gently, saying that intellectual debate was too competitive and thus not Daoist. I think he really lived his Daoism; Liu and the rest of us only thought ours.

But bring a child around us and he would erupt in glee, forgetting us all as he played. The wonderful writer Lu Xun once told of a teacher much like C, who "stared disdainfully upon a thousand athletes and bowed to serve as a horse for children."

The Banker's Tale

We even had a banker who came infrequently, chiefly for the xingyi. When I first started he volunteered to tell me of the C of an earlier period.

"C," the banker began, "is something of a secretive man, not given easily to confidences—you can learn little about him by asking him." I asked how the banker came to know the story.

The banker stiffened his back and tried to suck his sagging stomach in. "I may not look it now," he answered, "but I once practiced boxing. In fact, I was a boxing-brother of C's. Not of his caliber, of course, but still, a classmate. So I knew him as well as anyone. He didn't tell me this story. I saw it."

"C was teaching a few students in the western district of Beijing. I was there on bank business and stopped by to see him. We had a pleasant meal and then repaired to a nearby courtyard where he supervised the training of perhaps a dozen students, all men in their twenties. Things were going well, and I was taken with the celerity of C's movements as he corrected his tyros. Suddenly, through the gate stomped a big-chested fellow. He identified himself as Lai Mengshi and, sans ceremony or even courtesy, he insisted on a contest."

"C smiled. He insisted that Lai sit down and be served tea. Lai, a bulky man who towered over C, was little given to niceties and wanted neither a seat to rest on nor tea to sip. Only a fight would please him."

The banker's eyes twinkled, and he continued his account.

"But," C said to his glowering guest, "to be proper, a trial must have three things. First, a reason; second, form; and third, content. You want to divest it of the first two essentials. Tell me why you wish to fight and pay heed to the form, and then we can address the content."

Lai wrinkled his brow but would not sit. "I have heard you are an expert boxer, and I wish to test you."

C asked, "To test me or yourself?"

Lai responded, "I know my own ability well enough. It's you I want to try."

"Ah," C said, "but then why, if you are so sure of yourself, are you so belligerent?"

Lai spat an obscenity and shot back, "Boxing is belligerent; it is not tea drinking and smiles."

C shook his head saying, "No, friend. Tradition governs the form of boxing trials. It insists on at least a surface courtesy. Because you know nothing of the form, it would be better for you to go away. When you've learned it, return, and I will be happy to oblige you with a match."

The banker continued the tale, "Turning away from the enraged Lai, C gestured to me, and we began walking back to his house. All the while Lai cursed him. C's students were daunted by Lai's ferocity and stood somewhat abashed as their champion walked away."

"Most of them probably were embarrassed by what they took to be C's retreat. Even a man as educated as I had mixed feelings. Everything C had said was true. And yet, a bully like Lai—even then he had a wide reputation—deserved a beating, and a polite rejection of his challenge based on his ignorance of form seemed somewhat short of that."

"Well Lai, of course, passed the word around that he had buffaloed a frightened C. And I heard later that C lost some students because of it. But, with time, he got replacements and continued teaching."

"Fifteen years later—both C and I were past fifty then—I was again in Beijing and sought him out. He had not aged and was still thin as a rail, but what boxing! If xingyi was ever done better on this old earth, I have never seen it. His chopping hand arced like a swallow and fell like an iron tripod. And his crushing fist was so terrible that the students used pads lest, when he pulled the strike, it might inadvertently touch them."

"We were drinking wine in a small tavern when C's old nemesis, Lai, strode in with some friends. If the years had educated C, they had punished Lai. He had a pot, had lost too many fights and, soused, walked unsteadily. For him there had been no education in those years. He spied C and lurched over to us, berating C as he came."

"I've returned!" he yelled, "Now will you fight?"

C smiled and replied, "Lai, you are less equipped to fight now than you were fifteen years ago. You punish yourself enough without my assistance."

"As C was saying this, Lai struck surprisingly quickly and accurately. The punch caught C full on the jaw. His body wavered with the force of the blow—we were still sitting—but the smile never left him."

"You may strike again, friend," C said, "I will not resist you."

The banker continued his story, "Lai, beside himself with happiness, thought the offer over, but rejected it. He made a blustering exit speech to the assemblage and then shouldered his way out, flinging back, 'So much for the great C!' as he left."

"'Very fast,' I observed to C, 'for someone so over the hill.'"

"That time C talked a bit. Laughing, he said, 'Not fast; slow, too slow. I saw it from its inception in his poor brain. And because it was slow, it had no power.'"

"But why, then, did you accept it?"

"Because, if I had slipped it, I would have been accepting Lai's challenge. It was unworthy then; it is worse now. The man knows nothing of form. He must earn the right to contest. Otherwise it diminishes our entire tradition. This may seem stuffy to you, but it is important to me. And easily important enough to permit him one free shot."

Proper Timing

A somewhat similar story is told of C in which a famed Shaolin champion came forward to challenge him during a party at a friend's house. C deflected the challenge saying: "Another time since this is a social gathering where fighting should have no place."

The two didn't meet for another ten years and, when they did, C knocked his opponent out in the first minute. When friends asked why he hadn't done this at their first encounter, C answered succinctly with one of

Confucius' favorite expressions, "*shizhong*" (proper timing).

Regarding this, he told the story of an invasion by the Mongols. They sacked a town, and their leader took over the local magistrate's house. The defeated man was ordered to clean the house, cook, and wait upon the Mongol leader, who snarled, "Do you agree?" Without answering, the magistrate set about the chores. Twenty years later a friendly force retook the town, and the Mongol leader was killed. The old magistrate buried him, spat on his grave, and answered: "No." Shizhong—C lived by that idea.

Time and Other Boxing Elements

"Time is is-ness, a constant. It was here when the world wasn't. You can't shortcut or shortchange it. Half of the world's problems result from our inability to grasp this truth. Speed doesn't compress time; it merely contracts an action within time, thus creating the possibility for more activities to occur."

"That's interesting, and I quite agree, but isn't it generalization?"

"Perhaps, but it's one of those truths so obvious that it needs saying. To answer your question, if a course is marked off and we run it, the swifter of foot will win. In this instance speed is the only variable. But in boxing, there are many variables: space, terrain, attitude, posture, and so on. All of these can change from moment to moment."

"I understand that. But..."

"But it is still not responsive to your question?"

"Not quite. The Classics say that real boxing has no recourse to speed, power, or skill."

"Ah, and you wish to draw me out on an arcane matter of which I know little?"

"Yes, if it pleases you."

"All right. There is another element—the most important—in all this. It is profound, difficult to understand, but if comprehended aright, it is simple to do. It is summarized in one word—relax. I will make this brief because that is where truth resides. Everything begins and ends with and comes back to a quiet, concentrated mind. How to get it? By relaxing. Some get it from inside out; others, outside in."

Rule of the Root

I had heard tales of various internal masters who could levitate. But I had never seen such a thing. I asked C about it.

"It defies physical laws as we know them," he said. "Man with his head pushing up against heaven and his feet anchored in earth completes the cosmic circuit nicely. If he pushes higher and loses his root, would not the universe waver? Laozi says that one cannot stand on tiptoes forever."

He rubbed his chin reflectively, then continued. "I will only say that the physical is but one side of the universe. The more profound is the spiritual, the unseen or seldom seen aspect. So, yes, I believe it is possible. But, no, I have never seen it."

Then he proceeded to do what he had never seen, but at the other end. We were outside in the hard earth-packed courtyard, and we began practicing *tuishou* (pushing-hands). As always, I was entranced by his light arms, forever on me, owning me, but always bereft of strength. Utterly soft but completely controlling my insistent power. I asked how he could get so soft.

"The first rule is the root," he answered.

I looked down at his feet and was astonished to see that they had sunk in place to a depth of three or four inches. Did he push them, force them down? I wanted to know.

"I thought them down," was all he would answer, and we broke off the practice just then as two other students approached. I never saw him do it again.

On Love and Bugs

Though ordinarily C didn't talk much, a little wine sometimes lubricated him, and the words would flow. One of us once mentioned Mencius and his view on love. After some discussion, another addressed the master: what was his view on the subject?

His eyes twinkled as the words tumbled out in his grand Suzhou dialect (it is well said that the sound of a Suzhou couple quarreling is more beautiful than that of a Cantonese pair talking of love, so pleasing is the lilt of that dialect).

"Love is not something one has views about. One doesn't analyze or talk about love: one loves. I try to love everyone wholeheartedly, without stint. I love trees and rocks as well as the sentient. All parts of creation—the ten-thousand things—have energy, but of a different order. Love is at the heart of all things and, as all strive to return to the one, all these are worthy of our love and call it forth."

Once I strolled with him at Linhai Park, where the breezes in spring never stop their play with the flowers there. That day he displayed a nuance of that love. I noticed that as he walked he sometimes seemed to make a little hesitation. Curious, I watched and soon enough saw what it was. There were bugs all over the path, but he never stepped on one, even when his foot was falling and one chanced under it. His single-weightedness was so inbred that he would stop his foot in mid-fall and position it so as to miss the insect and would do it gracefully, without any strain.

I commented on it. "There are millions of insects; what does it matter if a few are destroyed?"

"Who knows?" he mused, "Perhaps a great deal. To extinguish any life is repellant to me. Did not the Mahatma—the Great Soul, Gandhi of India—say that one should not kill anything he could not recreate? We can't create; therefore, why should we stop life?"

As we arrived back at the park entrance, he went on, "It is curious how boys go about this business of stepping on bugs. In fact, I divide all boys (and men, who are merely obsolete boys) into three kinds. First, there are those who, like me, choose not to step on a bug. Next, there are those who are indifferent on the matter and step without a thought for the bug. Finally, there are boys—the worst kind—who not only step on a bug, but pause to grind it into the pathway. Remember: most of these boys become men."

Courtesy and Pride

My friend Lo, a professor of history at the university, also queried me about C.

"Your teacher must be a fine boxer."

"Yes," I answered, "superb. He has worked up a powerful synthesis of the three internal boxing arts: taiji, xingyi, and bagua. Even now that he is past eighty, I cannot match him."

"And did he teach you courtesy?"

"Yes, that is central, the core of his teaching. And I respect him greatly. In the beginning I was awed by him, but I tried not to be overcome. He taught courtesy as a cornerstone of the discipline. He was incredibly soft, but sometimes his pride was too strong. He has worked diligently on it. I'd say he is undefeated as a boxer, except for occasional bouts with his own ego. But give him credit; he has never stopped battling that foe. So I'd rate him as a brilliant boxer and a fine gentleman, but only a good man. C himself would have preferred it the other way round."

"I heard he mellowed some with the years."

"That's true," I said. "I recall once when he was in his seventies I knocked his staff out of his hands. I was younger, and he was a bit careless about me."

"What happened then?"

"Well, as you can imagine, there were cascades of laughter from the others. C retrieved his staff and with an imperious hand motioned them to silence."

"Yes," C told them, "Young Zhou has stolen my stick. But who else among you can do it? Not one of you! Therefore, from this day on, this diligent one who works instead of laughs will get special instruction."

"That was a kind thing for him to do," my friend said.

"Yes, it was. But the coin had two sides. When the others had gone home, he presented me with a huge smile which never left while, with a hundred blows, he knocked me all over the place: down halls, into walls, over chairs, and down stairs, as I romantically recall it. But at the time the 'special instruction' wasn't so romantic. It was rather a mad whirl of terrifying motion and a rain of blows amidst his sunshine. And next day there were the bruises. So, his mellowing was not a weakening, but a refining of his temperament."

"Perhaps," I mused. "But coming back to courtesy, he does indeed put great store by it. Another time he dilated on it when I said that much courtesy was of a ritual sort, unfeeling and impersonal. Since this smacks of insincerity," I asked him, "would it not be better never to use courtesy unless it is deeper than the superficial kind?"

"It's a difficult choice," C responded, "but I think I favor ritual over its absence. The ritual, you know, is not entirely bereft of sincere courtesy. It has at least a beginning of it in its makeup and so is something to build on. Often what starts out as conventional civility will deepen with time, the plow will crease the soil, and a seed may grow to fruition."

"But isn't ritual courtesy inherently a lie?"

"Not necessarily. It is a mode of current behavior with a promise of the future in it. The absence of courtesy, on the other hand, is nihilism having nothing but a bleak past and future."

Probing C further, I added, "As a corollary proposition: some philosophers argue that it is better to be hated than ignored since hate at least recognizes one as human."

"The nihilism escalates! If hate is countenanced at all as human, it is a humanity misdirected. The hatred of human beings is an aberration: it is death. Ask to be ignored, but not hated. If you are ignored, it in no way impairs your humanness; only that of the poor perpetrator. And that is his problem, not yours."

Violence, Fear, and Fantasy

We were alone one day. C began: "Laozi said 'Show me a man of violence who came to a good end and I will take him for my teacher.'" C insisted that the true master does not fight.

"We learn to fight," he said, "so that we never have to fight. It gives us the confidence to avoid fighting, knowing that, in an emergency, our discipline will see us through."

"The key, as I've said, has to do with relaxation. To relax unresistingly before an external force seems to go against nature, leaving us vulnerable. But if you can relax—and our training teaches this—then fear can be muted and your vital energy increased. This in turn will heighten your combative ability. Tension is the residue of fear. It is a way of hanging onto something that isn't there, a paranoia dealing with phantoms. So don't tense up—relax."

C went on, "I have seen much in this world and know a little of the Classics. Forgive me for saying it, but most boxing is ridiculous. The crude exertions and vulgar violences bore me, especially when boxers try to rationalize their idiocies as consonant with the teachings of the sages. I am offended also by protagonists of the inner school who all too often challenge and fight as promiscuously as these hardheads. Plus, these latter pretend to have skills that they say can't be explained by scientific principles. After decades of running these stories to ground, I've never met a believable case."

Then he sighed a bit wearily and shook his head.

"But enough of negativity. The day is pleasant; the birds are singing and the wisteria sighing. Having tea with a dedicated student is a privilege for me. Your words are direct. But why are they addressed to me? I am no fighter, much less one who can guess as to the truth of what you say. I can only sip this tea and be thankful for your presence."

My Wife Learns of C

By the time I married, I had trained under C for a decade. My wife wanted to know about him, of course.

"What manner of man is he?" she asked.

"Every man and no man. That is, all sorts of man."

"What do you mean?"

"Well, when you are with him, he is ordinary as rain. He talks and laughs, jokes and curses like the rest of us. He sometimes dresses plainly, even carelessly. And his bearing is so indifferent, he often looks like a coolie."

"So…?"

"But when you leave him and then reflect on him, he seems dignity itself and unusual as a rainbow."

"You mean as regards his technique?"

"Not at all. I mean all of him. But it's hard to explain. Part of it, I guess, is that he has no truck with pride. In talking with most people one resonates off their ego, but he gives you no ego."

"Well, what do you feel resonating, if not ego?"

"A man, my dear, a man."

L'Envoi

This master, this man, burning like a brilliant candle that never guttered, in the end, was extinguished by an errant night breeze.

The Chinese value a good death. And C's was. Somewhat weary of a life's accumulation of cares, he gently dozed off one evening and didn't awaken. His wondrous spirit simply subsided, and he died as gently as he had lived.

~ Zhou Yilai
1948

chapter 11

Again! Practicing for Perfection

by John Richard DeRose

In the practice for perfection, patience is learned.

All illustrations by Oscar Ratti.
© 2003 by Futuro Designs & Publications.

"Again!"

The voice wasn't very loud, yet it seemed to travel across the room, penetrating all the other noises, and finding the one man it was intended for. That one man rolled over onto his knees, struggled up onto his feet, and ran a sweaty hand through his tangled hair.

The voice repeated: "Again!"

The man adjusted his uniform and turned towards his opponent. The two men moved into their positions, this time reversing their previous roles: The first man became the thrower (*tori*), while the other man became the defender (*uke*). Gripping each other's jacket by sleeve and lapel, they moved into the defensive posture known as *jigotai*.

The first man was smaller and less muscular than his opponent, but he moved in a quicker and more decisive manner. In a succession of rapid movements, he began to practice forms. Stepping inward with his right leg, pivoting on the ball of his foot, and turning his body around 180 degrees, he placed his back against the lower chest and abdomen of his partner. His left foot followed the circular motion of his body, eventually planting near and parallel to his opponent's left foot. Meanwhile, his left hand pulled the right sleeve of the uke across the front of his rotated body, and his right hand tugged hard on the larger man's lapel. Then, suddenly, he stopped—reversing his movements and returning to his original position.

Again and again he repeated the initial maneuvers of the form, each time stopping before the actual throw. Finally, on the tenth and last repetition of the form, he followed through with the execution of the technique. He straightened his legs and pulled hard on the sleeve and lapel clinched tight in his hands. The larger man was lifted off his feet, carried over the back and shoulder of the tori, and dropped hard onto the orange mat.

As soon as the throw was completed, a voice drifted across the training hall and stung in the smaller man's ears.

"Again!"

Once again the two men switched positions, so it became the smaller man's turn to be thrown onto the matted floor. He landed on his right shoulder, rolled onto his back, and slapped his left palm sharply against the mat to absorb the shock of the fall. Before he could even regain his feet, the voice repeated the same word.

"Again!"

For the next 45-minutes, he continued to practice the same technique —over and over. He practiced with different partners and at different speeds, but it was always the same technique. At first he enjoyed learning and practicing the two-arm shoulder throw; it came easy to him, and he was good at it. His instructor noticed his ability with this particular maneuver and encouraged the repetitious practice of it. But now it was reaching the point of being ludicrous—nothing but three weeks of a bad dream, repeating itself over and over, and always followed by that same horrible word.

And now that word interrupted his thoughts once more.

"Again!"

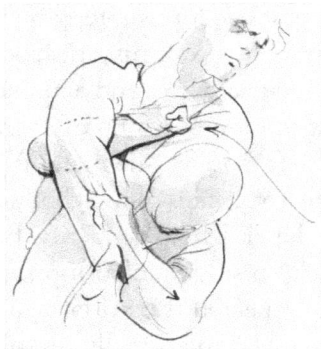

With a new partner he assumed jigotai, and once more went through the mechanics of the throw. He had reached a level of pure exhaustion, a point where his brain could no longer think of the individual parts of the technique; it simply allowed his body to move instinctively into the motion and against the fatigue of his aching muscles. His mind separated from his physical movements, until he could scarcely feel the weight of the other person's body being lifted over his own, or the shock of his weary self being lifted in turn and slammed onto the cushioned floor.

And the futility continued on and on, until he heard the familiar clap of hands that signaled the end of class.

The young man showered, changed his clothes, and walked quietly to the front door of the training hall. For a moment he hesitated, looking back at his instructor who was in the process of starting another class for more advanced students. He stood silently, watching the older man move through various techniques that belonged to those who had already passed his own level of ability. He searched the older man's face, trying to find an answer to the question he wanted, but was afraid, to ask.

He knew there had to be a reason—some reason why this man would condemn him to waste his time practicing a single technique over and over, until it could only be described by the Latin phrase: *ad nauseam*! But what was it? What could possibly be the purpose of such a ridiculous exercise? He searched the older man's face more intently, trying to look into his eyes, trying to find that answer—but seeing nothing.

Finally the instructor, feeling a cool breeze drift in through the open door, turned and looked at the puzzled student who was holding the door open. Their eyes met momentarily, each filled with a different question—one of depth, and one of simplicity. The younger man used that brief moment to try and discover some sort of dislike or perhaps even antagonism hidden deep behind the teacher's eyes; but there was nothing there, nothing to explain the purpose of all the ridiculous repetition. All he saw was the innocent look of a man wondering why the door was being held open.

The young man turned away and stepped outside.

The day's practice had bothered the young man more than any of the previous classes that he had suffered through, and the reason was simple—all too simple. The next day would be his first chance at a promotion; his first test to achieve a higher belt rank. He wanted this promotion, and he had looked forward to it since his first day in class over eight months ago.

When he started his study of judo and jujutsu, he knew that he was better than the other beginners. It was obvious, he moved with more precision and his reflexes were faster than any of his classmates. Compared to him, the other students were like children stumbling through their first steps that can lead to the maturity of an art. He seemed to possess a natural talent that caught everyone's attention—except his instructor's.

But things changed. He wasn't allowed to progress through all the various techniques that he had expected to learn. His classmates moved on, but he was forced to remain with a few basic throws and reaps that he was already naturally good at. Between three and four weeks were spent on each one of these individual movements, over and over, so there was never any time left to learn new material—those intricate maneuvers that might earn him the promotion that he wanted so badly.

He shook his head in disgust, and smiled a bitter smile. "I'll surprise them!" he said to himself. "I'll surprise all of them... and especially...." He grew quiet as his thoughts drifted across the strong features of his teacher's face.

The young man had a plan, a plan that he had put into action several weeks earlier. He could see the course that his formal instruction was taking—a course that guaranteed failure in the coming text. So he took matters into his own hands, arranging for some extra practice with a senior student in the backyard of his own home. He taught himself some of the advanced techniques that he had wanted so much to learn; those things that had been kept from his hungry mind and eager body.

In this private practice he moved up through the upper levels of this grappling art. He advanced beyond the simple throws and reaps, progressing

into combinations and tactical movements. He practiced sweeping, dropping, and grappling techniques. He taught himself the mechanics of arm locks and chokes, and felt that he could perfect them if given a variety of partners to practice on.

Of course, he never spent too much time on any one of these maneuvers, but that wasn't really necessary—not for him, not for someone with his natural ability. And now he was looking forward to the test; he was anxious to show his instructor how wrong his formal training had been—how wrong it was to hold him back from all that he could achieve.

It was Friday, and the training hall was filled with students from all the different classes. The young man saw people that he had never seen before: students from morning classes, evening classes, self-defense classes, women's classes, and children's classes. Suddenly he felt very proud of his ancestry, proud to be Japanese, and proud to be studying a Japanese art in the heart of the biggest city in all of Japan. Today would be his day, a day that would allow everyone a glimpse at his wonderful future in the world of his chosen art.

He sat quietly, his white belt and clean uniform as unsoiled and unruffled as his countenance. He watched as others took their turns in the center of the mat, pitting their skills against those of one of the assistant instructors. Each person was given the chance to demonstrate his skill and ability in a type of limited free-practice (*randori*) lasting three minutes. A variety of techniques were being used—some good and some bad—but all with the same enthusiasm for perfection and hope for victory. Win or loose, pass or fail, each student seemed pleased with his own performance and with the simple fact of having done his best. To the majority—this was enough.

The young man watched with a critical eye, judging each person's skill against his own—or at least, what he thought was his own. He could see every mistake, every imbalance, every inept movement that somehow snuck past the examiners' eyes. He couldn't understand why certain people were being promoted when their skills were obviously weak and ineffectual. For a moment, he thought that perhaps these students or the examination board were not as capable of seeing these mistakes as he was—and this thought bolstered his growing self-confidence and self-opinion of his own natural talent.

Finally, it was his turn, his chance to show these people how much he had accomplished in eight months—accomplishments he owed to himself, not to his instructor. As his name was called, he stepped onto the mat and walked towards his partner. The other man was much older and larger than he had expected, but it didn't matter; he was ready, ready to show everyone how this martial art was supposed to be performed.

He bowed to his seniors on the examination board, bowed to his partner, and bowed to the other students. On command, both men assumed jigotai and began circling each other in the center of the large mat. The young man started with an arsenal of offensive maneuvers, trying to down his opponent as quickly as possible—but nothing seemed to be working. The assistant instructor waited, knowing his role as simply the demonstration partner, allowing the young man to try his attacks and various strategies. But although the blackbelt remained inoffensive, he refused to give up easily to the incompetent techniques of the younger man; he stayed on his feet throughout the barrage of incomplete movements and amateurish combinations—and seemed to effect this defense with little skill or effort.

The seconds passed away, and an unfamiliar sense of panic appeared in the younger man's mind. Things weren't working the way he had imagined they would. His advanced techniques that were supposed to manifest his natural ability, instead turned soft and useless against someone with honest resistance. What was going to be his triumph was becoming his public failure, and the fear of failure—the kind of failure that makes men want to hide themselves from prying eyes—was creeping slowly into his troubled thoughts.

He moved around, shifting his weight and twisting his body, trying different ways to unbalance his opponent. He searched his mind, a mind that was cluttered with all the techniques and combinations that he had memorized in the last several weeks, but nothing was clear or ready for the situation. As soon as he thought of a maneuver for a particular position or movement, the position was gone or the movement had changed. There was not time to think, no time to carry out his pre-made plans. Each of his movements was followed by a counter-movement, the second blending into the first, until they appeared as one. His partner reacted to every action, not thinking or planing, but just doing—and becoming the art.

The young man was getting tired, wearing out from all the unnecessary and overextended effort put into each one of his attempted techniques. Around and around they moved, locked together by lapel and sleeve, moving on each other's slightest mistake in stepping or shifting. At last the young man saw an opening when his opponent leaned awkwardly to the left. Quickly, he stepped forward and slid his foot outwards, preparing for the execution of "floating drop" (*uki wasa*); but before he could finish positioning his body, he felt his own legs swept out form under him, followed by the sharp slap of the floor against his back.

The young man remained down for several seconds, collecting his senses, and trying to comprehend what had just happened. Then, he stumbled to his feet and once again assumed the initial posture. His attitude changed— he abandoned his offensive tactics and concentrated on the defense. The blackbelt saw this change in the younger man's behavior, and acted in accordance with his new role as offender. The situation was not the reverse, with the young man trying to defend himself against an array of maneuvers that his mind expected but that his body was unable to avert.

The blackbelt was using simple techniques, those techniques that a novice might be able to counter with a little speed and skill; but even these elementary movements resulted in the young man tumbling to the floor again and again. He was fighting his own body, refusing to listen to his instincts, trying to fight with techniques learned in his mind but not yet memorized by the fibers in his muscles or the cells in his nerves. He had become his own

worst enemy, defeating himself far more than the man who continued to throw his weary body over and over onto the faded orange mat.

The bell rang! The three minutes were up. He struggled into a standing position and faced his partner. Both men bowed to each other, then turned and bowed to the panel of examiners. The young man could see his failure etched across the faces of all those honorable judges. He could see it even more on the face of his demonstration partner—who turned quickly aside to hide the look of sympathy that crept over his features.

It was only three minutes—and yet it seemed to have lasted an hour. The young man was stiff and sore, but the greatest injury was the slaying of his pride. He turned away and started walking quickly towards the dressing rooms, hoping to disappear before any whispered remarks reached his ears.

What he heard was not a word, but a clap—the single clap of hands that was the signal from his instructor for attention. The young man stopped and turned slowly around. The instructor looked at the student, while the silence of the training hall stretched out each passing second—and then he lowered his eyes and spoke a single word. That word wasn't very loud, yet it traveled across the room and picked out the one man from whom it was spoken.

"Again!"

A soft murmur passed through all the students and spectators seated around the edge of the mat. The panel of judges simply looked at the instructor and laid down their pencils. The young man didn't move. He knew by the restless surprise of the other students that a second chance was never given, and he wondered why an exception was being extended to him. He had failed! His abilities were miserable and undeserving of a rank higher than he now possessed. So why? Why offer another chance to someone demonstrating such a complete lack of physical skill? There had to be some reason, some little insight, oblivious to himself but obvious to his teacher. He had to find it; he had to feel it; he had to use whatever it might be.

The assistant instructor stepped back onto the mat and moved to the center, motioning for his young partner to join him. The young man moved slowly into position, performing his bows and assuming his posture. His body was tired, his muscles were aching, and his mind was unable to think of the techniques that he needed to use. It was going to be another failure, another three minutes of absolute humiliation, just another confirmation of his total lack of talent in the art that he loved so much.

Suddenly, his partner moved in on him, grabbing at the back of his collar for some sort of reaping maneuver. Without thinking, the young man stepped inward, pivoted on the ball of his foot, and slid his back against the abdomen of the other man. In one continuous and circular motion, the senior partner was lifted up, carried over, and dropped gently onto the mat. A collective gasp ran through the people gathered around the two opponents. The blackbelt rolled away and quickly regained his feet, looking at his younger partner with a blink of surprise and a grin of satisfaction.

Once more the assistant instructor assumed his stance and attempted a different throw, only to be dropped to the floor by the very same technique, the technique that the young man had been practicing for the last three weeks. Again the blackbelt attacked, and once more he ended up on the mat—this time by a major outer reaping technique (*osotogari*), another one of the few basic movements practiced over and over by the young man during these first months of his training.

The young judo practitioner wasn't thinking, he wasn't planning any type of action; instead, he was allowing his body to utilize those motions that had become ingrained in his muscles and tissues. These half dozen techniques had been memorized by his body, not his mind; and they were being instantly applied at the very moment that they became needed. The constant repetition had given his body the ability to remember and put into practice those physical mechanics that his brain could only visualize in the abstract.

For the remaining part of the three minute period, the young man learned what his body could do by simply letting it perform as it was trained. Not all of his techniques were successful, and not all of his movements were completed, but even when he found himself on his back, he was still able to learn from the action that had put him there.

Now he understood what it all meant; he realized that it wasn't the number of techniques that was important, but rather the quality of the few. His instructor hadn't retarded his efforts to improve, but instead had picked those techniques that came the most natural to his physique, and then burned those few motions into the very substance of his instincts. The other members of his class had continued on to other instruction because the teacher hadn't yet found the best techniques for their individual abilities. It all seemed quite simple now, very clear and logical. He could see how it all fit together, and most of all—he could use it.

When the bell rang, he performed his bows with a different state of mind, and with a much richer sense of accomplishment. Before leaving the mat, he turned around and offered a special bow to his instructor, then moved to the ring of spectators and sat down among his fellow classmates. He knew that he could not accept the promotion if it were offered to him—for he felt that he had been granted a much greater reward by simply being allowed to test himself a second time. He felt that he had already received his promotion—a promotion in his skill; and it came in the form of a single, quietly spoken word: Again!

chapter 12

Samurai Geometry: A Story of Values

by Peter Graebner, M.A.

SAN GAKU: *San* to count, to reckon, to compute, to calculate; *Gaku* a fixed amount, number, value, a horizontal tablet.

All drawings are from the graphic novel series by Oscar Ratti and Adele Westbrook titled: *Tales of the Hermit.* ©2001 and 2002 Futuro Designs & Publications.

"Young monk, I understand little beyond battle. Since age seven when my father sold me to my Lord Ishida Mitsunari, I have known only training and war. Now I want more."

Kukai, the samurai, said these words to me many years ago. He spoke as he ascended onto the porch of our Zen temple, which had stood for more than two hundred years serving the unsatisfied.

I had watched him as he first approached our temple on the dusty road. We often saw samurai on the road then because of our proximity to Sawayama Castle. Lord Mitsunari required each warrior to walk in full armor from sunrise to sunset one day a week. A few stopped for tea on our porch. Kukai caught my attention; I had never seen a samurai who looked so fierce.

In addition to Kukai's fear-inspiring long sword, body armor, helmet, and fiery eyes, the wooden face armor covering his cheeks and chin was carved in an angry grimace, a death look frozen into the wood. His countenance radiated a clear message: "I have killed other men and I may kill you." Behind the fire in his eyes, I saw a hint of gentleness, and a great tension. Under his face armor I knew I would find a softer mouth than expected.

I had little personal knowledge of samurai, but my teacher had told me of these men. To bring his thoughts home to me, my teacher compared samurai warriors to Zen practitioners. He said that many samurai find themselves in accord with Zen. Whereas the Zen practitioner seeks enlightenment (*satori*) and rebirth, the samurai seeks everyday acceptance of death readiness. Both pursuits, he said, involve living while embracing death.

My teacher said many samurai suffered from observing themselves too closely and turning every war skill into a grueling self-discipline. He believed a samurai needed liberation from his focus on himself and his skills.

On the day we met, I took Kukai to the river, a short walk from the temple. We sat on the grassy bank at a bend in the river, above a deep, clear pool. Many fish gather at the bottom of this pool. Kukai remained tense. I asked him to listen to the fish breathe. He looked at me as if viewing a fool, but he tried to hear the breathing. I exaggerated when I told him that the noise of the fish breathing hurt my ears. He left abruptly. Uncertain he would ever return, I watched him walk down the road, as if for the last time, growing smaller and eventually melding with the dust of the road.

Overjoyed when Kukai arrived the following week, I suggested we find a way to quiet the raging monkeys of his mind. We tried sitting meditation (*zazen*). His bulging calf muscles prevented him from easily assuming the lotus position. I piled cushions under his buttocks until he managed to find a stable, although uncomfortable, position. Politely, he sat for an hour, but the tension in his eyes and body remained. I knew he could not gain harmony by sitting; something inside him battled against tranquility. I remembered the old adage, "Drinking a bowl of tea, I stopped the war." I told Kukai next week we would try something different.

When he arrived, we went immediately to the small hut behind the temple surrounded by our vegetable garden. We monks had carefully built the hut to appear refined yet rustic without a trace of affluence. We had thatched the roof using rice straw, laid bound straw mats on the floor surrounding the sunken fire pit, and framed the walls and sliding doors with opaque paper. The spare interior held only a small statue of Lord Buddha on a small box in one corner. One side of the box remained unpainted, to give our imaginations something to complete. We monks took our tea there with quiet conversation and contemplation.

Kukai and I removed our shoes, entered and sat facing each other across the fire pit. I prepared a charcoal fire in the pit, poured water into the squat brown soft-iron kettle. Once the water came to a boil, I whisked the finely powdered green tea in the ceramic bowl until it took on the texture and color of liquid jade. When tea and hot water touched, the aroma filled the hut. The moment the brewing process reached its perfect culmination, I formally poured. We drank slowly. I studied his face and movements to see if the tea provided him respite from his tension. I had failed again.

The next week we tried poetry. I explained the *tanka*, a form with five lines with syllable counts of 5, 7, 5, 7, and 7. Kukai tried hard. Although bright and clever, he could not lose himself in poetry. Again failure.

As soon as he arrived for our next weekly session, I confessed. I told him I had failed. When I suggested an older monk replace me, he said no. I had chosen sitting meditation, ceremonial tea, and poetry, and I wondered if I had simply made poor choices. I asked him what task, aside from anything related to war, had he ever enjoyed. He said he had enjoyed his sums.

I spent the next week in contemplation. I wondered if I could transfer Kukai's inner tension into some form of positive energy. I vowed to liberate Kukai from his focus on himself and his war skills. Perhaps a samurai could lose himself in numbers?

I had received training in numbers as a boy, and I had studied forbidden Dutch texts on my own. The temple kept many books in several languages, and a few dealt with numbers. I had studied equations and had gained a little experience with problems involving triangles and circles.

With Kukai during the next few weeks, I reviewed addition, subtraction, multiplication, and division. He carried work back to the castle after our sessions. It did not take long before he had mastered the four basic operations. He wanted more.

Our work with square roots led to solving equations that led to triangles and circles. At a point when our work involved drawing pictures, Kukai surpassed me. I lost my status as a teacher and assumed the role of observer. Without training, he understood the concept of a proof. He seemed immediately to sense the presence of certainty accompanying his work with proofs. I watched his eyes as he entered the heart of geometry, losing himself in proving the relationships associated with a triangle whose relative side lengths are three, four, and five. I could almost see the raging monkeys of his mind leave his body.

He began working on a situation involving four circles inscribed within a triangle. He played with the pattern of shapes until he had defined a problem to prove. The long side of the triangle he drew horizontal. The two short sides of arbitrary but different lengths joined above this horizontal. Inside the triangle he placed a large circle that touched all three sides of the triangle. At each inside corner, he placed a small circle. Each small circle touched two sides and the large circle. Kukai believed he could express the radius of the large circle in terms of the radii of the three small circles. He worked on his proof for two weeks. The unexpected arrived at the moment he completed his successful proof.

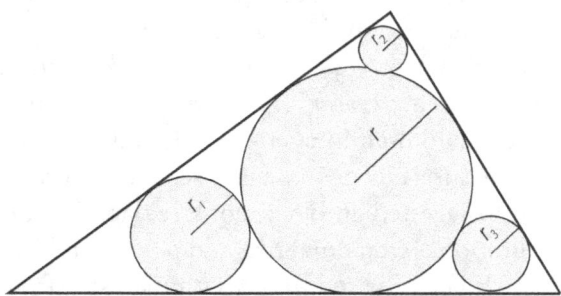

He raised his head and laid his brush on the table. His face took on a serene expression. He looked in all directions and I knew he saw everything as right, as right as his proof. Things, everyday things, he saw as right. I knew the remaining shadows and ghosts flickering in his mind had vanished.

I remembered my own enlightenment. One moment the universe seemed tawdry and the next moment I saw it all as right. Like the stars with no constellation badly arranged, everything stood correct, everything fit in place perfectly. In my body I had found the universe, its goal completely fulfilled in the immediate moment.

"I proved it," he said.

But his face said much more. I knew Kukai's eyes would never again look upon the universe as before.

"I must record this," he said. "Next week may I use tools and have some wood? And perhaps a few paints?"

That week I searched my heart for the relationships among Lord Buddha, samurai, enlightenment, geometry, and death readiness. A warrior finds conflict in war and moves toward a resolution, a solution. Perhaps finding a solution to a problem compares to finding one's spiritual path; in both cases, one can lose oneself. My teacher once described life without Lord Buddha as bondage. Perhaps a proof may serve as a torch to light the way in the search for a path to freedom.

Kukai built a thin wooden tablet 180 centimeters by 90 centimeters—we commonly used the Dutch units of length. After varnishing the entire tablet, he carefully defined the frame, the triangle, the large circle, and the three small circles with black ink. In formal script, beneath the horizontal longest side of the triangle, he wrote out the relationship he had proven:

$$r = \sqrt{r_1 r_2} + \sqrt{r_2 r_3} + \sqrt{r_3 r_1}$$

After we hung his tablet in the eaves beneath the temple's wind-worn roof, Kukai suggested we go to the river. Before we reached it, he paused. He said the sound of the breathing fish hurt his ears. With a formal bow to me, he announced he could not work at the temple for a time as he believed a big battle was brewing. I wanted to change the direction of our discussion, because I experienced a painful premonition.

"Did you make the tablet to honor the Lord Buddha?"

"No. I make a statement: See if you can prove this."

Unfortunately my premonition of his death in battle proved correct—I never saw Kukai again.

The battle, fought in the small mountain valley encircling the village of Sekigahara, realigned the universe. The fighting that occurred on October 21 in the Western year 1600, changed Nippon and it changed me. I arrived with my brother monks after the killing. We offered prayers for the dead and consolation for many of their loved ones who gathered near the Nakasendo Road. Thousands of bodies, half of them headless, along with hundreds of dead horses, covered the plain. Working alongside the villagers, we formed many piles of bodies. We chanted prayers as we burned each pile. I chanted prayers for Kukai, but I did not find his body. Over the last 70 years, the stench of the burning bodies has never left my nostrils.

Weeks after the battle, a friend of Kukai's—surprisingly articulate for a masterless samurai (*ronin*)—took refuge in our temple. He had fought at Sekigahara and escaped with Lord Mitsunari to Mount Ibuku. He described the politics and the battle to the assembled monks in exchange for a week's food and lodging. I can still hear his words:

The death of Toyotomi Hideyoshi, whose steel grip on Nippon had brought a rough peace, sparked a fierce rivalry between two warlords. Nippon could not contain the two warlords, the first my Lord Ishida Mitsunari, an impoverished aristocrat slavishly devoted to Hideyoshi, and the second, the Lord of Kanto Plain, Tokugawa Ieyasu, who descended from the Minamotos. One of these burning ambitions had to perish, along with thousands of others.

In a cold midnight rain my Lord Mitsunari led us in darkness to the village of Sekigahara. Our scouts reported Lord Ieyasu advancing behind us westward along the Nakasendo Road. My Lord Mitsunari ordered his army spread along the high ground west of the village: Mount Matsuo to the southwest, Mount Tengu directly west of the village, and Mount Sasao to the northwest.

Lord Mitsunari placed himself and his personal troops, including me, on the crest of Mount Sasao at the extreme left flank of his army. If the fog lifted, I knew we would see Sekigahara in the distance at dawn. My Lord Mitsunari's first order sent samurai to scout an escape route. His second order established barricades at the foot of Mount Sasao manned by archers.

At dawn the fog disappeared and everything happened at once. We saw the vanguard of Lord Ieyasu's army occupying the village. Soon the pounding of his giant war drums reverberated throughout the mountains, and at the blast of his deep-throated war horns, one of his lead units attacked our center.

Soon all Ieyasu's lead units attacked along our entire front. Directly opposite our position on Mount Sasao, Lord Nagawasa's forces formed the extreme right flank of Lord Ieyasu's army. These men attacked uphill toward us.

Before mid-day, Nagawasa led his men around our barricades to attack our flank. Meanwhile, some leaders who began the battle on the side of my lord went over to the enemy. Lord Mitsunari ordered Kukai to lead our counterattack down the mountain, but only assigned him a few samurai and a few archers.

Vastly outnumbered, Kukai led his men directly into the center of Nagawasa's samurai. He forced the enemy back toward the barricades for a short time, but they rallied. Kukai acted as rear guard for the retreat of his men and he helped his wounded men to safety. He carried one of his men on one shoulder, while continuing to swing his great sword. None of Nagawasa's samurai would approach Kukai. A volley of arrows finally brought him down.

My Lord Mitsunari used the time provided by Kukai's action to escape. We fled to Mount Ibuki where my lord told us to disband and hide. I avoided capture, but my Lord Mitsunari and many of my fellow samurai did not.

I knew Kukai well, a fellow samurai, a complex man who in his last act used his long-sword more to preserve life than to take life. He spoke well of all the monks of this temple.

I experienced great sorrow when I heard of Kukai's death. I had experienced much death then at my young age, but before I wept for Kukai, death had always seemed distant. Now in my 90th year, I must face my death just as Kukai faced his. He died young—a samurai's destiny—but not before he experienced his awakening and his release from bondage. And not before he bestowed upon me the gift of death readiness.

The days of the samurai have passed now, just as my days must pass. Every morning for 70 years I have raised my eyes to see Kukai's work hanging by hooks under the eaves. His clear signature on the tablet, "Samurai Kukai," rests alongside an invisible statement:

SEE IF YOU CAN PROVE THIS.

chapter 13

From the Tatami Mat to the Printed Page
Author Barry Eisler Keeps His Fiction Real

by Brian R. Sheridan, M.A.

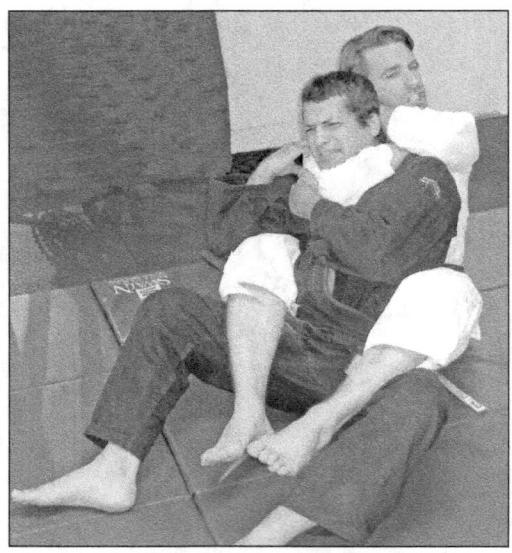

The author puts a choke on his friend and "awesome teacher," Dave Camarillo. www.davecamarillo.com. *Photograph courtesy of Barry Eisler.*

Introduction

There are authors who write fight scenes involving the martial arts and some who use martial artists as their protagonists. Only a handful can make it believable. Fewer have been able to gain critical acclaim and sales like Barry Eisler, the author, and martial artist, who created the "John Rain" series. His novels feature an assassin who uses judo to stay alive, and each book is full of no-holds-barred fight scenes. They appeal to not only martial artists but millions of readers who don't know a kata from a katana. But after seven novels, Eisler is taking a break from *Rain*. His new book, *Fault Line* [2009, Ballantine Books], will hit bookstores in March. It is expected to be no less realistic than his previous work and feature all of the excitement and action readers have come to expect.

The New Jersey born Eisler became interested in the martial arts as a youngster. As he puts it, he loved "acquiring knowledge people weren't supposed to have." His official biography notes that it led him to "a lifelong study of martial arts, including western boxing and wrestling, Japanese judo and karate, and Brazilian jiujitsu; a library of books on esoteric subjects such as methods of unarmed killing, lock picking, breaking and entry, spy craft, and other areas that the government would prefer only a select few to know."

After college and law school at Cornell University, Eisler joined the Central Intelligence Agency and worked as a covert operative. The agency trained him, and in return, he spent three years working in the Directorate of Operations. He left the spy world in 1993. Eisler then fulfilled his love of Asian culture by moving to Japan for a year. It gave him the opportunity to train at the Kodokan, the birthplace of modern judo. The "John Rain" character began taking shape there, in Eisler's imagination and on paper.

Putnam published his first novel, *Rain Fall* in hardcover in July 2002. Eisler describes Rain as living "a life of meticulously planned anonymity." Rain was trained by U.S. Special Forces and served in Vietnam. He's further described by Eisler as: "a cool, self-contained loner—and he has built a steady business over the past twenty-five years specializing in death by 'natural causes.' He is also a man struggling with his own divided nature: Japanese/American; soldier/assassin; samurai/ronin."

Rain Fall received glowing reviews. *The Boston Globe* raved that "Eisler provides a cracklingly good yarn, well written, deftly plotted, and surprisingly appealing..." *The London Times* called the book "...an original, adrenalin-filled romp through an exotic cultural landscape with an engaging murderer as a guide..." A similarly well received second book, *Hard Rain* [2003, Putnam], followed. In all, seven "John Rain" thrillers have topped bestseller lists around the world. They all have garnered praise for transcending the spy thriller genre with realistic action sequences and well-developed, multifaceted characters.

Eisler's anti-hero may also gain a whole new audience with his first appearance on the big screen. Sony Japan is releasing a Japanese-language adaptation of *Rain Fall* in April 2009. Max Mannix wrote and directed the film. Gary Oldman, the only Western actor in the cast, co-stars with Kippei Shiina as Rain. Eisler is expecting worldwide distribution, though there is also talk of a future Hollywood version.

Last year, Eisler, with his wife and daughter, moved back to Japan. The move allowed him to dip back into the culture that permeates his writing. He will be visiting the U.S. extensively this year, promoting *Fault Line*. Eisler also keeps in contact with his readers through his blog, "The Heart of the Matter," and the forums at his official website www.BarryEisler.com.

In the following interview, Eisler discusses why realism is important to him and his passion for the martial arts.

Barry Eisler Interview
Conducted by Brian R. Sheridan

- YOU WRESTLED IN HIGH SCHOOL AND THEN TRAINED IN JUDO. WHY DO YOU PREFER THE GRAPPLING ARTS OVER OTHER STYLES?

  I'll probably get in trouble saying this, but karate is karate no matter the style. It is punching and kicking. My primary interest in the martial arts has always been for their self-defense value. I believe if you don't train as reasonably close to "live" as you can, you probably are not going to get a lot of self defense value out of the art. I like the grappling arts because you can train them live. You can argue what "live" means because no martial art is exactly like a real fight or real combat. It is a question of degree. But in the grappling arts, jujitsu, wresting, judo, you are really mixing it up and feel a struggle. Having been in a few fights myself, it is not a bad facsimile. This is just my opinion; I know people in the martial arts will violently disagree with all of this, and I respect that people have different ideas.

- HOW DID YOU BEGIN TRAINING IN JUDO?

  There were some 4th-dan black belts from the Kodokan at the Cornell business school. I became friendly with these judokas, and I really liked what they did. I was totally unfamiliar with any kind of submission holds or armbars, and so I started playing around with judo on my own.

- WHAT LED YOU TO THE KODOKAN?

  Training at Cornell was only twice a week, so I couldn't train the way I wanted. When I was in the CIA, I decided to study Japanese. Then I left the CIA, I still really wanted to go to Japan to continue with the language and my judo training. It was a dream come true to train at the Kodokan. I read about the place, and it was everything I dreamt about.

- HOW WAS YOUR EXPERIENCE THERE?

  The only way the Kodokan can disappoint is if you are expecting a traditional Japanese building. About twenty years ago, they built this new building that is seven stories tall. What makes it special is that you have an amazing depth of talent in the teaching. All of the instructors are 3rd, 4th or 5th-dans. They are not part time—judo is their thing. In addition to that, you have people coming to train from all over the world. They are united by their passion for judo. The atmosphere was part of the reason why I loved it so much. Everyone is there out of love. They found a way to get there no matter how far away they lived. They dropped whatever they were doing in their life to move to Tokyo and train in judo. I knew a guy from Malaysia who was working in a gas station. I met a guy from the Philippines who worked in a bowling alley. People ended up living together in tiny rooms with shared bathrooms, whatever it took so they could train at the Kodokan. It created an atmosphere of excitement, devotion, and dedication. I loved being a part of it.

- DID THEY TREAT YOU DIFFERENTLY AS A WESTERNER? HOW WERE YOU TREATED?
  There were many Westerns there for training. I found my experience there, as it was throughout Japan, if you treated people with respect then they treated you with respect. I was trying to learn the language, the culture, and judo, and I think my excitement came through. I was training five or six days a week….two or more hours at a time. When they see how devoted you are, they treat you with respect.

- WHAT IS ONE THING THAT THE MARTIAL ARTS HAVE TAUGHT YOU?
  The real essence of strategy isn't fighting your way out of a situation. It is seeing a situation far enough in advance so you can avoid it entirely. Anyone who has done any sort of jujitsu, judo, or other submission wrestling, knows you can reach a point where you are so boxed-in, you have no options and there is no escape. The point is not to get into that position. Your defense begins before you find yourself in an inescapable situation.

- HOW DID YOU CREATE A CHARACTER AS COMPLEX AS JOHN RAIN?
  Rain Fall was my first try at a novel. I never wrote anything before with a martial arts angle. The idea for a story and a character involving judo came to me while I was training at the Kodokan. Rain is a combination of some people I have known, but no one specific person. I am not sure where he came from. When people meet me they say they are surprised I am a warm, approachable kind of guy, because Rain is so cynical and bitter.

  People expect me to be dourer, given the character I write. I have cynical elements to my personality, but it is not my dominant trait. Those elements of cynicism are leavened by more of a sunny, optimistic outlook. With Rain, the cynicism grew unrestrained.

- RAIN HAS BEEN CALLED A RONIN AND A SAMURAI. WHAT LED TO TAKING THAT APPROACH, AND DO YOU CONCERN YOURSELF WITH RAIN MAINTAINING

THE SAMURAI CODE?
While living in Tokyo, I was reading Eiji Yoshikawa's novel about Musashi, and reading a fascinating book by swordsman Dave Lowry called *Autumn Lightning: The Education of an American Samurai* [2001, Shambhala], so samurai matters were on my mind. But the martial aspects were less an influence than was the notion of service to a larger cause.

On one level, Rain is the ultimate loner and cynic, but on a deeper level, he longs to believe in something, to be part of something, and the contradiction between those aspects of his character is part of what drives the stories.

- WHY ARE YOU SO CONCERNED WITH BEING ACCURATE IN YOUR MARTIAL ARTS SCENES? MOST READERS PROBABLY COULDN'T TELL THE DIFFERENCE.
Just by inclination, it was important for me from the beginning to try to make everything look as real as I could get it. I have become increasingly concerned about that as the series has gone along. It is almost a "branding" issue for me. I want my readers to be able to trust me when I describe a place, or a martial arts technique, or some spycraft. I want my readers to be confident that I am describing those things realistically. I do a lot of research from on-site visits, to discussions with experts, as well as drawing on my own experiences. It is the brand I am trying to create where a fictional character is dropped into non-fictional settings and circumstances. My readers seem to like that. I'm not saying you have to do that—it is fiction. You can make up any rules you want, as long they are internally consistent. The rules I try to establish in the books are the rules that you find in the real world. The back-stories are inspired by today's headlines. So when you read even the back-stories, I want you to not only think "Wow. This could happen," but also "This probably IS happening."

- WHAT HAS BEEN THE RESPONSE FROM MARTIAL ARTISTS TO YOUR WRITING?
I am pleased to say most of the responses I get from martial artists are ones that say "you've obviously done your homework and know what you are talking about." They say they find it refreshing since most fiction is not realistic. It is flattering to get that feedback from experienced martial artists who recognize the diligence that goes into those sequences and appreciate it.

- ANY FAVORITE FIGHT SCENES OR ACTION SEQUENCES THAT YOU ARE PROUD OF WRITING?
There is one in *The Last Assassin* [2006, Putnam] where Rain and Dox (a sniper that Rain has cautiously teamed with) fight two sumo wrestlers. I'm proud of that because it is both extremely exciting, but also hilariously

funny. It is not an easy balance to bring off since those emotions—suspense and excitement on one hand and hilarity on the other—tend to be oppositional. I'm proud that I was able to pull it off.

I have noticed that anyone under extreme stress might find it can elicit an inappropriate emotion. You might laugh at a funeral, for instance. Well-trained, experienced men who have dealt with the kind of danger Rain and Dox have faced realistically could react with a laughing fit to relieve enormous tension.

- THE "JOHN RAIN" SERIES HAS A LARGE FOLLOWING OF READERS OUTSIDE OF THE MARTIAL ARTS COMMUNITY. ARE YOU CONCERNED ABOUT BEING LABELED AS A GENRE WRITER?

You don't want to write just for an exclusive audience. If no one but martial artists want to read your books, that is not a big enough market to live on. I don't think about this when writing the first draft. When I go back and rewrite a scene, however, I think 'Okay, martial artists will be reading this but also people who are not interested in martial arts. So how much detail do I need to use?' I usually just write so I please myself first with as much detail as I find interesting. I am also conscious of the people who are not into the mechanics of a [martial arts] style. People like that can just skim the scene and get right to the part where the character gets his neck broken. They don't need to know everything.

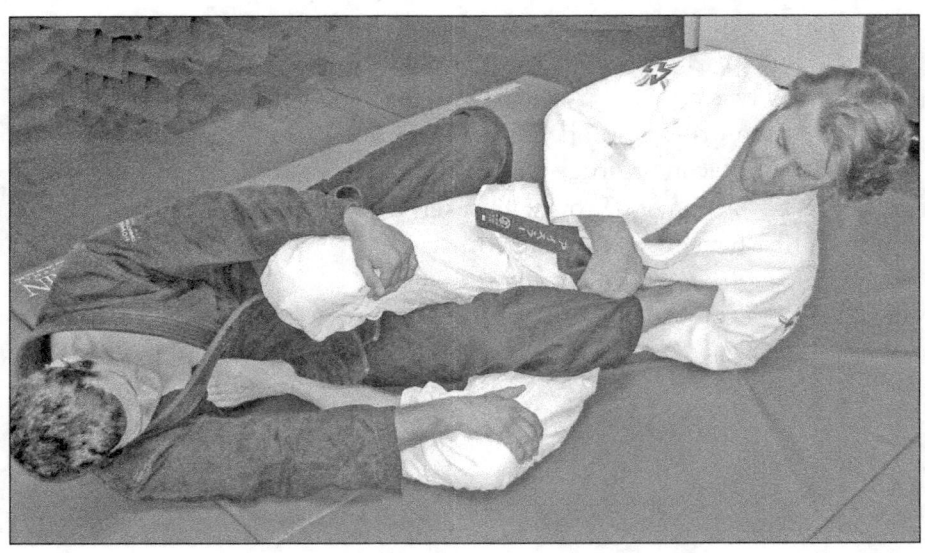

Eisler gets some hands-on grappling experience with instructor Dave Camarillo.

- WITH THE *RAIN FALL* MOVIE COMING OUT, ARE YOU CONCERNED ABOUT LOSING YOUR CHARACTER IF IT BECOMES A SUCCESSFUL SERIES LIKE "JAMES BOND"?

   Not at all—because the movie is not my project, not my art. It is someone else's interpretation of characters and a story I invented. I just recognize the movie people are free to do whatever they want in their interpretation and that's cool with me. I am sure there will be things I would have done differently, but that is not the point. I'm sure their John Rain will be different than mine. I find it interesting to see someone else's interpretation of my books. In many ways, it may be like a musician who writes a song and then hears someone "cover" it. It is probably not the way you sang the song yourself, but you might find it an interesting rendition. Overall, I'm thrilled with the movie. For me to dislike it, the filmmakers would have to make some horrendous mistakes, like changing Rain's gender or lose the mixed-race angle entirely, because that's essential to the character.

- YOUR NEW BOOK, *FAULT LINE*, IS A NON-JOHN RAIN BOOK. WHAT IS IT ABOUT?

   The book is about two brothers—one, a black ops soldier; the other, a Silicon Valley lawyer—who hate each other and haven't spoken since their mother, their surviving parent, died seven years earlier. When the younger brother, Alex, gets caught up in a murderous conspiracy surrounding an invention he's tried to patent, he's desperate enough to call on the last person he thought he'd ever ask: his big brother, Ben. Resentful and reluctant, Ben travels from Istanbul to Silicon Valley, where the tension between them is tuned to a fever pitch by the presence of the only other person who knows about the invention—Sarah Hosseini, a beautiful Iranian-American attorney who both brothers desire, despite suspecting she has an agenda of her own. To survive the forces arrayed against them, they'll first have to survive each other.

> "The real essence of strategy isn't fighting your way out of a situation. It is seeing a situation far enough in advance so you can avoid it entirely."
>
> – Barry Eisler

- CAN WE EXPECT SOME MARTIAL ARTS SCENES?
  You can, but they are more "more down and dirty." With Rain, he is such a well-trained, well-practiced martial artist, but yet he has also all of this combat and street experience, which combines to make a deadly package. He uses real martial arts techniques that martial artists can recognize. Ben is a former high school wrestler and college football player who is now an undercover military operative. Again, there is that combat experience, and a killer instinct, which make for great action sequences. He uses very practical techniques, but there is nothing fancy about it. I will keep it realistic as possible to show how violence between these types of professionals can go down.

- WHAT IS THE FUTURE FOR JOHN RAIN?
  Right now, I'm working on a sequel to *Fault Line*. After that, I can definitely see returning to Rain's world along a number of possible storylines, one of which might be a prequel, an origin of John Rain story. How did Rain become who and what he is? Fragments of that story have been told, but never the whole thing, and I think it would make a great book.

Note
For Eisler's book titles discussed in this article, see his website (www.barryeisler.com).

chapter 14

Arthur Rosenfeld: Martial Artist & Storyteller

by Thomas H. Bailey, Jr., L.M.P., A.P.

Left: Rosenfeld with custom made, folded Damascus steel broadswords in Chen form posture: Full Circle with Chop. Right: One of many variations of color and design of the pen and sword logo. *Photographs courtesy of Arthur Rosenfeld.*

Hidden beside the quiet dead end of a street in Lighthouse Point, Florida and along the Intracoastal Waterway, you will find a park little-known by most South Florida residents. It is frequented on the weekend by neighborhood locals; camouflaged youth marching to war in the woods with paintball guns, by parents and little ones heading to the playground, and by groups of picnickers and campers. It is also home to a group of women and men who gather every Saturday morning at 9 a.m. for hours of training. They will lunge forward and backward and sideways and stretch, punch and kick, and do it over and over. They study a very challenging movement system that teaches them how to develop profound postural and body movement awareness and mechanics. They learn to relax and release tension physically, mentally…maybe spiritually. They also learn to kick butt and to develop the temperament to avoid doing so. They train in the blazing sun and hell-like heat and honey-thick, sticky humidity of August or cool, breezy winter mornings. They follow ancient ideas for working out and living life: balance, moderation, consistent effort, avoiding excess, expending 70% energy and keeping 30% in reserve, and building up energy instead of depleting it. They train in the ultimate Chinese martial art—taijiquan.

Their teacher is a man who has experienced the life changing effects of the training. With over thirty years in martial arts and over thirteen years in this specific one, he is, among other things, a master level practitioner and teacher. He is also a Yale graduate, son of a world-renowned physician, lover and breeder of rare geckos, tortoises, snakes and frogs, and was for a time a student at Cornell Veterinary School. He is a father, husband, practical joker, blogger, pharmaceutical industry consultant, expert lecturer on chronic pain, connoisseur of fine chocolates, cigars, loose leaf teas, knives, swords, firearms, and motorcycles.

You may have see him on Fox News demonstrating the virtues of taiji. You may have read his blogs for *Basil & Spice*, the *Huffington Post*, *Reuters*, or the *Wall Street Journal*, and you might have read his best selling non-fiction work or one of his critically acclaimed novels. Through all his activities, achievements, vocations, hobbies, and passions, Arthur Rosenfeld is always a storyteller.

He desires to write and tell stories that "leave a residue that colors the way you look at life." He mentions J.R.R. Tolkien, Fyodor Dostoevsky, Dashiell Hammett, Gabriel Garcia Marquez, Jim Thompson, George Simenon, Mark Helprin, and Albert Camus as writers who have shifted his perspective through the myths they create. Myths, he says, are the "sweet packaging of wisdom." It is wisdom he relentlessly pursues, and it is his constant pursuit of myth and wisdom that leads him on his search for the ultimate martial art.

Martial Arts

Rosenfeld's serious martial arts training began in 1980 in Santa Barbara. He studied Tang Soo Do there, then Chinese Kenpo in Ed Parker's lineage. He moved to San Diego and took up Choi Lai Fut with Frank Primicias, then White Crane Gongfu in Ithaca, New York. Later, in Connecticut, he spent years practicing Wing Chun Kung Fu in Moy Yat's (teacher to Bruce Lee) lineage. In 1990 he moved to Los Angeles and studied xingyiquan with a senior student of Kenny Gong, a well-known New York City teacher and acupuncturist.

Settling in South Florida in the mid-1990s, Rosenfeld continued his search for a teacher who would "blend physical practice with wisdom" and by chance, discovers Master Max Yan (Yan Gaofe, b. 1967), senior student of Chen Taiji Grandmaster Chen Quanzhong (b. 1925). After a breakfast meeting, Yan quietly invited Rosenfeld to practice in the rain. Rosenfeld smiles as he recounts how effortlessly and often Yan put him on the wet pavement, and how he is suddenly hit with the understanding that in this smiling, smaller and younger man, he has finally found his teacher, and his martial art, Chen style taijiquan.

Rosenfeld describes Yan as a "transcendent intellect residing in an athletically gifted body; a character who walks the talk of the Dao better than anyone

I've ever met, genuinely embodying and living the tenets of esoteric Chinese philosophy in a rare and magical way. He does a finer job of walking his talk than anyone I know, of keeping his physical and emotional equilibrium, of actually living the Eastern teachings in the context of the speed and greed culture we call the Western world."

His relationship with his teacher exposes him to the great modern masters of Chen Taiji. His home has been guest quarters for Chen Taiji Grandmaster Chen Quanzhong. Through Yan, he has also hosted Master Chen Zhenglei (one of "Four Tigers" of Chen Taijii), and met and trained with Masters Li Enjiu and Zhu Tiancai (another one of the "Four Tigers"). His story of meeting Chen Quanzhong in the late 90s is filled with his typical child-like exuberance. Rosenfeld describes Chen's then 72 year-old body as "that of a powerful athlete half his age." He recounts the "sublime subtlety of the grandmaster's movements, the vertiginous feeling I had when placing my hand on Chen's chest and watching it move all the while feeling nothing but a ghostlike presence under my fingers". He has great respect for all the Chen masters, but still considers Quanzhong—whose lineage traces back to Chen Fake (1887-1957) and forward to Yan and Rosenfeld—the most formidable practitioner he has met.

As his own proficiency grew, he established Pen & Sword Tai Chi as a philosophy school with a major in martial arts in clear contrast to what he considers the usual path of martial arts schools that merely pay lip service to philosophy. He believes the art of taiji to be the physical manifestation of Daoist thinking, the famous book by Laozi, the *Daodejing* in motion. He chooses two symbols, the tip of a fountain pen to represent his writing and the broad sword to represent the weapons of the Chen system. The school name and its logo link his two passions into one goal, to convey Chinese wisdom to Western minds.

Rosenfeld has forty different translations of the *Daodejing* on his shelf at home. When asked how so many "intellectuals" view Laozi as the first libertarian and an advocate of anarchy, while others, like spiritual teacher Ekhart Tolle, view him as the author of "one of the greatest spiritual books ever written," Rosenfeld replies that, just as atomic energy can be used for the low purpose of warfare or the high purpose of powering a city, the knowledge in the *Daodejing* can be used for a low purpose such as justifying anarchy, or a high purpose such as the self-actualization of a human being. According to Rosenfeld, the handbook offers information on multiple levels and has been used to guide China's ancient rulers and inspire other writers, such as Sunzi and his *Art of War*.

"As much as I enjoy practicing taijiquan the martial art, its ultimate use is to create a physical laboratory with which to test and develop the philosophical understanding and life path of taiji and Daoism," he says. Rosenfeld uses this mind/body mix to coach individuals and groups to find new solutions, to minimize conflict, regain purpose, and shed old habits and restrictions. He sees achieving personal equilibrium as the martial art's highest goal, and the ultimate purpose of the life strategy as well.

Evading jump performed by the author as he simultaneously positions himself to strike with the "Reclining Moon Blade" (*yan yue dao*), usually called the *guandao*.

The Literary Life
In the same way that he cast about for the most rewarding martial practice, Rosenfeld has pursued various literary disciplines and genres. Beginning with stories in national magazines such as *Vogue* and *Vanity Fair* while an undergraduate, he moved on to a book about exotic animals as pets, motorcycle reviews for the major bike magazines, and detective fiction.

January 2000 brought critical acclaim for his novel of magical realism *A Cure for Gravity*. Among those who wrote endorsements for the book were Neil Simon, Larry Gelbart (M*A*S*H, Tootsie), Jack Parr (Tonight Show), and *New York Times* bestselling author Barbara Taylor Bradford. The following year brought more attention for *Diamond Eye*, a novel about a United States Postal Inspector that enjoys the distinction of being the first novel to be promoted and sold by the Federal Government when it was featured on the US Postal Service's website.

As his taiji study deepened, Rosenfeld began to realign more of his writing, teaching and lecturing with Daoist ideas. *The Truth About Chronic Pain* explored the social, cultural, psychological, religious, and spiritual dimensions of suffering through a Daoist lens, challenging patients and caregivers and the public alike to approach the issue with compassion and honesty, and without prejudice. The book has been used in nursing and medical schools and was a finalist in the prestigious Books for a Better Life award.

In the new millennium Rosenfeld has created a genre he calls Gongfu Noir. Inspired by his love of the traditional martial arts novels of China (*wuxia*), Rosenfeld creates a literary blend of Daoist ideas, martial arts action, Chinese history, and American crime fiction. YMAA, the leading American martial arts publisher of books and DVDs, ventured into fiction for the first time and published the first Gongfu Noir novel, *The Cutting Season* (2007). The story of Xenon Pearl, a South Florida neurosurgeon turned sword-wielding vigilante, the book was followed by a sequel, *Quiet Teacher* (June 2009), in which Pearl explores his previous lives, pursues more martial arts training from his Chinese nanny, and deepens his understanding of his violent compulsions.

Between the two Xenon Pearl novels came *The Crocodile and the Crane*, which chronicles the lives of a pair of Daoist immortals, brother and sister, who have lived for 3000 years and now face an apocalyptic plague threatening the very existence of mankind. All three novels deal with understanding one's true nature, how the actions we take and the choices we make affect all of those we touch, and in that process, come back to touch us. They deal with the yin and yang of our inner workings bad/good, wrong/right, and the limited human understanding that creates such polarizing judgments.

His novels are rich with action, suspense, western medicine, acupuncture, Chinese herbal medicine, sword wielding, taiji principals, detestable villains, and reincarnation. Reviews are strongly positive, and readers eagerly await Rosenfeld's current project, a novel of Chinese history and philosophy that he describes as his most ambitious literary project so far. While writing it, Rosenfeld continues to apply Daoist principals and great story telling to his blog writing, to his taiji group class, private taiji lessons, and to corporate consulting.

In his goal to expose more people to the philosophy of taiji, Rosenfeld also travels the country teaching seminars on Chen Taijiquan as the learning tool for taiji the way of living. He will soon be adding exotic locale international vacation/seminar packages to his schedule. If all this were not enough, he is the recipient of an educational grant from a major pharmaceutical company and is producing documentary videos on taiji and meditation. The intention for the videos is to educate medical doctors to the scientifically proven health benefits of taiji and meditation, and how these Eastern traditions may help patients' health and well-being. The videos include interviews with leading research scientists from University of California at Irvine and at Davis, Harvard Medical School, Massachusetts Institute of Technology, University of Vermont, and the University of Arizona. The videos also feature demonstrations of Chen taiji by Rosenfeld and his students. Throughout all of his projects, he blends storytelling with teaching, believing that, like myths, storytelling sugar-coats the "lesson" and helps others to most easily grasp the precepts of taiji and Daoism as a way of life.

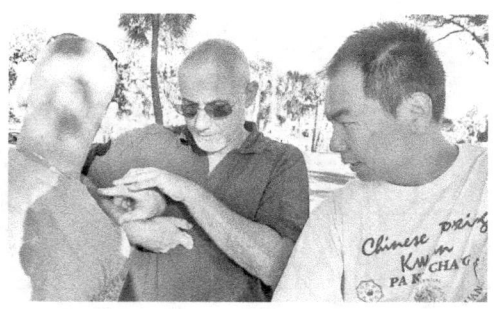

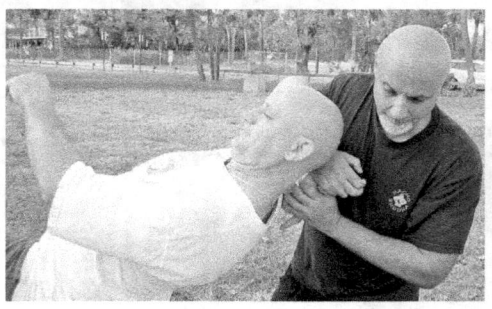

Rosenfeld working on joint-locking techniques with the author, under the guidance of Master Yan. Martial arts training helps bring realism into Rosenfeld's novels.

In his personal life he and his accomplished wife raise their nine-year old son, who decided last summer that he wished to quit his study of Brazilian Jujitsu to focus full-time on his Japanese karate class. When Rosenfeld reminded his son that quitting is not a path to choose, his son replied, "Dad, it isn't about that, Sensei teaches me about Japanese culture, and stories to make us good people as well as responsible practitioners and my jujitsu teacher only teaches me how to beat people up."

There is no moment when the storyteller is as happy as when he proudly tells his newest, favorite story, about his boy.

chapter 15

Fighting Heroes: The Core Values of the Xia Tradition in Early China

by Albert Dalia, Ph.D.

All artwork by Jungshan Ink. • http://jung-shan.blogspot.com

Rise and Ideals of the Xia

Wuxia xiaoshuo and *pian* (which I translate as "heroic fiction" and "heroic cinema," but are traditionally rendered as "martial arts" fiction and cinema) have been the mainstays of Chinese popular entertainment. Their increasing popularity in the world of globalized entertainment is well known. As both a traditional China scholar and a wuxia novelist, I have an interest in this popular genre. In this chapter, I would like to briefly consider the historical origins of the genre's characters.

While contemporary Chinese wuxia novelists seem to deal only with the Yuan (1280-1368 CE), Ming (1368-1644), and Qing (1644-1911) dynasties, in both my academic and fiction work, I never venture much past the Tang (618-907). Actually, I prefer the first century or so of the Tang, its "golden era." And for wuxia literature, the Tang is a seminal period, for it is with the Tang that Chinese fiction takes a big leap with the rise of the short story. However, to consider the rise of the *xia* ("martial heroes") in Chinese history, we need to go back to the Warring States Period (475-221 BCE).

As of this writing, the seminal work in English on this subject is the late Professor James J. Y. Liu's (1926-1986) wonderful, little book, *The Chinese Knight-Errant* (1967). Even though the book is out of print, I will frequently quote from it because it will be more easily accessible for this audience than articles and books written in Chinese for this audience.

The primary meaning of the character *xia* in ancient China was "to use strength to help people." It became synonymous with the word "chivalry." The character xia came to describe this class of fighters/heroes, as their chief characteristic was the use of their strength to help others. The character *you*, to roam, to wander, was appended to *xia*, becoming the combination, *youxia*, as these fighters did tend to wander over the land, helping others. In my fiction, I have translated *youxia* as "wandering blades," since I write about heroes who use bladed weapons. From this, wuxia comes to be literarily translated as "martial use of strength to help others" or, perhaps, "martial chivalry." In English we use it to refer to the "martial arts" genre of literature and cinema.

In China, as far as we know, the character xia used this way first appears in the writings of the eminent legalist philosopher Han Fei (韓非; ca. 280-233 BCE) under the heading "Five Vermin." This would not seem to be an auspicious start for the reputation of these fighters. Han Fei, being an advocate of strict authoritarian rule known as "legalism," considered both the Confucians and the xia dangerous to the state. He wrote, "[T]he Confucians with their learning bring confusion to the law; the knights with their military prowess violate the prohibitions." Further, that "men who wield swords, attack, and assassinate are violent and extreme people, but society regards them as upright and courageous men, bandits and men who conceal traitors should be condemned to death, but society regards them as men of honor" (Lai, 1999: 89).

The greatest influence on later wuxia fiction, however, was the *Records of the Grand Historian* (*Shi ji*), by the grand historian Sima Qian (145-86 BCE). He was China's greatest historian, and perhaps a man who shared some of that wuxia ethic in his determination to carry out his father's vision of a grand history of China. Sima Qian honorably defended the reputation of a defeated general against the unfair accusations of the emperor. For this the emperor condemned him to death.

The law at that time was that death sentences could be commuted through a cash payment or through suffering mutilation. Sima Qian didn't have the money and underwent the humiliation and pain of castration rather than death. He did this so he could live to carry out his father's dream for their family to compose a history of China. Sima Qian lived to finish the *Records of the Grand Historian*. It set the standards for not only all the subsequent histories written in China, but was also influential in the rise and composition of fiction during the Tang dynasty. His writing not only provided the form that Tang fiction would take (the use of character development and narrative line), but also provided a fertile subject for those early short stories—the adventures of the xia are found for the first time in Chinese literature in the Tang *chuanqi* ("accounts of remarkable things" or, more simply, "tales of wonder") literature.

"*Sha*" (kill): artwork by Jungshan Ink.

In his *Records* Sima Qian initiated the biographical form as a historical genre. "Among these biographies, the chapter entitled 'Biographies of Wandering Knights' (*Youxia liezhuan*) probably had the most influence on later knight-errant fiction" (Lai, 1999: 88). What was Sima Qian's opinion of the xia?

Unlike the legalist philosopher Han Fei, who gives us the first mention of the xia in writing, Sima Qian has a different take on their actions when he writes:

> Now, as for the knights-errant, though their actions were not in accordance with the rule of propriety, they always meant what they said, always accomplished what they set out to do, and always fulfilled their promises. They rushed to the aid of other men in distress without giving a thought to their own safety. And when they had saved someone from disaster at the risk of their own lives, they did not boast of their ability and would have been ashamed to brag of their benevolence. Indeed, there is much to be said for them. Besides, distress is something that anyone may encounter from time to time.
> – Liu, 1967: 14

"Blood Fist": artwork by Jungshan Ink.

So writes the historian who suffered castration for his integrity! We can see here that early definition of xia as "to use strength to help people."

Regarding the xia's social origins, Professor Liu considers three scholarly opinions: 1) They were unemployed peasants and artisans, commoners who became professional warriors. 2) They were men without property, but not exclusively of lower social origin, and some could have been nobles who lost their status. 3) They were not a special social group, but simply men of chivalrous temperament.

Liu is inclined to this last view and concludes, "I suggest it is best to regard the knights-errant not as a social class or a professional group but simply as men of strongly individualistic temperament, who behaved in a certain way based on certain ideals" (Liu, 1967: 4).

Professor Liu writes (1967: 4-6) that in reading the literature of this early period, he has found eight basic ideals that are related to the xia: 1) altruism, 2) justice, 3) individual freedom, 4) personal loyalty, 5) courage, 6) truthfulness and mutual faith, 7) honor and fame, and 8) generosity and contempt for wealth. I will follow Professor Liu's discussion, since his book is hard to find, and add my own comments where possible.

EIGHT BASIC VALUES HELD BY THE XIA

1. Altruism

"Altruism" is Professor Liu's translation of the Chinese character *yi* (義). This was also a main concept in the teachings of Confucius (551-479 BCE), who lived in the Warring States Period, which we are discussing. He was one of those wandering scholars seeking to impress the warring states with their solutions, along with "our" wandering blades—whose "solutions" tended to be more direct. The early Confucian yi is frequently translated as "righteousness."

Liu points out that the modern Chinese philosopher Feng Yulan believed that yi, as understood by the xia, "means doing more than what is required by common standards of morality." And he quotes this example, "[T]o bestow a kindness and not expect a reward is moral; to bestow a kindness and to reject any reward is supermoral." So yi in this context is understood as a type of "supermorality" (p. 4).

However, there are other understandings of yi. An interesting interpretation is that given by an old friend from the University of Hawaii, Roger T. Ames, in his translation with Henry Rosemont, Jr., of *The Analects*, that ancient collection of Confucius' teachings. These two scholars look at the variants of this character recorded from the Shang dynasty (ca. 1766-ca. 1050

BCE) and conclude that "morality" is not quite the correct sense of the character (Ames & Rosemont, 1999).

Ames and Rosemont argue that "appropriate" or "fitting" are closer English equivalents to yi in this historical/intellectual context. They explain:

> Yi, then, is one's sense of appropriateness that enables one to act in a proper and fitting manner, given the specific situation ... It is because yi is the sense of appropriateness that makes relationships truly meaningful in a community of mutual trust, that Confucius says, "making good on one's word (*xin*) gets one close to appropriateness"
>
> – Ames & Rosemont, 1999: 54-55

I think that this interpretation, while directed at the early Confucian use of the term, might find significant resonance with the xia ethic. Sima Qian, as pointed out above, observed that although the xia tended to flaunt the rule of propriety, they were true to their word. Can we say, then, that their actions, while possibly contrary to contemporary rules of propriety, were "appropriate" to the situation at hand—as they understood it? In other words, their sense of yi was relative, situational.

2. Justice

Liu believes that the xia's sense of "appropriateness" (using the Ames/Rosemont interpretation) springs from their sense of justice, which (and this is significant in a Confucian society) "they placed above family loyalty." He gives moving examples from this period in the story of the wandering blade, Kuo Hsieh (ca. 127 BCE) (pp. 4-5). I will summarize Liu's translation, which is from Sima Qian's historical record.

Kuo Hsieh was from Honan province. His father was a wandering blade who was executed by Emperor Wen (reigned 179-157 BCE). As a young man, Kuo was spiteful and killed many who offended him. "He avenged the private wrongs of his friends at the risk of his own life, concealed those on the run from the law, robbed people and even tombs, and illegally coined money. All of these crimes he committed countless times, but he either managed to escape or was pardoned because of an amnesty." As he grew older, he reformed, but remained revengeful. Yet when he would save someone's life, he didn't boast about it. Many times he would act as an objective arbitrator in various types of disputes. Government authorities, however, tired of disturbances centering on Kuo or his retainers, brought charges against him, arguing that, "Kuo Hsieh is a commoner who indulges in knight-errantry and wields great power. He would kill for a slight offence ... he deserves the penalty for high treason."

Kuo and his entire family were executed (Liu, 1967: 37-40). There is one incident from his life that is worth recounting here from Liu in full detail:

> Once, Kuo Hsieh's sister's son, relying on Kuo's influence, forced another man to drink beyond his capacity. The latter grew angry, killed the young man, and ran away. Kuo's sister, angry that the killer had escaped, said, "My brother is known for his altruism [or "appropriateness" of behavior], yet now he can't even find the murderer of my son!" So she left her son's body in the road and refused to bury it, so as to shame Kuo Hsieh. Eventually Kuo found out who the killer was, and the latter, in desperation, came to see him voluntarily and told him the whole truth. Kuo said, "It was my nephew's fault; you were quite right to kill him." So he let the killer go and quietly buried his nephew. All those who heard about this admired him for putting fairness above family loyalty, and more and more men came to follow him.
> – Liu, 1967: 38

Kuo's behavior would not qualify him for a model citizen's award. At best he might be characterized as an outlaw or a minor gangster with a conscience, of sorts. It is interesting, however, that Liu cites Kuo's dealing with the murder of his nephew as an example of the xia "sense of justice." And that it is from this "sense of justice" that their "altruism" springs.

What interests me as a novelist is that Kuo's behavior regarding "justice" for his nephew seems to fit well with the "appropriateness" definition that I cited for the term *yi* ("altruism" in Liu's translation). Kuo dealt with his nephew's murderer in what he felt was the "appropriate" manner, or to quote Sima Qian, again, "not in accordance with the rule of propriety," that is, not in accordance with common social norms.

3. Individual Freedom

It seems to me that the key to xia behavior is the ideal that seems most antithetical to the Chinese social/cultural norm as it came to be defined by Confucianism—individual freedom, or individualism. While this is the third ideal in Liu's list, I would put it at the top. As Liu explains it:

> Not only did the knights manifest their rebellious nature in openly defying the law while attempting to see justice done, but they also showed their non-conformity in daily life by living in what would nowadays be called a Bohemian manner and paying little attention to social conventions.
> – Liu, 1967: 5

Could this be why wandering-blades tales are so attractive to their Western fans? Possibly, but don't forget that this genre is also the most popular genre in East Asia too! These men, and women (!), were very individualistic. Li An captures that well in Zhang Ziyi's character in *Crouching Tiger, Hidden Dragon*. But this is not new. We have seen this same characteristic in countless martial arts movies. And in the literary tradition, swordswomen date back to at least the Tang dynasty.

Further, the various martial arts forms are the very expression of individualism, as are many of the arts in East Asia. Those of you who practice martial arts know from your own experience that your teachers are very individualistic and that although we are all trained with a sense of community in our movements and in our interactions with our fellow students and teachers, these skills breed a certain sense of self-confidence. And those who practice with paint or calligraphy brushes share in this same experience—the discipline makes us strong enough as individuals to control our egos (hopefully), yet also strong enough to know how to express ourselves when necessary—or dare I say, when "appropriate"! And this can be in social situations or on rice paper.

Artwork by Jungshan Ink.

Thus, on a certain level, we can understand the xia values as expressions of individualism. This is not to say that the followers of Confucius and the other schools at the time were not individuals, rather that their expressions of individualism were different. Traditionally a follower of Confucius would rather wield a calligraphy brush than a sword to redress grievances. But like the xia, they would not hesitate addressing a grievance. The first emperor of China, Qin Shihuangdi (259-210 BCE), buried alive Confucian scholars who opposed him and executed xia who attempted to assassinate him (the movies *The Emperor and The Assassin* and, to a lesser extent, *Hero* are based on incidents recorded by Sima Qian). Both groups were threatening enough to his oppressive rule that he felt it necessary to eliminate them.

4. Personal Loyalty

Liu believes that the xia's sense of personal loyalty transcended their loyalty to their ruler/state or their parents/family. This particular aspect of xia values was in sharp conflict with Confucian tradition, which taught that the five social relationships (ruler-subject, father-son, husband-wife, elder brother–younger brother, between friends) were the basis of civilized society.

Xia culture placed the emphasis on *zhi-ji*, a sense of "loyalty," which short-circuits the five relationships. Hamm (2004: 13) gave the sense of this value when he quoted Yu Rang, noted in Sima Qian's record of the assassin: "A man will die for one who understands him, as a woman will make herself beautiful for one who delights in her."

A variation on this type of loyalty is the famous story of Bo Ya, a musician from this ancient period, who destroyed his lute when Zhong Ziqi died. According to Bo, Zhong was the only person who could understand his music, the only one who could intuit the musician's heart. This sense of loyalty is known as *zhi-yin*, which a modern Chinese dictionary would translate as "intimate friend."

This special sense of friendship or appreciation was the basis of social relationships for the xia. Such relationships, from a Confucian perspective and that of the state, could threaten the foundation of society. Thus, we find xia like Kuo Hsieh helping escaped criminals and avenging wrongs done to his friends or going against his family in letting his nephew's killer go unpunished. Xia friendship could be seen to undermine orthodox Chinese social order, thus Kuo Hsieh's eventual execution by the state.

5. Courage

This should be obvious and needs no further comment except to pass on Liu's remark that the xia's cavalier attitude toward death "almost suggests they did not much care for life" (p. 5). I think that is a bit extreme. My reading of their biographies suggests they had a larger-than-life enjoyment of being alive, but that they were not attached to it.

Artwork by Jungshan Ink.

6. Truthfulness and Mutual Faith
To quote Sima Qian again, "They always meant what they said, always accomplished what they set out to do, and always fulfilled their promises." Liu says that they would even go as far as committing suicide to show their sincerity (pp. 5-6).

7. Honor and Fame
Liu says that this value is connected to the previous one. He quotes our Grand Historian, Sima Qian: "[T]hey disciplined their action and cherished their honour so that their fame spread all over the empire." Liu feels that if they were not entirely motivated by "altruism," "then their only selfish motive was their desire for fame" (p. 6).

8. Generosity and Contempt for Wealth
Liu argues that the xia had no problems with accepting or refusing money from friends, because they didn't have a strong sense of ownership. They could live lavishly and share with their friends, or live modestly and share with the poor (p. 6).

Based on James Liu's study, it is clear that later Chinese writers, first in the Tang dynasty, developed the wuxia literary genre from these early Chinese heroes and the stories handed down about their exploits. It is from that literary tradition that the cinematic tradition developed. These early ideals are powerful influences on what comes later, not only in the Chinese literary tradition, but also in wuxia cinema.

Further, these ideals were not limited to China. In the Boston University Writing Program, I teach a class devoted to the East Asian hero/heroine—the class emphasizes a mix of Chinese and Japanese film. My students and I have discovered that these ideals have remained potent for the last two millennia, crossing over from traditional Chinese literature into the media of film and then being globalized by contemporary entertainment trends. The regional influence of the Chinese wuxia tradition also influenced the warrior traditions found in those cultures adjacent to the Chinese core culture area. It seems that altruism rising from a sense of justice is at the heart of these values. Yet this sense of altruism derives from a strong notion of individualism, and it is this sense of individualism in this culture complex that is the basis of my course title: Paradox of the Hero/Heroine in East Asian Cinema and Fiction. How does a cultural region that is defined by its emphasis on group cohesiveness give rise to and pay respect to heroes who exhibit such a strong sense of individualism? If a culture's heroes represent its highest standards of behavior, then what does this heroic tradition tell us about East Asian culture? Further, beyond the East Asian region, what explains the global fascination with this ancient heroic tradition?

References

Ames, R. & Rosemont Jr., H. (1999). *The analects of Confucius: A philosophical tradition*. New York: Ballantine Books.

Hamm, J. (2004). *Paper swordsmen: Jin Yong and the modern Chinese martial arts novel*. Honolulu: University of Hawaii Press.

Lai, S. (1999). From cross-dressing daughter to lady knight-errant: The origin and evolution of Chinese women warriors. In Sherry J. Mou (Ed.), *Presence and Presentation: Women in the Chinese Literati Tradition*. (pp. 77–107). New York: St. Martin's Press.

Liu, J. Y. (1967). *The Chinese knight-errant*. London: Routledge and Kegan Paul.

Credit for Artwork

Featured artwork by illustrator Jungshan Ink., http://jung-shan.blogspot.com

index

13 Rue Madeleine (movie), 39
Above The Law (movie), 35, 43 note 7
aikido, 2, 9-10, 22, 33, 35, 39, 43
altruism, 196, 198, 201
Art of War (book), 188
Autumn Lightning: The Education of an American Samurai (book), 182
Bad Day at Black Rock (movie), 29, 41
baguazhang, 147-148, 158
The Big Brawl (movie), 105
Billy Jack (movie), 34-35, 105, 122, 128
Black Belt (magazine), 73, 78, 82-84, 92, 141
Blood On The Sun (movie), 43
bokken (wooden sword), 138-140
Bond, James, 6, 12, 34, 36, 130, 184
Bright Lights, Big City (novel), 15, 26
Bronson, Charles, 40
bullying, 45-58
Cagney, James, 39, 43
Campbell, Joseph, 1, 25 note 2
Carradine, David, 79-80
Central Intelligence Agency, 26 note 13, 35, 39, 179-180
CFW Enterprises, 88, 92
challenging a master, 20, 65, 140-143, 150, 153-154, 160
Chan, Jackie, 34, 88-90, 105, 128-132
Chapman, Tracy, 1, 25 note 1
Chen, Fake, 188
Chen, Quanzhong, 187-188
Chen, Zhenglei, 188
China (book), 20-21, 24
The Chinese Knight-Errant (book), 183
Chow, David, 78-79
Chow, Raymond, 118, 121-124, 128, 130
Choy Li Fut (Cai Li Fo), 20
Combat (magazine), 7
Confucius, 147, 155, 193, 196-198, 200
contempt for wealth, 196, 201
courage, 6, 59, 193, 196, 200
The Crocodile and the Crane (book), 190
Crouching Tiger, Hidden Dragon (movie), 199

Cruise, Tom, 130
Cusack, John, 41-43
The Cutting Season (book), 190
Daodejing (book), 188
The Devil's Brigade (movie), 38
dianxue (acupoint hitting), 108-116
Dragon: The Bruce Lee Story (movie), 34, 39
Drunken Style, 150
Dudikoff, Michael, 129
Eisler, Barry, 178-185
eight basic values held by the xia, 196
Elleston, Trevor, 11, 26 note 12
Ellison, Ralph, 18
The Emperor and The Assassin (movie), 200
Enter The Dragon (movie), 34, 117-118, 123-125, 127, 129-130
Fairbairn, W.F., 38
fame, 106, 126, 196, 201
Fault Line (book), 178-179, 184-185
Fists of Fury (movie), 60, 122-123
Fitzgerald, F. Scott, 1, 3
Five-Animal Style, 74, 81
Fleming, Ian, 1
The Flight of the Phoenix (book/movie), 11
Fox Volant of the Snowy Mountain (book), 109
Game of Death (movie), 125, 127
Gardner, John, 20-21, 25 note 6
generosity, 196, 201
Gluck, Jay, 7
Goju-ryu, 15-16, 96
Golden Communications, 130-131
Golden Harvest, 118, 121-124, 127-128, 130-131
Goldfinger (movie), 1
Gong, Kenny, 187
grappling, 43, 97, 101-102, 165, 180, 183
Green Beret Special Forces, 26, 38
guandao, 189
hakama, 135, 138
Hall, Adam, 11-14, 26 note 12
Han Fei, 193, 195
Hapkido, 34, 129
Hard Rain (book), 179

Hero (movie), 200
hero concept, 4-6, 13, 30, 32, 36, 125, 129, 193, 202
Hideyoshi, Toyotomi, 176
honor, 6, 193, 196, 201
Hung, Sammo, 90, 118, 128-132
Hunt, David, 9-11,
Hunter, Stephen, 25 note 6, 36
Huo, Yuanjia, 60, 62-68, 70, 146-147
Ieyasu, Tokugawa, 176
Inosanto, Danny, 91-92
Inside Karate (magazine), 71, 84
Inside Kung Fu (magazine), 71, 82, 84, 86, 88
Iron and Silk (book/movie), 36
Jeet Kune Do, 126
kendo, 7, 138, 142
kenpo, 7, 13, 16, 97, 187
The Killer Elite (movie), 38
Jingwu Men Academy, 60
Johnson, Charles, 18-24, 27 ntoe 19
judo, 2, 7, 33, 39, 43, 50, 52, 58, 79, 162-170, 178-181
justice, 42, 196-198, 202
The Karate Kid (movie), 39, 105
katana, 138
kickboxing, 94-95, 97-102, 105, 107
Kodokan, 179-181
Koyama, Shojiro, 13
kumite, 2, 36
Kung Fu (TV), 78-80, 82, 122
Kwoon (book), 20, 27 note 21
Laozi, 152, 156, 160, 188
The Last Assassin (book), 182
Lee, Ang, 36-37
Lee, Bruce, 10, 16, 23, 34, 39-40, 60, 81, 83, 97-98, 117-118, 122-130, 132, 136, 187
Lee, Jason Scott, 81
Lefiti, "Tiny" Haumea, 75
Leong, Albert, 81
Lew, James, 81, 83
Lewis, Joe, 91
Li, Bruce, 91
Li, Enjiu, 188
Li, Jet, 132
life energy (ki/qi), 34, 109, 115, 160, 186
Liu, James J. Y., 193

Lowry, Dave, 182
Lu Xun, 152
Lung Sihung, 37
The Magnificent Seven (movie), 30
The Man from Hong Kong (movie), 130
The Manchurian Candidate (movie), 40-41
Mannix, Max, 179
Mantis Supply Company, 83
Martial Arts and Combat Sports (magazine), 71, 130
Martial Law (TV), 105, 118, 130-131
The Matrix (movie), 1, 130
McInerney, Jay, 15-18
Merriman, Chuck, 96, 98
Middle Passage (book), 18
Mifune, Toshiro, 48
Mission Impossible II (movie), 130
Miyamoto, Musashi, 138, 182
Mizong Yi (Lost Track [boxing] Art), 62-64, 66-67
Mok-Gar (Mo Family), 75
Morgan, Andre, 117-134
Mulan, 8
mutual faith, 196, 201
Nadeau, Robert, 10
Norris, Chuck, 98, 105-106, 118, 122, 129
O'Donnel, Peter, 5-8, 25 note 9
Office of Strategic Services, 39
Oldman, Gary, 179
Oxherding Tale (book), 20
Pai, Daniel K., 96-97
Pai Lum Kung Fu, 96
Parker, Ed, 87, 89, 97, 187
Pelecanos, George, 15, 26 note 17
personal loyalty, 196, 200
Primicias, Frank, 187
proper timing (shizhong), 154-155
push-hands, 37, 156
Pushing Hands (movie), 36-37
Qin Shihuangdi, 200
qinna (locking), 150
Quiet Teacher (book), 190
Quiller Memorandum, 12
Quiller Salamander (book), 13
Rain (book), 178
Rain Fall (book/movie), 179, 181, 184
Ransom (book), 15, 17-18
randori, 2, 166

Records of the Grand Historian (book), 193-194
Redemption (movie), 106
Rhee, Jhoon, 125
Rosenfeld, Arthur, 186-191
Rozan, S.J., 8
Ruddy-Morgan Organization, 118, 131
san gaku, 171
Sanders, Steve, 91
Sarchanowski, Ron, 88-91
Schwartzenager, Arnold, 98
Seagal, Steven, 10, 35, 38-39, 43 note 7, 129-130
Sekigahara Battle, 175-176
The Seven Samurai (movie), 30
Shaolin, 33, 73-74, 81
Shaw Brothers, 121-122, 128
Shi, Nai'an, 59
shinai, 138
Shotokan karate, 12-13, 15, 44 note 8
Shuai Jiao (Chinese wrestling), 149
Silva, Henry, 40-41
The Silver Mistress (book), 7
Sima, Qian, 59, 193-195, 197-198, 200-201
Sinatra, Frank, 40-41
Sorbel, Kevin, 81
Springsteen, Bruce, 1, 25 note 2
Star Wars (movie), 33-34
Sunzi, 188
sword taking (tachi-dori), 140
Tae Bo, 105
taekwondo, 2-3, 8, 31, 33, 44 note 7, 73, 76, 125, 129
Taguchi, Todd, 83
taijiquan, 2-3, 20, 22, 35-38, 147-148, 151, 158, 186-190
Tales from the Water Margin (book), 59
Tales of Chivalrous and Altruistic Heros (book), 59-60
Tang Soo Do, 187
truthfulness, 196, 201
Ultimate Fighting Championship, 93, 97, 101
Uyehara, Mito, 83
Under Siege (movie), 38
Urquidez, Benny, 100-101
Van Damme, Jean-Claude, 91, 105, 129-130
Walker, Texas Ranger, 118, 131
Wallace, Bill, 100-101
Wang Yu, Jimmy, 128, 130-131
Warring States Period, 193, 196
Warrior Dreams (book), 25 note 3
White Crane, 187
Wilson, Don, 94-107
Wing Chun, 39, 86, 129, 187
The Woman Warrior (book), 8
Wong, Ark Y., 73-75, 81
Wong, Curtis (Huang Fulin), 71-93
Wong, Douglas, 72-73, 75-77, 79, 81, 90
Wong, Harry, 83
Woo, John, 89, 128, 130-131
wuxia, 60, 190, 192-193, 202
xia (martial heros), 60, 192-195
xia's social origins, 196
Xiang Kairan, 59-60
xingyiquan, 147, 152, 154, 158, 187
Yamashita, Tadashi, 83, 88-89, 91
Yan, Max (Yan Gaofe), 187
Yang, Chengfu, 2, 25 note 5
Yang, Jianhou, 148
Yeoh, Michelle, 132
Yip Man, 39
Yoshikawa, Eiji, 182
youxia (**wandering blades**), 193
zazen (sitting meditation), 172
Zhu, Tiancai, 188
Zhang Ziyi, 199

www.ingramcontent.com/pod-product-compliance
Lightning Source LLC
Chambersburg PA
CBHW071436080526
44587CB00014B/1869